INTERVENTIONS: NEW STUDIES IN MEDIEVAL CULTURE
Ethan Knapp, Series Editor

FICTIONS OF EVIDENCE

Witnessing, Literature, and
Community in the Late Middle Ages

Jamie K. Taylor

THE OHIO STATE UNIVERSITY PRESS
COLUMBUS

Copyright © 2013 by The Ohio State University.
All rights reserved.

Library of Congress Cataloging-in-Publication Data

Taylor, Jamie K., 1975–
Fictions of evidence : witnessing, literature, and community in the late Middle Ages / Jamie K. Taylor.
    p. cm. — (Interventions: new studies in medieval culture)
Includes bibliographical references and index.
ISBN 978-0-8142-1223-3 (cloth : alk. paper) — ISBN 978-0-8142-9324-9 (cd)
1. English literature—Middle English, 1100–1500—History and criticism. 2. Witnesses in literature. 3. Witnesses. 4. Witness bearing (Christianity) I. Title. II. Series: Interventions : new studies in medieval culture.
PR255.T39 2013
820.9'001—dc23
                                2012044198

Paper (ISBN: 978-0-8142-5695-4)
Cover design by AuthorSupport.com
Text design by Juliet Williams
Type set in Adobe Minion Pro

contents

Acknowledgments		vii
List of Abbreviations		x
Introduction	Witness Testimony and Literary Production in the Later Middle Ages	1
Chapter One	The Face of a Saint and the Seal of a King	24
Chapter Two	Silence, Testimony, and the Case of Susanna	55
Chapter Three	Neighbors, Witnesses, and Outlaws in the Fourteenth and Fifteenth Centuries	86
Chapter Four	*Piers Plowman*, Book, and the Testimonial Body	115
Chapter Five	Witnessing, Presence, and Lollard Communities	151
Coda	Witnessing the Middle Ages	189
Works Cited		199
Index		213

acknowledgments

I AM FORTUNATE to have many colleagues and friends who have shown me innumerable kindnesses while I researched and wrote this book. It is a true pleasure to express my gratitude to them.

My first teachers of medieval literature and culture, Bruce Holsinger and Beth Robertson, have continually encouraged my work since I met them over a decade ago, and I will always be grateful for their guidance and support. My thinking about witnessing emerged during my early graduate work at the University of Pennsylvania, and Rita Copeland, Emily Steiner, and David Wallace helped me shape my beginning thoughts about medieval law into the questions that are at the heart of this book. Kevin Brownlee always offered a kind word and sage advice, as did Liliane Weissberg, Marina Brownlee, Emma Dillon, and Nancy Bentley.

Special thanks go to Jonathan Eburne, who gave thoughtful feedback on the entire manuscript, and Hester Blum, who helped me think about its larger conceptual stakes. William Chester Jordan talked medieval witnessing with me and solicited thoughts from his colleagues when I asked him for advice; I want specifically to thank Richard Helmholz and Paul Hyams for sharing their work and thoughts on testimony with me. Vance Smith and Larry Scanlon both took the time to help me think more deeply and sharply about Langland, and an early conversation with Maura Nolan helped me focus on some core questions about medieval testimony.

I am also grateful for the insightful comments and thoughts from many colleagues, acquaintances, and friends, many of whom are probably not even aware that our discussions found their way into the book: Candace

Barrington, Andreea Boboc, Chris Bradley, Cristina Cervone, Andrew Cole, Holly Crocker, Celeste Dinucci, Bob Edwards, Carey Eckhardt, Kasey Evans, Frank Grady, Marissa Greenberg, Jon Hsy, Stephanie Gibbs Kamath, Kathleen Kennedy, Nenette Luarca-Shoaf, Jana Mathews, Tim McCall, Justine Murison, Chris Oze, Keith Poniewaz, Shyama Rajendran, Masha Raskolnikov, Jessica Rosenfeld, Martha Schoolman, Matt Shoaf, Stella Singer, Paul Strohm, Amy Vines, and Caitlin Wood. A friendly group of early modernists welcomed me into their works-in-progress group, and they offered sharp feedback on several pieces of this project: thanks go particularly to Alice Dailey, Matt Kozusko, Zack Lesser, Laura McGrane, Nichole Miller, Shannon Miller, Kristin Poole, Lauren Shohet, and Eric Song.

I am lucky to have found myself in a friendly department at a collegial institution, and I am very grateful for the support and encouragement of my colleagues and friends at Bryn Mawr College: Linda-Susan Beard, Elaine Beretz, Peter Briggs, Kim Cassidy, Catherine Conybeare, Anne Dalke, Ignacio Gallup-Diaz, Marianne Hansen, Jennifer Harford Vargas, Jane Hedley, Gail Hemmeter, Maud McInerney, Hoang Nguyen, Ray Ricketts, Bethany Schneider, Rosi Song, Kate Thomas, Karen Tidmarsh, Michael Tratner, Elly Truitt, and Sharon Ullman all deserve thanks for their generosity, support, and good cheer. Particular thanks go to the unbelievably energetic Katherine Rowe, whose enthusiasm and expertise have been invaluable for this project, and to Bryn Thompson, who helped this book materially and otherwise with her trademark elegance and grace. Louisa Foroughi cheerfully double-checked a few Latin translations, and Kersti Francis was indispensable in the final stages of this project.

At Bryn Mawr, support for this book came from a Junior Faculty Research Leave, the Helen Taft Manning Fund, and a Faculty Research Grant. Outside of Bryn Mawr, some of the research for this book was conducted with support from an Andrew W. Mellon Huntington Library Research Grant. I want to thank the librarians at the Beineke Rare Book Library, Princeton University's Rare Books and Special Collections, and the University of Pennsylvania's Rare Book Library. I am also grateful to AnnaLee Pauls, Charles Greene, and Paul Needham at Princeton for their help with the image included in this book.

Ethan Knapp and the anonymous reviewers for The Ohio State University Press were thorough, generous, and thoughtful readers of the manuscript, and the book has benefitted enormously from their engagement with it. I am especially grateful for Malcolm Litchfield's encouragement and guidance throughout the publication process, and for Maggie Diehl's and Kristen Ebert-Wagner's editorial acumen.

I delivered versions of parts of this book as talks at the University of Toronto, Villanova University, the Delaware Valley Medieval Association meeting at Bryn Mawr College, the Modern Language Association meeting in San Francisco, the International Medieval Congress at Kalamazoo, and the New Chaucer Society. Part of chapter 3 appeared in *English Language Notes* 48.2 (Fall/Winter 2010): 85–97. Copyright © the Regents of the University of Colorado 2010. All rights reserved. Reprinted by permission.

I am most grateful for the ongoing support and love of my family, especially of my parents, Ronald and Patricia, and my sisters, Lara, Meredith, and Dana. And finally, my wonderful husband, Andrés, and my lovely son, Javi, are the greatest joys of my life. This book is dedicated to them.

abbreviations

CCSL   *Corpus christianorum series latina*
CHMEL   *Cambridge History of Medieval English Literature*
EETS   *Early English Text Society* (e.s., extra series)
EHD   *English Historical Documents, 1189–1327*, ed. Harry Rothwell. London: Eyre and Spottiswode, 1975.
JEGP   *Journal of English and Germanic Philology*
MLQ   *Modern Language Quarterly*
PL   *Patrologia Latina*, ed. J-P. Migne. Paris, 1844–64.
PMLA   *Publications of the Modern Language Association of America*
SAC   *Studies in the Age of Chaucer*
STC   *Short-Title Catalogue*
YLS   *Yearbook of Langland Studies*

introduction

Witness Testimony and Literary Production in the Later Middle Ages

WITNESSES were integral to a wide range of devotional and legal practices throughout the Middle Ages. As the crowds at martyrs' trials, the audiences of mystery plays, and the readers of saints' lives, they were repeatedly invoked in the traditions, rituals, and texts that shaped and articulated the ideals of Christian communities to testify to the sanctity and efficacy of Christian doctrine. Likewise, in ordeal trials, last wills and testaments, and writs of complaint, witnesses attested to the integrity of a law-abiding community. This book focuses on both devotional and legal witnessing practices in the later Middle Ages, arguing for the centrality and the plasticity of witnessing in fourteenth- and fifteenth-century English culture. It describes witnessing as a diverse set of customs and procedures that sought to produce and authenticate different communities and kinds of authority. The swearing of an oath, the communal experience of a miracle, the oral testimony of a defendant, and courtroom documents alike provided religious and secular officials ways to construct and police doctrinal, customary, and royal communities. Yet witnessing practices could also be used to dispute or reframe, rather than shore up, doctrinal and legal communities. For example, as chapter 3 explores, outlaws sometimes deployed witnessing discourse to authorize communities that lived beyond the disciplinary reach of the crown. Likewise, as described in chapter 5, some Lollards used fifteenth-century depositional formulae to imagine a coherent community of heterodox believers even as ecclesiastical officials sought to censure such communities through the strategic use of testimonial rhetoric.

In particular, this book illustrates that witnessing practices offered medieval vernacular writers a language and a framework to examine the various ways devotional, moral, legal, or ethical obligations to one's community might be understood and to challenge how the authority to determine those obligations could be asserted.[1] Writers such as Chaucer and Langland, as well as lesser-known theologians such as John Waldeby and William Thorpe, depicted episodes of witnessing in their work to explore the overlaps and tensions between different kinds of legal or doctrinal communities. Accordingly, they imagined their own literary productions both attesting to and critiquing ecclesiastical and legal modes of community-formation and -articulation.

The late medieval witnessing ideals and practices this book explores emerge from a long history of devotional and legal forms of testimony. In the earliest martyr stories, for instance, witnesses are key to describing the communal experience of divine judgment, and they do so through the double testimony of the martyr's tortured body and the witnessing audience. Crucially, this audience of witnesses includes both eyewitnesses who are present at the event and readers of the legend. To take one example, the third-century martyrdom of St. Perpetua establishes a continuum of witnesses that imagines Perpetua's body as the central, spectacular expression of steadfast faith that can assemble and unite a Christian community, present and future. For her devotion to a Christian god and her defiance of her pagan father, Perpetua is first scourged in front of a crowd and then attacked by an angry bull. When the bull fails to kill her, her neck is cut with a sword. At least one description of her martyrdom begins with a prologue that calls upon readers to be quasi-witnesses to her steadfast faith:

> The deeds recounted about the faith in ancient times were a proof of God's favor and achieved the spiritual strengthening of men as well; and they were set forth in writing precisely that honor might be rendered to God and comfort to men by the recollection of the past through the written word.[2]

---

1. For discussions of witnessing practices and community-formation, particularly in the sixteenth century, see Andrea Frisch, "The Ethics of Testimony: A Genealogical Perspective," *Discourse* 25.1 (2004): 36–54. For a discussion of witnessing practices and travel literature, see Mary B. Campbell, *The Witness and the Other World* (Ithaca, NY: Cornell University Press, 1988).

2. "Si uetera fidei exempla et Dei gratiam testificantia et aedificantionem hominis operantia propterea in litteris sunt digesta ut lectione eorum quasi repraesentatione rerum et Deus honoretur et homo confortetur." *The Acts of the Christian Martyrs*, trans. Herbert Musurillo (Oxford: Clarendon, 1972), 106.

The text presents itself as a diachronic tool that can produce a devotional community across time and space, imagining the martyrdom of St. Perpetua as an event that must be witnessed both by the crowd at her trial and by future readers. Indeed, the prologue reinforces the link between the eyewitnesses who saw Perpetua's brutal death and the text's readers. "And so, my bretheren and little children," the prologue says, "that which we have heard and have touched with our hands we proclaim also to you, so that those of you that were witnesses may recall the glory of the Lord and those that now learn of it through hearing may have fellowship with the holy martyrs and, through them, with the Lord Jesus Christ."[3] The prologue promises that the sense of fidelity to Perpetua will transfer from the intimate experience of the eyewitnesses—those who "have heard and have touched with our hands"—to the more distant knowledge of those who have heard about the martyrdom, and then to the even more distant knowledge of those reading the text. Witnessing thus expands to encompass a wide range of audiences, from observers to listeners to readers; those immediately present at her trial and death and those detached from it can equally claim to have "witnessed" her martyrdom, and by extension, to have experienced the divine wisdom of God.

The story of St. Perpetua demonstrates the importance of witnessing in producing devotional communities as well as its flexibility to accommodate those unable to observe martyrological suffering firsthand. Indeed, in this and other martyrologies, the act of attesting to one's faith must be performed publicly and spectacularly: the body of the martyr is a touchstone that unites the witnesses watching her suffering with the "witnesses" reading the descriptions of that suffering. Similarly, following the logic of communal witnessing depicted in martyrologies such as St. Perpetua's, medieval mystery plays constructed witnesses out of their audiences so that they could attest to the miracle of Christ's resurrection, offering testimony based on the eyewitness "evidence" offered by dramatic reenactment. Thus, for example, in the Wakefield Resurrection play, Christ repeatedly implores the audience to "behold" his body and, in doing so, to recognize the fullness of his love:

And therfor, thou shall understand,
In body, hede, feete, and hand,
Four hundreth woundys and five thowsand

3. "et nos itaque quod audiuimus et contrectauimus, annuntiamus et uobis, fratres et filioli, uti et uos qui interfuistis rememoremini gloriae domini et qui nunc cognoscitis per auditum communionem habeatis cum sanctis martyribus, et per illos cum domino nostro Iesu Christo...," *Acts of the Christian Martyrs*, 106–7.

> Here may thou se;
> And therto neyn were delt full even
> For luf of the.[4]

This play asserts that because the audience can "see" the wounds on the actor playing Christ, they can also access the magnitude of Christ's grace. Similarly, in the Chester Emmaus play, Christ presents himself to Thomas and makes him believe that he has risen again by saying, "Yea, Thomas, now thou seest me." He addresses his disciples and the audience at the same time, imploring them both to recognize the play as testimony of Christ's divine power: "Christ geve you grace to take the way / Unto that joy that lasteth aye!" (273–74). These plays construe Christian witnessing as a hybrid of individual eyewitness experience and communal knowledge and faith, unifying members of the audience by insisting the plays be understood as the common experience of watching doctrinal history unfold before their eyes. Each member of the audience becomes an eyewitness to Christian eschatology and can thus consider him- or herself as a member of a community that already knows and believes the "evidence" rehearsed on the stage.[5]

For such witnessing claims to operate effectively—that is, to construct and rehearse a community's integrity—the testimonies of belief must be considered accurate and authentic. Thus, it was crucial that the multiple forms that witnessing could take (eyewitnessing, listening to a sermon, seeing a play, reading a text) be rendered parallel modes of testifying. For example, to authenticate his *Life of St. Cuthbert,* Bede explains how he relied on all kinds of testimony:

> what was done in the Church throughout the province of the Northumbrians, from the time when they received the faith of Christ till this present, I received not from any particular author, but by the faithful testimony of innumerable witnesses, who might know or remember the same; besides what I had of my own knowledge. Wherein it is to be observed, that what I have written concerning our most holy father, Bishop Cuthbert, either in this volume, or in my treatise on his life and actions, I partly took, and faithfully copied from what I found written of him by the brethren of the Church of Lindisfarne; but at the same time took care to add such things

---

4. "The Resurrection of the Lord," in *Medieval Drama*, ed. David Bevington (Boston: Houghton Mifflin, 1975), 280–85.

5. See Sarah Beckwith, *Signifying God: Social Relation and Symbolic Act in the York Corpus Christi Plays* (Chicago: University of Chicago Press, 2001). For a discussion of the intimate relationship between legal witnesses and medieval drama, see Jody Enders, *Rhetoric and the Origins of Medieval Drama* (Ithaca, NY: Cornell University Press, 1992).

as I could myself have knowledge of by the faithful testimony of such as knew him. And I humbly entreat the reader, that if he shall in this that we have written find anything not delivered according to the truth, he will not impute the same to me, who, as the true rule of history requires, have laboured sincerely to commit to writing such things as I could gather from common report, for the instruction of posterity.[6]

Here, Bede asserts that "faithful testimony" can be found in a wide range of sources, from letters to hearsay to his own personal experience. Indeed, the accuracy of his report depends not on an individual author, he says, but on "innumerable witnesses," whether human or documentary.

However, although Bede implies that different forms of testimony can be considered equally accurate in his narrative of the life of a saint, he issues a caveat that he ought not be blamed for any mistakes. This caveat turns on the "true rule of history" (*vera lex historiae*) that envisions "common report" and "faithful testimony" as fundamental to historical veracity. For Bede, testimony asserts its authenticity when it can be gathered into a historical account that seems accurate. In other words, Bede claims here that he is reporting the testimony accurately, rather than vouching for the accuracy of the testimony itself. Indeed, when Bede imagines "the faithful testimony of innumerable witnesses" to signify multiple kinds of testimonies, including ecclesiastical letters and eyewitness claims, he implies that testimony is as useful for tracking communal memory and belief as for accurately describing a historical event.[7] We see a similar rhetorical move at the beginning of Geoffrey of Monmouth's *History of the Kings of Britain*, in which he claims that the deeds of British kings have been handed down to him through oral tradition, "just as if they had been committed to writing, by many peoples who had only their memories to rely on."[8] The equation of oral testimony, memory, and written document in both Bede and Geoffrey of Monmouth suggests that the requirements of accurate reportage did not strenuously distinguish between personal experience and documented history, and that testimony could confirm the beliefs of a community as well as offer historical accounts on its behalf.

6. Bede, *The Ecclesiastical History of the English Nation*, ed. J. A. Giles (London: Henry G. Bohn, 1849), 3.

7. Roger Ray, "Bede's Vera Lex Historiae," *Speculum* 55.1 (1980): 14. See also Andrew Rabin, "Bede, Dryhthelm, and the Witness to the Other World: Testimony and Conversion in the *Historia ecclesiastica*," *Modern Philology* 106.3 (2009): 375–98.

8. "laudis constarent & a multis populis quasi inscripta iocunde & memoriter predicarentur." *The Historia Regum Britanniae of Geoffrey of Monmouth*, ed. Robert Ellis Jones (London: Longman, Green, and Co., 1929), 219.

Indeed, as Geoffrey of Monmouth shows, the witnessing rhetoric used to rehearse Christian unity and history was likewise important in the formation of geopolitical and legal communities, and a wide range of texts imagine witnessing as an opportunity to examine how one might attest to the concatenation of divine and state authority. For example, as Andrew Rabin has demonstrated, Wulfstan deployed forms of legal witnessing to envision an integrated model of Christian unity and English law. Rabin argues in particular that the *Sermo Lupi ad Anglos* locates the homily's poetic subject "at the nexus between the interior moral obligations of the Christian self and the public legal responsibilities of the English ðegn," suggesting that the *Sermo* posits witnessing as the fullest expression of the individual's ordered relationship to the state and, in turn, the state's ordered relationship to the divine.[9] Many medieval romances similarly describe witnessing as an important way to assert the state's link to God. Marie de France's *Lanval*, for example, depicts the power of sworn testimony to determine the outcome of the slander case against Lanval. The Queen accuses Lanval of having no interest in women after he denies her advances on account of his love of another; because he has promised that he will not reveal his love for his lady, it looks as if his defense will be severely hampered and the Queen's slander will stand for truth. During the trial, however, he denies under oath that he has insulted the king's honor, and his lady then comes to court to testify that Lanval never propositioned the Queen. With the exculpatory evidence provided by those two testimonies, the king's barons quickly free Lanval, determining that "Lanval had successfully answered the charge."[10] This text, like any number of romances, including *Amis and Amiloun, Le chevalier de la charrette,* Guillaume de Dole's *Roman de la rose,* and *Tristan,* repeatedly illustrates the necessity of testimony both to the heuristic work of legal trials and to the drama of the story. More pointedly, such trial episodes demonstrate that witnessing was thought to be a way to restore the king's authority and the unity of the realm.

Twelfth- and thirteenth-century romances such as *Lanval* or Guillaume de Dole routinely include trial scenes that focus on treason, whether imagined as sexual transgression against a queen, slander, or plots against a king or a close kinsman.[11] Such trial episodes often represent witnessing as crucial to

9. Andrew Rabin, "The Wolf's Testimony to the English: Law and the Witness in the *Sermo Lupi ad Anglos*," *JEGP* 105.3 (2006): 389.
10. "N'I a un sul ki n'ai jugié / que Lanval a tut desraisnié." *Lais de Marie de France*, trans. Laurence Harf-Lancner (Paris: Lettres Gothiques, 1990), 627–28. For an English translation, see *The Lais of Marie de France*, trans. Robert Hanning and Joan Ferrante (Durham, NC: Labyrinth, 1978).
11. See Stephen D. White, "The Problem of Treason: The Trial of Daire le Roux," in *Law, Laity,*

the legal proceedings that rely on ordeal (that is, a trial by battle or bodily test of guilt).[12] In fact, even after ordeals were officially denounced by the Church in 1215 (discussed below), romances depicted ordeal trials as spectacular and foolproof ways of rooting out treason, asserting that the witnesses of those ordeals ought to be understood as metonymic stand-ins for the community as a whole. For example, the fourteenth-century romance *Athelston* describes the fate of four kinsmen, one of whom, Athelston, ascends to the throne after the king dies without an heir. He appoints his kinsmen to various posts: one becomes the earl of Dover, another the earl of Stone, and the third the archbishop of Canterbury. Jealous when Athelston becomes close with the earl of Stone's family, the earl of Dover tells Athelston that the earl of Stone is plotting against him. Athelston resolves to kill the earl of Stone and his family, pursuing his punishment with blind rage until a series of trials by fire establishes their innocence and the earl of Dover's guilt. Significantly, each time the ordeal trial is performed, *Athelston* repeats the phrase "that sawgh the lordes of the land." (It occurs three times in an 812-line romance.) And at the end of the romance, the text asserts, "alle men myghten see with yghe" that the real traitor has been revealed and order restored.[13] In *Athelston,* diegetic and extradiegetic eyewitnesses alike function as members of the community who can attest that the threat has been averted, that justice has triumphed, and that the unifying authority of the king has been affirmed.

Thus, the diverse forms and practices of witnessing—whether personal experience, hearsay, ordeal trial, oral testimony, or written documents—were designed to produce a unified devotional or political community. Witnesses were called upon to provide accounts of events that revealed divine or royal judgment, and those accounts produced narratives that spoke to communal obligations, hierarchies, and rules. However, even as witnessing was recognized as fundamental to constructing and protecting legal, ideological, or doctrinal communities, literary portrayals of witnessing often constructed it as a way to highlight and trouble shifting ethical, legal, and doctrinal boundaries. Specifically, this book outlines how vernacular writers used depictions and discussions of witnessing to critique the modes of authority designed to

---

and Solidarities: Essays in Honor of Susan Reynolds, ed. Pauline Stafford, Janet L. Nelson, and Jane Martindale (Manchester: Manchester University Press, 2001), 95–115.

12. For a discussion of the importance of witnesses in understanding cases of injury, wrong, and "the king's peace" in Angevin and early common law, see Paul R. Hyams, *Rancor and Reconciliation in Medieval England* (Ithaca, NY: Cornell University Press, 2003), esp. chapters 4 and 5.

13. *Athelston,* in *Four Romances of England,* ed. Ronald B. Herzman, Graham Drake, and Eve Salisbury (Kalamazoo, MI: Medieval Institute, 1999); "that sawgh the lordes of the land" repeated at lines 589, 613, and 643, and "alle men myghten see with yghe" at line 803.

produce and protect differences between, for example, orthodox and heterodox doctrinal communities, or between law-abiding subjects and outlaws. Indeed, witnessing was an important way fourteenth- and fifteenth-century legal thinkers, ecclesiastical officials, and vernacular writers alike sought to expose the overlaps and fissures between various kinds of authorities and communities: between local justice and royal law, for example, or between lay and clerical claims of access to the divine Word.[14]

Indeed, testimony does not operate as a fully "historical" discourse, insofar as it cannot provide a perfectly accurate or "factual" account of an event. Nor does it operate as a purely inventive or "fictional" discourse, insofar as it operates according the assumption of fact or accuracy. Its liminal status between the historical and the imagined, or between the factual and the fictional, means that witness testimony can be fruitfully taken up by literary scholars and particularly, as I discuss below, by medievalists. Derrida's reading of Maurice Blanchot's *The Instant of My Death*, a first-person account of a man's near-death experience at the hand of Nazis, captures the importance of the "literary" at the heart of testimony: "In essence a testimony is always autobiographical: it tells, in the first person, the shareable and unshareable secret of what happened to me, to me, to me alone, the absolute secret of what I was in a position to live, see hear, touch, sense, feel."[15] Derrida articulates a central paradox in testimonial discourse: testimony both exposes an event and reveals the impossibility of articulating that event fully. A radically first-person discourse, witness testimony must nonetheless speak to larger, communal truths, whether legal, historical, or ideological. Yet because testimony cannot extract itself from the limits of the individual witness's perspective, it is for Derrida particularly linked to "the possibility of fiction, simulacra, dissimulation, lie, and perjury—that is to say, the possibility of literature" (29).

Indeed, the literary possibilities inherent in testimony emerge especially when it attests to distinctions between individual recollection and historical authenticity. In their work on the testimony of Holocaust survivors, Dori Laub and Shoshana Felman focus particularly on the relationship between psychoanalytic and historical testimony, recognizing "how issues of biography and history are neither simply represented nor simply reflected, but are reinscribed, translated, radically rethought and fundamentally worked over

---

14. For a discussion of the relationship between customary "folklaw" and official forms of statute and royal law in the fourteenth century, see Richard Firth Green, *A Crisis of Truth: Literature and Law in Ricardian England* (Philadelphia: University of Pennsylvania Press, 1999).

15. Jacques Derrida, *Demeure: Fiction and Testimony*, trans. Elizabeth Rottenberg (Stanford, CA: Stanford University Press, 2000), 43.

by the text."[16] For Laub and Felman, the gaps between individual memory and history in the survivors' testimony point to the friction between individual experience and communal truth. Those gaps also suggest the possibility of resistance against accepted communal knowledge or belief. Recalling one witness who testified about an Auschwitz uprising, Laub explains that the woman claimed with surety that four chimneys had been blown up, but in fact it had been only one. Laub argues that rather than offer factual evidence, the witness testified to the "bursting open of the very frame of Auschwitz," such that she "is breaking the frame of the concentration camp by and through her very testimony: she is breaking out of Auschwitz even by her very talking. She had come, indeed, to testify, not to the empirical number of the chimneys, but to resistance, to the affirmation of survival, to the breakage of the frame of death.... This was her way of being, of surviving, of resisting" (62). Laub points out here that testimony emphasizes the vexed relationship between individual experience and historical truth, and more crucially, she suggests that by paying attention to this vexed relationship, we allow for the possibility of resistance and critique, recognizing the ways testimony might operate as a critical response to the rules, obligations, and oppressions that can shape a community.

Taking up Laub's claim that an individual's testimony can function as critique or resistance of communal truths, Felman reminds us that to testify is more than to report a fact or an event: "Memory is conjured here essentially in order to *address* another, to impress upon a listener, to *appeal* to a community" (204, emphasis in original). Kelly Oliver similarly argues that witnessing is always structured as a dialogic relation with another. For Oliver, this means that witnessing foregrounds the ethical obligations required of individuals by their communities *and* that it permits those obligations to be reshaped and rearticulated. Because witnessing requires addressing another and being addressed, she suggests, it offers the possibility of empathetic, intersubjective engagement with another and thus the possibility of a community that coheres around mutual ethical responsibility rather than authoritarian systems of duty and punishment.[17] Thus, in their different ways, Derrida, Laub, Felman, and Oliver all define witnessing as a discourse that both attends to and remakes historical events, such that testimony can construct as well as critique communal experiences and obligations. They

---

16. Dori Laub and Shoshana Felman, *Testimony* (New York: Routledge, 1992), xiv. See also Dominick LaCapra, *History and Memory after Auschwitz* (Ithaca, NY: Cornell University Press, 1998).

17. Kelly Oliver, *Witnessing: Beyond Recognition* (Minneapolis: University of Minnesota Press, 2001).

also usefully explain that testimony is structured by a tension between two sometimes irreconcilable acts: on one hand, testimony can recount an event, narrating what a witness has seen with his or her own eyes or heard with his or her own ears, but on the other hand, testimony can bear witness to a truth that cannot always be verified, such as faith or repressed trauma.[18]

Witnessing has thus been understood by contemporary theorists as a discourse that must be read with a recognition of its mutual engagement with fact and fiction, and this hermeneutic imperative guides this book's investigation of medieval testimony. Indeed, medievalists have long focused on the vexed relationship between historical truth and literary invention, particularly in terms of authorial voice and what constitutes "evidence" from the medieval past. In his classic article on Chaucer's narratorial persona, for example, E. Talbot Donaldson warns readers of the *Canterbury Tales* not to mistake Chaucer-the-pilgrim for Chaucer-the-author, and to mistake neither for historian or reporter.[19] In response, H. Marshall Leicester argues that the *Tales*' verisimilitude invites the reader to confuse the voice of a pilgrim with a "real" person, and, by extension, to think of the voice of Chaucer-the-pilgrim as that of a "real" author. As he puts it, "All these views demand that the voice in a text be traceable to a person, a subject, *behind* the language, an individual controlling and limiting, and thereby guaranteeing, the meaning of what is expressed."[20] Yet, he continues, "Chaucer" does not exist apart from his utterances, and the search for an authorial presence is mere fantasy.[21] The status of the author and/or narrator is a critical topos in medieval literature, and any examination of witnessing, including this one, implies an interest in the authority of the speaker: that is, it implies an interest in the complex interface between historical or biographical evidence and literary expression. Indeed, how medieval authors and their texts both offer and obscure access to the past, and how the "literary" and the "historical" might be defined and seen to interact, are persistent, key issues for scholars of the Middle Ages. This book takes up these issues with a particular focus on late medieval testimonial practices, exploring how literary depictions of witnessing present us with opportunities to examine complex relationships between historical accuracy and literary invention, between evidence and narrative, between event and expression.

---

18. See Kelly Oliver, "Witnessing and Testimony," *Parallax* 10.1 (2004): 79–88.

19. E. Talbot Donaldson, "Chaucer the Pilgrim," *PMLA* 69.4 (1954): 928–36.

20. H. Marshall Leicester, Jr., "The Art of Impersonation: A General Prologue to the *Canterbury Tales*," *PMLA* 95 (1980): 213–24.

21. George Kane refers to such a search as "the fallaciousness of free biographical inference." *Chaucer and Langland: Historical and Textual Approaches* (London: Athlone, 1989), 7.

In investigating late medieval witnessing, then, this book attends both to the historical particularities of fourteenth- and fifteenth-century witnessing practices and to the interpretive commitments of critical work on testimony. It reveals the importance of witnessing to legal, devotional, and political models of community-formation in the fourteenth and fifteenth centuries, paying special attention to how English political and ecclesiastical authorities built upon and wrestled with statutory law. Specifically, this book demonstrates that late medieval vernacular writers took advantage of the complex claims to authority available in witnessing practices to explore how legal and devotional communities could be constructed, destroyed, and reformulated. In doing so, they drew on witnessing practices to examine increasingly blurred boundaries between clerical and lay, Latinate and vernacular, oral and written. By reading texts such as the *Pistel of Swete Susan*, *Piers Plowman*, and the *Testimony of William Thorpe* with legal and devotional witnessing practices in mind, this book offers a picture of late medieval culture that actively negotiated the "oral" and the "documentary" rather than describes a culture in which oral practices and interactions of old were supplanted by written or documentary ones.

Critics of medieval English culture will be familiar with the claim that literate culture can be viewed as an evolutionary step away from the oral cultures that preceded it from Walter Ong's seminal *Orality and Literacy*, which, despite its important assessment of communicative practices, nonetheless offers a somewhat teleological view of the relationship between oral cultures and written literacies. Ong still exerts some pressure on accounts of the development of scribal technologies, vernacular literacies, and documentary forms, though his assertions have been widely challenged and nuanced.[22] Mark Amodio, for example, has advocated that medieval scholars examine the Middle Ages via an "oral–literate nexus," in which they can recognize the performative dynamics of an oral poetics within the literate productions of Middle English texts. Doing so, he argues, would demonstrate that orality and literacy were interdependent rather than competing forces in post-Conquest England.[23] Similarly, Janet Coleman has shown that listening remained critical to medieval reading practices, even in an increasingly documentary culture.[24]

---

22. For an account of the endurance of Ong's work in medieval studies, see Janet Coleman, "Aurality," in *Middle English*, ed. Paul Strohm (Oxford: Oxford University Press, 2007), 68–85.
23. Mark Amodio, *Writing the Oral Tradition: Oral Poetics and Literate Culture in Medieval England* (Notre Dame, IN: University of Notre Dame Press, 2004).
24. Janet Coleman, *Public Reading and the Reading Public in Late Medieval England and France* (Cambridge: Cambridge University Press, 1996).

In studies of late medieval law and literature specifically, scholars have tended to focus on literacy and written documents. This is no doubt due to the legacy of legal records from the period, which are, not surprisingly, made up of such documents as official depositions, writs of complaint, and last wills and testaments. Moreover, following M. T. Clanchy's groundbreaking work on twelfth-century developments in legal apparatus and literacy, much of the scholarship on the relationship between medieval law and literature concentrates on a burgeoning culture of official documents and texts.[25] This work sees new kinds of bureaucratic writing emerging out of and nurturing the growing literacy in legal procedures and languages among lay communities. Scholars such as Steven Justice, Emily Steiner, and Wendy Scase have persuasively shown that the upsurge in lay literacy and the efflorescence of legal and bureaucratic documents in the later Middle Ages were mutually supportive. Moreover, as these scholars have shown, bureaucratic language and documentary form infiltrated vernacular texts, which in turn deployed these new vocabularies for ideological—and sometimes transgressive—purposes.[26] Such criticism has significantly broadened our picture of late medieval literacy and culture, depicting a world in which official and quasi-official documents softened the distinctions between clerk and layperson or between elite and "rustic."[27]

By tracing multiple practices of witnessing in fourteenth- and fifteenth-century England, this book builds on this scholarship, focusing especially on the status of bodily and vocal testimony in a culture increasingly inundated with written documents. Indeed, what is striking about the texts considered here is that they repeatedly depict the literate practices of official culture in conversation with "archaic" forms of evidence that rely on the body or the voice as their probative media. Literary explorations of witnessing take as their objects of investigation the testimonial media of juridical and religious witnesses: the tortured body of the martyr, the vocal testimony of the oath-taker, the documentary formulae of witness depositions. This book shows that Middle English writers imagined creative and dynamic interactions between bodily evidence, spoken testimony, and written text. For the authors this book studies, witness testimony functions as a flexible and vibrant discourse through which they can test the limits of witnessing

25. M. T. Clanchy, *From Memory to Written Record: England, 1066-1307*, 2nd ed. (Cambridge, MA: Blackwell, 1993).

26. Steven Justice, *Writing and Rebellion: England in 1381* (Los Angeles and Berkeley: University of California Press, 1994); Emily Steiner, *Documentary Culture and the Making of Medieval English Literature* (Cambridge: Cambridge University Press, 2003); Wendy Scase, *Literature and Complaint in England, 1272-1553* (Oxford: Oxford University Press, 2007).

27. See David Aers, "*Vox Populi* and the Literature of 1381," in *CHMEL*, 432-53.

to shape legal and doctrinal communities and communal obligations. In depicting witnessing as a crucial but flexible mode of community-formation, these authors critique the value of written documents as carriers of stable and legible authority, even as they rely on the documentary formulae and literate technologies of legal and bureaucratic texts.

Although each chapter focuses on the specifics of witnessing practices and formulae, a more general sketch of the history of witness testimony in English legal practice here will help contextualize some of the ideas described above. Witnesses were necessary for all sorts of legal procedures and transactions throughout the Middle Ages, from corroborating property transfers to attesting to the age of a minor at the time of a crime. Before 1215, legal actors known as "compurgatory witnesses" were primarily used as oath-helpers who could ratify for a judge the truth of the defendant's oath. In such forms of proof, the accused would take an oath of innocence and call upon several upstanding members of the community to testify not to the facts of the case per se, but to the accused's reputation and standing in the community. As Richard Firth Green has pointed out, this system depended on ethical relationships within a local community, in which truth (or "trouthe") was understood as communal agreement, rather than something more akin to "fact."[28] The system of compurgatory witnessing took seriously the perlocutionary nature of the oath, which constituted a form of proof that produced an inflexible contract between God and the swearer. Accordingly, God (as well as the saint upon whose relics the oath-taker swore) also became a witness, testifying to the truth of the case through the mouth of the oath-taker.[29]

If compurgation were unsatisfactory (because a compurgator failed to repeat the oath verbatim, for example, or because the compurgator did not have sufficiently solid social standing in the community), litigants could turn to battle, duel, or ordeal trial. These violent legal procedures were considered a last resort, used only when compurgation failed or when "open proof" (*lex aperta*) was required, as in cases of homicide or treason.[30] Trial by battle is precisely what it sounds like: two parties physically fought to determine the outcome of a case, often to the death but sometimes just to the satisfaction of a judge. Duel followed the same format and was used specifically in property disputes.[31] Ordeal trials proceeded a bit differently. Rather than pit two

28. Green, *A Crisis of Truth*, 100–103.
29. Paul R. Hyams, "Trial by Ordeal: The Key to Proof in the Early Common Law," in *On the Laws and Customs of England: Essays in Honor of Samuel E. Thorne*, ed. Morris S. Arnold et al. (Chapel Hill: University of North Carolina Press, 1981), 92–93.
30. Robert Bartlett, *Trial by Fire and Water: The Medieval Judicial Ordeal* (Oxford: Oxford University Press, 1988).
31. Nicole Clifton, "The Romance Convention of the Disguised Duel and the Climax of *Piers Plowman*," YLS 7 (1993): 123–28.

contesting parties against one another, ordeal put the accused through a series of physical tests designed to harness and make manifest the *judicium Dei* upon the body of the accused. A trial by hot iron, for example, required that the accused hold in his hands a red-hot piece of metal that had been blessed by a priest, then proceed through a public marketplace and drop the iron at the altar. Three days later, the priest would examine the accused's hands for signs of guilt, registered as blisters, red marks, or scabs.[32] Constructed as a legal ritual in which the community functions as a witnessing audience, ordeal trial relied on two complementary testimonial media. First, it relied on the body of the accused as the canvas upon which God could testify and offer his divine judgment. Second, it constructed the members of the accused's community as a single-voiced witness that could attest that the *judicium Dei* revealed during the procedure corroborated its beliefs and customs.

In the twelfth and thirteenth centuries, both ecclesiastical and common law maintained that testimony was a crucial, even fail-safe, form of proof. With the revival of legal study at the University of Bologna in the twelfth century, canonists turned to Roman legal models to outline testimonial practice, using what legal historians call Roman-canonical procedure, a hybrid jurisprudential field that reconfigured classical proceduralists such as Justinian within the spiritual mandates of Church law. Following Gratian's *Decretum*, canonists repeatedly claimed that witnesses offering vocal testimony were the best mode of proof, better than either written documents or the bodily "proof" offered in ordeal or battle.[33] Using both Roman law and Scriptural axiom as bases, canonists such as Gratian adopted the principle that two witnesses constituted full proof in ecclesiastical courts, and ecclesiastical law developed a sophisticated system of admitting and interrogating witnesses based on this evidentiary ideal.[34] Tancred's *Ordo judicarium*, for example, explains thoroughly that the two witnesses must take an oath and swear that they do not give testimony for money or out of friendship or hate.[35] It also

32. Rebecca V. Colman notes that there is a disturbing lack of quantitative precision in ordeal trial records. It is not at all clear what physical criteria would indicate guilt or innocence, so it seems that priests had enormous interpretive power to determine the outcome of these cases. "Reason and Unreason in Early Medieval Law," *Journal of Interdisciplinary History* 4.4 (1974): 589.

33. Charles Donohue, Jr., "Proof by Witnesses in the Church Courts: An Imperfect Reception of the Learned Law," in *On the Laws and Customs of England*, 127–58.

34. R. H. Helmholz, *The Oxford History of the Laws of England*, vol. 1 (Oxford: Oxford University Press, 2004), 338–41. For a discussion of the use of two witnesses, see Bernard Jackson, "Susanna and the Singular History of Singular Witnesses," *Acta Juridica* 37 (1977): 37–54.

35. *Pilii, Tancredi, Gratiae, Libri de iudiciorum ordine*, ed. Friedrich C. Bergmann (Bottingen, 1842), 3.8. For a discussion of hate and spite in legal disputes, see Hyams, *Rancor and Reconciliation*, 175–83.

insists that witnesses describe only what they have seen and heard personally. Hearsay was to be admitted only in very particular cases.[36]

Whereas twelfth-century ecclesiastical law codified the reliance on witness testimony in Church matters, Angevin legal reforms in common law conceptualized witnessing as a way to support the crown's control over legal communities. The twelfth century has long been marked as a critical moment in English legal history, when the operations of local courts were centralized under the aegis of royal administration.[37] In 1166, Henry II sent itinerant royal justices to the counties and shires to hear criminal cases, instituting an inchoate form of jury trial in which groups of twelve local representatives (called "assizes") would give their assessment of the case to royal judges, who would then rule.[38] When the *Tractatus de legibus et consuetudinibus regni Anglie qui Glanvilla vocatur* (known simply as "Glanvill"), the earliest common law treatise, surfaced around 1189 to outline the procedures for the use of juries and other legal standards of royal justice, it proposed trial by assize as a possible alternative to battle.[39] Indeed, when Glanvill specifically offers the choice between trial by battle or by assize, it considers the evidentiary certainty provided by witnesses used in battle and those who offer narrative testimony in assize to be complementary forms of proof. In cases of land disputes, for example, Glanvill states that for a battle, the complainant must come to court with a "champion" who can corroborate the complainant's claims, and he insists repeatedly that the champion must be "a suitable witness who heard and saw the facts" (*per idoneum testem audientem et uidentem*) (II.3). Alternatively, if the defendant chooses a trial by assize, then the "neighborhood" is called to testify to what they already know about the case: "recourse must be had to the neighborhood, whose verdict shall be conclusive" (*ad uisnetum erit recuperandum et eius uerodicto credendum*) (II.6).

Thus, for Glanvill, those who testify in battle and those who testify to the assize authenticate their authority in much the same way: they offer their eye- and ear-witness knowledge of facts on behalf of their community. Significantly, Glanvill saw the community as both a testimonial and judging

---

36. Donohue, "Proof by Witnesses," 131.
37. See, for example, F. W. Maitland and Frederick Pollack, *The History of English Law Before the Time of Edward I*, 2 vols. (Cambridge: Cambridge University Press, 1899). For an excellent summary of historians' emphasis on Angevin legal reforms and a nuanced reading of them, see Hyams, *Rancor and Reconciliation*, 155–86.
38. For a discussion of Henry II's role in constructing a new system of royal justice, see Bruce O'Brien, "Forgery and the Literacy of the Early Common Law," *Albion* 27.1 (1995): 1–19.
39. Most scholars agree that this text was likely not written by Ranulph de Glanvill, Henry II's chief justiciar. For a discussion of its authorship, see G. D. G. Hall's introduction to *Tractatus de legibus et consuetudinibus regni Anglie qui Glanvilla vocatur*, ed. and trans. G. D. G. Hall (Oxford: Oxford University Press, 1993). Hereafter cited parenthetically within the text.

body, since "in proportion as the testimony of several suitable witnesses in judicial proceedings outweigh that of one man, so this constitution relies more on equity than does battle; for whereas battle is fought on the testimony of one witness, this constitution requires the oaths of at least twelve men" (II.7). On one hand, then, witnesses were to testify "objectively," narrating facts and events they had seen with their own eyes and heard with their own ears. But on the other hand, witnesses were also to offer testimony on behalf of the community and judgment according to their communal beliefs. Used for multiple purposes and in multiple forms in both ecclesiastical and common law, witnessing was fundamental for asserting the customary, legal, and ethical contours of community, whether that community was understood as a local group of eyewitnesses who could attest to a *judicium Dei* or a twelve-person jury that could represent a communal accusation.

In 1215, the Fourth Lateran Council explicitly articulated the function and procedures of witness testimony in the service of shoring up the beliefs and customs of Christian community. Scholars have widely acknowledged the long-term effects of the Council's famous *Omnis utriusque sexus* decree, which required annual auricular confession to one's parish priest. The decree invigorated the production of texts that were designed to instruct both the laity and lower clergy on basic spiritual knowledge, and it helped develop new discourses of confession and instruction that sought to manage a relationship between the individual penitent and a larger doctrinal and spiritual community.[40] However, despite scholarly focus on the Council's decree about confession, the Council's document speaks much more frequently about witness testimony.[41] Indeed, it begins by establishing the unity of the Church through a citation from John 5: "Thus we read in the canonical letter of John: *For there are three that bear witness in heaven, the Father and the Word and the holy spirit, and these three are one;* and he immediately adds, *And the three that bear witness on earth are the spirit, water and blood, and the three are one,* according to some manuscripts."[42] The assertion of witnessing as a foundational principle of Christian unity inaugurates the Council's list of decrees, which was itself designed to cement the practices of a doctrinal community.

40. See, for example, Marjorie Curry Woods and Rita Copeland, "Classroom and Confession," *CHMEL*, 376–406; and Katherine C. Little, *Confession and Resistance: Defining the Self in Late Medieval England* (Notre Dame, IN: University of Notre Dame Press, 2006).

41. John W. Baldwin, "The Intellectual Preparation for the Canon of 1215 Against Ordeals," *Speculum* 36 (1961): 613–36. For a somewhat different take on the demise of ordeal trial as a result of the Fourth Lateran Council, see Hyams, "Trial by Ordeal," 101–4.

42. *Decrees of the Ecumenical Councils*, vol. 1, ed. Norman P. Tanner (Washington, DC: Georgetown University Press, 1990) 231.

The two decrees from the 1215 Council that focus specifically on witness testimony helped articulate important ways of thinking about the relationship between an individual witness and his or her doctrinal community. Canon 18, *Qualiter et quando,* which prohibited priests from blessing the instruments used in ordeal trial, sought to detach divine judgment from human processes of evidence and inquiry. Its procedural effect on witness testimony in English law was to institute inquisition as the most common court procedure, shifting away from accusation and denunciation.[43] Unlike inquisition, accusation required an individual complainant to initiate and carry out a prosecution; the complainant had to be of good standing in the community, and women, minors, excommunicates, and reputed criminals were barred from beginning court proceedings.[44] If the accuser failed to prove his case, he would suffer the same punishment meted out to convicted criminals. Denunciation followed the same process, differing only in that it required a Church official first to admonish the accused in an attempt to prevent a formal trial. Both accusation and denunciation relied on oaths to verify the truth of the complainant's accusations, and compurgatory witnesses were used by the complainant and by the defendant to support their reputations and corroborate their oaths.

Unlike either accusation or denunciation, inquisition did not require an individual complainant. Instead, based on the *Qualiter et quando* decree, a judge could initiate criminal proceedings based on *publica fama*, in which widespread acknowledgment of the crime took the place of individual accusation. Crucially, this shift made it possible to conceptualize an entire community—rather than an individual—as a complainant. Indeed, as the decree makes clear, rumors swirling around the community should not be taken lightly: "the superior should carry out the duty of his office not as if he were the accuser and the judge but rather with the rumor providing the accusation and the outcry making the denunciation."[45] Rather than issuing from the voice of a single accuser, a complaint emerged from the general public, and its truthfulness resided in the perceived unanimity of the community.[46] The recognition of a communal accusatory voice rendered compurgatory

---

43. H. A. Kelly, "Inquisition and the Prosecution of Heresy, Misconceptions and Abuses," in *Inquisitions and Other Trial Procedures in the Medieval West* (Hampshire: Ashgate Variorum Series, 2001), I.439–51.

44. Helmholz, *History,* 605–8.

45. "et si rei poposcerit qualitas, canonica districtio culpam feriat delinquentis: non tamquam sit actor et iudex, sed quasi deferente fama vel denunciante clamore, officii sui debitum exequatur." *Decrees,* 238.

46. Hence the phrase *ex frequenti et clamosa insinuatione,* typically used in defamation records. See Helmholz, *History,* 610.

witnesses obsolete, since it assumed all members of the community spoke with one voice against the defendant. Thus, through the *Qualiter et quando* decree, rumor (or, more precisely, public outcry) acquired sufficient legal status to initiate proceedings against someone.

In addition, Canon 38, the *Quoniam contra falsam* decree, required that scribes (as the decree puts it, either a public official or "two suitable men") compile written records of court proceedings. The canon stipulates that the judge keep the documentation for himself as well as furnish copies to each party upon request, in case disputes should arise about his handling of the case. In essence, the *Quoniam contra falsam* suggests that written documents can obviate both judicial misbehavior and misinterpretation. Consequently, as Richard Helmholz points out, it called into question the effects of oral pleading and testimony by suggesting that a written document could offer stable, enduring, and even inarguable evidence of judicial *acta*.[47]

In terms of witnessing, then, the Fourth Lateran Council illustrates two crucial issues that resonate both for later medieval jurists and for vernacular writers. First, the idea that trial could proceed based on "public outcry" gave rumor and gossip legal force, and vernacular writers often probed the legal and doctrinal ideal of a unified, evidentiary communal voice. Chaucer, for example, illustrates his worry about the power of rumor when he yokes "fals and soth" together in the House of Rumor.[48] Second, requiring legal documentation suggested that legal documents could supplant the ethical truths to which a community tacitly consented through local, customary practices. (Notably, many vernacular writers found work in clerks' offices or the Office of the Privy Seal, and the bureaucratic language of the documents they produced there often found its way into their poetry.) Yet for writers such as William Langland or the anonymous author of the *Pistel of Swete Susan*, the ideal of an accurate and stable written text became a point of contest as they tried to negotiate the various ways their own works would be copied, cited, and transmitted, even used as "evidence" for a range of unanticipated ideological purposes.

Thus, witnessing—construed both as communal belief and as written instruments of the court—was crucial to the Fourth Lateran Council's sense of a unified doctrinal community. Witnessing and its written instruments

---

47. Richard Helmholz, "*Quoniam contra falsam* (X 2.19.11) and the Court Records of the English Church," in *Als die Welt in die Akten kam*, ed. Susanne Lepsius and Thomas Wetzstein (Frankfurt: Vittorio Klostermann, 2008), 31–49.

48. *House of Fame* 2108–9, in *The Riverside Chaucer*. For a discussion of gossip in late medieval vernacular writing, see Susan E. Phillips, *Transforming Talk: The Problem with Gossip in Late Medieval England* (University Park: Pennsylvania State University Press, 2007).

were likewise crucial to statute law's sense of a unified political community. To take one important example, Henry de Bracton's mid-thirteenth-century *De legibus et consuetudinibus Angliae* imagined a coherent program of statute law and attempted to collate the complicated system of writs used in English criminal and civil procedure. It explained both how "suits and pleas are decided according to English laws and customs" as well as instructed the reader in "the art of preparing records and enrollments."[49] Bracton claims that his compilation will serve both the legal expert and the untrained layperson: "The general intention is to treat of law that the unskilled may be made expert, the expert more expert, the bad good and the good better, as well by the fear of punishment as by the hope of reward" (2.20).

Like Glanvill, Bracton offers defendants the choice of being tried by battle or by assize, replicating Glanvill's argument that a 12-person jury is more dependable than individual witnesses, because it relies on multiple oaths that promise to adhere to the truth. He also, like Glanvill, explains the mixed role of juries as both judging and testimonial entities: while juries are to present their *veredictum* to royal justices, they must also report criminal activity going on in their local communities: "And let them be told in private that if anyone in their hundred or wapentake is suspected of some crime they are to arrest him at once if they can. If they cannot, let them give his name, and the names of all those who are under suspicion, privately to the justices in a schedule and the sheriff will be ordered to arrest them at once and bring them under arrest before the justices, that the latter may do justice upon them" (2.329). Yet despite his careful explanation of how assize trials work, Bracton is tentative about the way testimony among various authorities might differ. He insists that credible witnesses must be able to give specific information, carefully outlining the facts to which any complainant must attest, such as the year, place, date, day, and hour of the event, as well as what he or she knows by "his own sight and hearing." The complainant must also "be consistent in what he says and in all circumstantial details" (2.388).

However, one notable exception to Bracton's requirement of consistency is the official documents used in court. He states that sometimes, particularly in cases of homicide, coroners' rolls and the sheriff's records differ because an accuser might forget the details of his story out of fear. Or perhaps, Bracton suggests, the sheriff who recorded the story has died and his rolls have gone missing (2.395–96). In these cases, the story with the most supporting documentary evidence should prevail in court, and other docu-

---

49. Henry de Bracton, *De legibus et consuetudinibus Angliae*, trans. Samuel E. Thorne (Cambridge, MA: Harvard University Press, 1968), 2.20.

ments ought to be dismissed. Bracton also worries about the possibility that the voice of the community could initiate legal proceedings, since "uproar and public outcry are at times made of many things which in truth have no foundation and thus the idle talk of the people is not to be heeded" (2.404). Distinguishing between legal clamor and "idle talk" (*vanae voces populi*) is the task of the judge, who must carefully examine the twelve jurors about the source of the suspicion. Defendants have the right to remove anyone from the jury they feel is acting out of enmity or revenge. For Bracton, then, witnessing is a necessary but imperfect mode of establishing legal truth and, by extension, community unity. He sees the pitfalls of oral testimony as well as those of written documents, but he also recognizes how important witnessing is to legal procedures and to policing the communities served by those procedures.

This outline of testimonial philosophies and practices is merely a snapshot of the range of issues that emerge in an analysis of medieval witnessing. Each chapter discusses specific witnessing practices with respect to the texts it analyzes, exploring how particular modes of testimony inform the texts' explorations of community-formation and -discipline. Altogether, these chapters depict witnessing capaciously, thinking of witnessing as practices that register and critique communal obligations and systems of authority. However, examining the wide implications of witnessing necessarily means this book cannot consider in detail all of the contexts it touches upon. For example, this book repeatedly returns to the problem of mediation and presence: that is, it explores how witnesses often functioned as intermediaries between divine truth and a skeptical community. Mediation and presence is a critical and complex issue at the heart of fourteenth- and fifteenth-century Wycliffism and Lollardy, and chapters 2 and 5 examine how the idea that clergy can act as mediators between God and an individual believer is articulated as a problem of witnessing in vernacular poetry and in fictionalized legal documents. But this book cannot treat fully the complicated theological and philosophical traditions surrounding mediation and presence. Rather, it seeks to show that witnessing is an important part of those traditions. Likewise, while this book demonstrates that witnessing was important to establishing the authority of the crown to trump local customary practices (as examined in chapters 1 and 3), it cannot discuss in detail the complex developments of royal law and parliamentary privilege in the fourteenth century. This book seeks instead to demonstrate that testimony and witnessing are central to a range of debates and controversies ongoing in the fourteenth and fifteenth centuries. With the many implications of witnessing in mind, this book concentrates on two critical issues at the heart of medieval witnessing: the production of legal and doctrinal communities and the truth-claims available in different witnessing media.

The first three chapters focus on the first of these issues, on how legal and doctrinal communities were asserted, disciplined, and reconfigured. All three specifically examine false witness, a concern that emerges in a wide range of texts, from pastoral manuals to royal statutes to lyric poetry. The ubiquitous worry about perjury, muddled oaths, and blasphemy in the fourteenth and fifteenth centuries points to more generalized anxiety about the failure of the mechanisms designed to harness the word of God on behalf of ecclesiastical and secular order. Episodes of false witness depicted in vernacular literature expose how the systems of power that depend on a declared intimacy with the divine might rest on flimsy claims, and these episodes thus explore how legal and ecclesiastical authorities could be resisted.

Chapter 1, "The Face of a Saint and the Seal of a King," examines the various kinds of witnessing practices used to produce a "nacioun" in Chaucer's *Man of Law's Tale*. This chapter argues that, though told by a sergeant of law, the *Tale* dramatizes the failure of legal inquiry, material evidence, and bureaucratic documents to construct and protect a unified Christian community. Its retelling of the hagiographical story of Constance, a saintly woman who endures numerous tortures without ever losing her faith in divine justice, depicts at its center Constance's public trial for a murder she did not commit. Chaucer uses a knight's false oath to elevate divine judgment over legal inquiry and to demonstrate how divine intervention into legal proceedings can convert a pagan king into a Christian one. Later, when the king's pagan mother forges royal letters to condemn Constance, Chaucer animates the widespread worry that the king's word can be easily manipulated. In doing so, he upholds the sanctity of the divine Word over and against the legal and political systems that work to authenticate the royal word by attaching it to the divine. That he does so through a lawyer's tale illustrates his ambivalence about the power of the law to produce and convey the communal beliefs upon which a Christian "nacioun" relies.

Chapter 2, "Silence, Testimony, and the Case of Susanna," examines how the depiction of false witness in the Scriptural story of Susanna works both to shore up and to critique doctrinal assertions of Christian female obedience. As told in the Book of Daniel, Susanna is falsely accused of adultery by two Church Elders and condemned by a legal trial; at the last second, the prophet Daniel saves her after she prays silently to God. After tracking the muffling of Susanna's voice in early patristic commentaries on the Book of Daniel, this chapter focuses on the *Pistel of Swete Susan*, an English alliterative version of the tale from the 1390s. It argues that the *Pistel* actively engages with the strategies of silence deployed by the early Church fathers who sought to translate Susanna into an exemplar of female obedience and chastity. The *Pistel* exposes the legacy of silence in the Susanna story and considers how her silence might be understood as a kind of testimony under English rape and adultery laws. The *Pistel*, this chapter shows, draws upon the Susanna story's long-term interest in silence, testimony, and doctrinal community to focus on contemporary legal procedure in England, probing the complex relationship between English statute law and Christian community.

Together, the first two chapters outline the ways that worries about perjury presented literary writers with opportunities to depict how an exemplary witness can resist corruptible legal models of authority to authorize a Christian community. Chapter 3, "Neighbors, Witnesses, and Outlaws in the Fourteenth and Fifteenth Centuries," focuses on the refusal to testify, a form of false witness different from, but no less worrisome than, perjury. This chapter explores how religious officials, jurists, and poets exploited the multiple registers of the Scriptural requirement to bear witness against one's neighbor. Tracing the term "neighbor" in thirteenth- and fourteenth-century pastoral treatises and common law, this chapter shows that the legal neighbor poses a challenge to the ideal of Christian unity emphasized in the Scriptural precept to "love one's neighbor." This challenge is foregrounded in a little-studied exemplum included in John Waldeby's collection of Sunday sermons, in which Waldeby excoriates a community for failing to testify to a rash of murders in the area, accusing them of "turning God into an outlaw." By contextualizing his exemplum with statutory laws on false witness, pastoral calls to neighborliness, and late medieval outlaw literature, this chapter argues that Waldeby suggests that a community united by its fidelity to the king and one united by spiritual responsibility to one another may be at odds.

These first three chapters all demonstrate how witnessing shapes, defends, and breaks community bonds, examining particularly how portrayals of false witness illustrate the centrality of witnessing in both formulating and critiquing doctrinal and legal communities. The final two chapters turn to the authoritative rhetoric of witnessing media, investigating the distinctions and similarities of claims made by the testifying body, voice, and document. William Langland's sustained investigation of witnessing is the subject of chapter 4, "*Piers Plowman,* Book, and the Testimonial Body." This chapter examines Langland's scenes of witness testimony throughout his poem, prominently displayed in the complaint of Peace against Wrong, in Lady Mede's trial, and, more surprisingly, in his discussion of grace in the third vision as well as in the famous pardon scene. In these scenes of witnessing, Langland negotiates the experiential claims of the eyewitness and the iterability of Scriptural citation, conceptualizing personification as a fulcrum between the two. His investigation of witnessing, personification, and material texts culminates in his peculiar personification, Book. As a vocal text with a body, Book poses challenging questions about the authoritative rhetoric of the martyrological body, material texts, and the divine Word. The chapter ends by examining how Langland's exploration of witnessing and textuality in *Piers Plowman* resurfaces in fifteenth- and sixteenth-century Langlandian texts, which deploy witnessing for overtly reformatory ends.

The fifth and final chapter, "Witnessing, Presence, and Lollard Communities," examines witnessing practices in the heated debates surrounding Scriptural access and vernacular literacy at the turn of the fifteenth century. Focusing on the staged interrogation between Archbishop Arundel and William Thorpe, this chapter tracks how the particularities of heresy inquisition—*inquisitio heretice pravitatis*—provide Thorpe a structure and vocabulary by which he can resist Arundel's attempts to trap him into abjuring his heterodox beliefs. For Thorpe, the interplay between his own presence in the interrogation room and an absent audience who will "witness" the truth of his beliefs offers him strategies to create an extralegal "deposition" that exceeds the circumstances of its production and the constraints of its genre.

Although these five chapters take the literature of fourteenth- and fifteenth-century England as their main objects of investigation, they also suggest that the multiple portrayals of witnessing in the later Middle Ages might help us conceptualize how we understand the differences and overlaps between a fictional story and an evidentiary one: that is, how we understand literary and historical evidence. This book thus ends with a coda that traces the uses of textual and historical "witnesses" in New Philology and New Historicism, parsing how this vocabulary conveys a certain access to the Middle Ages and a kind of historical accuracy. Analyzing medieval witnessing, this book suggests, challenges us to consider critically how we authenticate scholarly evidence and determine the truth of the work that we do.

one

The Face of a Saint and the Seal of a King

CHAUCER'S MAN OF LAW takes seriously his role as a *narrator,* the medieval Latin term for both someone who enters legal pleas and a teller of stories. Indeed, the Man of Law insists he is not a poet, but a lawyer, insulting Chaucer as a silly rhymer: "'I kan right now no thrifty tale seyn / That Chaucer, thogh he kan but lewedly / On metres and on rymyng craftily, / Hath seyd hem in swich Englissh as he kan / Of olde tyme, a knoweth many a man.'"[1] He then claims that he will "speke in prose," as is befitting a lawman such as himself (II.96).[2] However, despite his assertions regarding his own authority to tell the kind of story he wants to tell—presumably, a lawyerly one, rather than a literary one—the Man of Law finds himself subject to the Host's requirement to tell an entertaining tale. In fact, throughout the *Canterbury Tales,* the Host reminds the pilgrims that the storytelling game is structured by his organization and command, not theirs. In the Man of Law's introduction, the Host explicitly reminds the Man of Law that he has assented to the Host's sovereign judgment:

1. II.46–50. All citations from the *Canterbury Tales* are from the *Riverside Chaucer* and will be cited parenthetically by fragment and line number.
2. For a discussion of the possible multiple registers of prose here, particularly given that the Man of Law uses rime royal, see A. S. G. Edwards, "'I Speke in Prose': *Man of Law's Tale,* 96," *Neuphilologishe Mitteilungen* 92 (1991): 469–70.

"Ye been submitted, thurgh youre free assent,
To stonden in this cas at my juggement,
Acquiteth yow now of youre biheeste;
Thanne have ye do youre devoir ate leeste." (35–38)

The Host's establishment of his sovereignty over this ad hoc community of pilgrims here not only insists on his status as judge; it more broadly inaugurates a vision of sovereign law and community-formation that the Man of Law himself goes on to parse in his *Tale*. Indeed, sovereignty and community are central preoccupations throughout the *Canterbury Tales*.[3] Written at the end of the fourteenth century, when Richard II sought to shore up the coercive authority of the crown even as various legal and bureaucratic institutions emerged to mediate between its sovereign power and the commons, gentry, barons, and peasants, the *Canterbury Tales* repeatedly depicts and explores how sovereign law might be asserted and protected.[4] The Man of Law's story in particular deconstructs the complicated ways sovereign authority can both foster and threaten communal sensibilities, focusing on the production of an English "nacioun," which the Man of Law fantasizes to be a community united by divine justice and protected by the sovereign rule that relies on divine justice.

Curiously and significantly, the Man of Law depicts the requirements and consequences of sovereign law through a well-known hagiographic tale that turns on the treachery of false witness. In this story, the obedient and patient Constance is sent by her father from Rome to Syria to marry the Muslim Sultan there, but his mother ships her off to sea in a rudderless boat. After she lands in Northumberland, her steadfast devotion converts the Northumbrians as well as their pagan king, Alla, who marries her. But after a trial for murder (of which she is falsely accused), Constance is again shipped away in a rudderless boat. Miraculously, she returns to Rome, where she is reunited with her father and with Alla. Repeatedly tested by false accusations, fallible systems of evidence, and unjust punishments, Constance remains patient

---

3. For example, the *Tale of Melibee*, which the Man of Law was perhaps slated to tell in early versions of the *Tales*, depicts at length Melibeus's deliberations about how to assert his authority to punish the thieves who have broken into his house and beaten his wife and daughter. Likewise, the *Wife of Bath's Tale* overtly depicts women's desire for *soveraynetee*, while the *Clerk's Tale* illustrates Walter's right to sovereign power over Griselda even as it critiques the severity with which it is performed. See Donald C. Green, "The Semantics of Power: *Maistrie* and *Soveraynetee* in *The Canterbury Tales*," *Modern Philology* 84.1 (1986): 18–23.

4. Nigel Saul, "The Kingship of Richard II," in *Richard II: The Art of Kingship*, ed. Anthony Goodman and James Gillespie (Oxford: Clarendon, 1999), 37–57.

throughout her ordeals, sure of her devotion to God and steadfast in her belief that divine justice will prevail.[5]

Specifically, the Man of Law uses the repeated scenes of false witness at the heart of the Constance story to assert the importance of faith in shaping and expressing the sanctity of a community and to explore how a sovereign leader must relinquish his earthly legal power to the authority of divine justice.[6] Indeed, though the story provides an exemplary model of womanly obedience and Christian faith in Constance, the Man of Law's focal interest in his exploration of nation-building is Alla, the Northumbrian king who defies his mother, his culture, and his religion to marry Constance and produce a Christian heir to his throne. As a sovereign lord, Alla is the "primary organizing figure around whom divergent groups build or contest alliance," insofar as he functions as the figure through which the Man of Law can conceptualize how Muslim and pagan communities might be subsumed under the aegis of Christian law.[7] In other words, the Man of Law produces in Alla the image of a Christian sovereign that can turn away from a pagan past and transform a "strange nacioun"—the phrase the Man of Law uses to describe Syria—into one that adheres to divine law. The *Man of Law's Tale* thus explores both how sovereign legal authority can shape a doctrinally bound, divinely sanctioned "nacioun" and how culturally and ideologically distant communities—in this case, Muslim Syria and pagan Northumberland—can be transformed into nations that work according to Christian principles of obedience.[8] The scenes of false witness depicted in the *Tale* illustrate that witnessing is a critical tool in shaping a community whose sovereign authority

---

5. See Robert M. Correale's contribution to *Sources and Analogues of the "Canterbury Tales,"* vol. 2, ed. Robert M. Correale and Mary Hamel (Cambridge: D. S. Brewer, 2009), 277–350.

6. Joseph E. Grennen, "Chaucer's Man of Law and the Constancy of Justice," *JEGP* 84.4 (1985): 498–514.

7. Patricia Clare Ingham, *Sovereign Fantasies: Arthurian Romance and the Making of Britain* (Philadelphia: University of Pennsylvania Press, 2001), 9.

8. Many scholars have convincingly demonstrated that the *Man of Law's Tale* fundamentally, and in multiple ways, explores tensions around cultural difference and proximity: the proximate difference between Islam and Christianity, between England and Rome, and between masculine, institutional forms of religious hierarchy and feminine, extrainstitutional modes of devotion. These studies illustrate that the *Man of Law's Tale* depicts racial, cultural, and religious difference in order to stage a series of conversions to reassert what Paul Strohm has called the Man of Law's "complacently pious" set of Christian values. See Susan Schibanoff, "Worlds Apart: Orientalism, Antifeminism, and Heresy in Chaucer's *Man of Law's Tale*," *Exemplaria* 8.1 (1996): 60–96; David Wallace, *Chaucerian Polity: Absolutist Lineages and Associational Forms in England and Italy* (Stanford, CA: Stanford University Press, 1997), 182–211; Kathy Lavezzo, "Beyond Rome: Mapping Gender and Justice in the *Man of Law's Tale*," *SAC* 24 (2002): 149–80; Elizabeth Robertson, "The 'Elvyssh' Power of Constance: Christian Feminism in the *Man of Law's Tale*," *SAC* 23 (2001): 143–80; and Paul Strohm, *Social Chaucer* (Cambridge, MA: Harvard University Press, 1989), 167.

stems from divine justice, one that can claim a Christian heritage and erase its non-Christian ancestry.

The urgency of these scenes draws, in part, upon the many Scriptural precepts that describe witnessing as a way to construct and protect Christian community. Indeed, it would be difficult to overestimate the Scriptural preoccupation with giving testimony and bearing witness as a way of formulating doctrinal unity. For example, Hebrews 12:1 describes saints who can testify to God's perseverance as a "cloud of witnesses" (*nubem testium*), while Acts repeatedly calls the apostles Christ's witnesses (*testes*). Likewise, Luke requires that witnesses confirm the resurrection of Christ, linking together preaching and witnessing: "And he said to them, Thus it is written and thus it behooved Christ to suffer and rise again from the dead on the third day, and that penance and the remission of sins should be preached in his name to all people, beginning in Jerusalem, and you are witnesses to these things."[9] Giving and hearing testimony is fundamental to affirming and repeating one's faith, and one also bears witness to one's faith by listening to sermons, remembering Christ's suffering, and attending Mass. Moreover, witnessing binds members of a community together by offering them opportunities to attest to collective beliefs. The Man of Law depicts witnessing as a way to draw together a unified "nacioun" that is bound by its subjects' mutual Christian faith and dedication to a sovereign leader. Strikingly, he envisions such community unity by critiquing legal models of witnessing as fallible and divisive.

In the *Tale*'s first scene of false witness, a treacherous knight accuses Constance of a murder he himself has committed. Although all the physical evidence points to her guilt, Constance's pale face, a face of innocence and steadfast faith, belies the knight's accusation. The second episode of false witness occurs after Alla has converted and has married Constance. It depicts the king's pagan mother, Donegild, repeatedly sending counterfeit royal documents to Alla while he is away at war in Scotland to frame Constance for producing a "monstrous" heir to the throne. Taking up the crisis of false witness, sovereign power, and divine justice dramatized in the first episode, this extended scene conceptualizes false witness not as courtroom perjury, but rather as the manipulation of royal documents and official seals, a crime that was understood to be treasonous false witness by the second half of the fourteenth century. By staging the falsification of royal documents, this episode plays upon contemporary fears about the fallibility of the royal word

---

9. Luke 26:46–48: "Et dixit eis quoniam sic scriptum est et sic oportebat Christum pati et resurgere a mortuis die tertia, et praedicari in nomine eius paenitentiam et remissionem peccatorum in omnes gentes incipientibus ab Hierosolyma vos autem estis testes horum."

and bureaucratic documents at the hands of forgers. The *Man of Law's Tale* thus yokes together two distinct forms of false witness—courtroom perjury and forged documents—to consider how false witness, in its many forms, is a threat to divine justice and Christian sovereignty. Reading these two episodes together reveals the Man of Law's overall project to portray multiple kinds of false witness as real dangers to the ability of sovereign law to shape Christian community and protect its boundaries, and, by extension, to register how crucial witnessing is to building a divinely sanctioned "nacioun."

False Oaths, Bloody Knives, and Constance's Pale Face

The *Man of Law's Tale* begins in Syria, where a company of merchants tells the story of the Roman emperor's beautiful daughter, whom they encountered during a trade trip. When they returned to Syria, the story goes, they described Constance so vividly to the Sultan "that al his lust and al his bisy cure / Was for to love hire while his lyf may endure" (II.188–89). Wanting to marry Constance based on her reputation alone, the Sultan consults a "privy conseil," which argues that it cannot imagine that a Christian prince would permit his daughter to wed a Muslim, since "ther was swich diversitee / Bitwene hir bothe lawes" (II.220–21). Undeterred, the Sultan agrees to convert rather than lose Constance, and he convinces his barons to do the same. When word of his conversion gets back to the Roman emperor, he agrees to send Constance to live in Syria as part of a peace-keeping strategy between the two nations. Though she weeps that she will be sent to a "strange nacioun," away from friends and family, Constance nonetheless reluctantly agrees to go, telling her father, "'Allas, unto the Barbre nacioun / I most anoon, syn that it is youre wille'" (II.281–82). Syria is thus established as a "nacioun" that is alien and barbarous, distant from the Rome she knows. Nonetheless, when she arrives, "she peyneth hire to make good contenance" and perform dutiful obedience to her father (II.320). Upon Constance's arrival in Syria, the Sultan's mother, enraged that her son has converted, puts together a welcome feast for the new queen only to brutally kill the Sultan and the converted Christians and ship Constance out to sea in a rudderless boat.

The abruptly truncated episode in Syria establishes the tale's overall concern with the necessity of constructing and articulating an English "nacioun" based on Christian belief and, by extension, of contending with a threatening power whose royal authority and sense of community is not shaped by Christian virtue. The Syrians' "strangeness" and "barbarity" indicate both their distance from the Roman world from which Constance hails and the

Man of Law's dismissal of the Syrians as a people truly worth imagining as a kindred "nacioun." Geraldine Heng reads the sudden ending of the Syrian episode as an assertion of the radical difference of Syria from England and Rome: "Both Syria and English Northumberland might be heathenish foreign lands to a Christian 'Roman' princess," Heng writes, "but Syria—the 'Barbre nacioun'—unlike England, presents the prospect of a penultimate alienness, an alienation beyond the pale, by virtue of the race and color of its constituents, even when the aliens have been Christianized."[10] Indeed, the Man of Law focuses his attention on those communities that might be successfully absorbed into a Christian "nacioun," rather than on a truly "alien" nation that cannot be made to attest to the righteousness of a Christian community. Thus, when the next episode mirrors and amplifies the Syrian story in an extended episode of false witness, it suggests that pagan Northumberland is close enough to Christian sovereign law to merit extended treatment, such that the Man of Law can imagine it as a community that might someday bear witness to Christian truths and divine justice.

After the Sultaness ships Constance away from Syria, Constance lands under an unnamed castle in Northumberland, where a constable comes upon her and takes her in to live with him and his wife, Hermengild. As the story details Constance's transformative effect on the constable and his wife, it also offers a short geohistorical narrative of Britain, saying that no Christians lived in Northumberland anymore, having fled to Wales and leaving the pagan "olde Britons" in the region. Yet according to the Man of Law, Christianity still lurked on the edges of Northumberland: "But yet nere Cristene Britons so exiled / That ther nere somme that in hir privetee / Honoured Crist and hethen folk bigiled / And ny the castel swiche ther dwelten three" (II.547–50). The suggestion of Christians living "in hir privetee" in pagan Northumberland sets up the central issues that govern the ensuing episode of false witness: that is, how witnessing might construct and monitor the boundaries of a properly English, Christian "nacioun." To imagine a narrative in which a nation of Christians can be imagined, sanctioned, and protected, the Man of Law stages an elaborate episode of perjury that establishes Constance, the faithful Christian and daughter of Roman royalty, as Northumberland's preeminent witness to divine truth. Significantly, this episode uses two contradictory forms of witnessing to establish divine justice as the foundation for Christian nationhood. On one hand, the embodied testimony of the Christian martyr serves as a critical backdrop for this

---

10. Geraldine Heng, *Empire of Magic: Medieval Romance and the Politics of Cultural Fantasy* (New York: Columbia University Press, 2003), 233.

scene. Specifically, Constance's "good contenance," which she had tried to assume when she landed in Syria, is registered here as her "pale face," and it functions as a powerful site of Christian conversion.[11] On the other hand, the Man of Law explores the legal authority of King Alla to testify as both inquisitor and judge, ultimately presenting his legal authority as a secondary, earthly model of witnessing that must harness divine justice to authorize itself.

When Constance is discovered by the constable, he finds he can understand her, even though she speaks "a maner of Latyn corrupt," and he takes her home to care for her (II.519). After living with her a short while, the constable and Hermengild find they are so taken with Constance's diligence that they are filled with a powerful feeling of grace and convert to Christianity. The Man of Law tells us that Constance's face is the initial locus of her power to convert: "She was so diligent, withouten slouthe, / To serve and plesen everich in that place / That alle hir loven that looken in hir face" (II.530–32). Likewise taken in by her beautiful face, a young knight finds himself overwhelmed with love for her, though Constance rebuffs his persistent advances. Stung by Constance's rejection, one night the knight kills Hermengild and plants the bloody knife in Constance's bed to frame her for the crime. The next day, when the constable finds his wife dead and Constance unable to explain what happened, he goes to King Alla to report the murder. The constable then also admits how he found Constance on the shore and took her in. Alla immediately recognizes Constance as "so benigne a creature," an innocent defendant who must stand a trial like a lamb being led toward its death. Yet as the sovereign legal authority in Northumberland, he must initiate legal proceedings, during which the false knight gives seemingly incontrovertible firsthand, eyewitness testimony that Constance committed the murder.

The ensuing scene of perjury depicts multiple sites of witnessing and truth-telling: the body of the condemned functions as a witness to God's justice, for example, and physical evidence, oaths, and the probative claims of a communal voice likewise compete for the authority to expose the truth, both legal and divine. The contradiction between divine law and human testimony crystallizes in the image of Constance's face, which the Man of Law has already established as a site that can express obedience to sovereign law, stir Christian grace, and even inspire conversion. When the trial begins, a crowd gathers to watch their beloved Constance be tried for the heinous crime, and

---

11. See Robertson's discussion of the power of Constance's face to convert others in "The 'Elvyssh' Power of Constance," 162–63.

she moves slowly through the crowd, headed toward what looks like certain doom. Significantly, the Man of Law takes a moment here to address his fellow pilgrims. "Have ye nat seyn somtyme a pale face," he asks,

> Among a prees, of hym that hath be lad
> Toward his deeth, wher as hym gat no grace,
> And swich a colour in his face hath had
> Men myghte knowe his face that was bistad
> Amonges alle the faces in that route?
> So stant Custance, and looketh hire aboute. (II.645–51)

This narratorial intrusion is peculiar to Chaucer's version of the tale: neither Nicholas Trevet nor John Gower includes it in his version of the Constance story. Examining this momentary departure from the narrative, Carolyn Dinshaw notes that Constance's pale face is one of many Chaucerian pale faces that denote despair. For example, Palamon's face drains of blood when he sees Emily for the first time in the *Knight's Tale*, and Criseyde pales when she learns she will be traded to the Greeks in *Troilus and Criseyde*.[12] Dinshaw argues that Constance's paleness not only registers her anguish; it must also be understood relative to the cultural and religious differences of the once-heathen Northumbrians, so that this particular stanza works to locate her Christian innocence in her facial pallor. As Dinshaw asserts, in the *Man of Law's Tale*, "paleness is marked white Christianity" (22).

Constance's face certainly offers an obvious visual of her Christian patience and virtue, drawing upon the medieval commonplace that links whiteness to Christian innocence. In addition, the Man of Law's particular focus on the face in this stanza—as Dinshaw points out, he uses the word "face" four times in these seven lines—suggests his desire to counter the false legal testimony that could condemn Constance by asking the pilgrims to imagine the face of an innocent, one that can provide a kind of moral testimony that transcends courtroom practices and exposes divine truth rather than legal proof. Significantly, in a wide range of medieval texts, faces attest both to the possibility of divine revelation and to the way divine wisdom can be obscured in human systems of testimony. When a face does offer access to

---

12. Carolyn Dinshaw, "Pale Faces: Race, Religion, and Affect in Chaucer's Texts and Their Readers," *SAC* 23 (2001): 19–41. See also Heng, who argues that in the Constance narrative, "the recognition of racially marked differences of color and bodies is articulated through the authoritative, masterful grammar of religious difference; simultaneously, religious difference itself is articulated through the grammar of physiognomy, color, and genealogy, posited on normative bodies and the norm of human whiteness." *Empire of Magic*, 232.

divine knowledge, it often embodies the sublime fear and awe encountered by the witness who sees the divine face. For example, Langland's dreamer begins his search for "kynde knowyng" with Holy Church, noting that when he first saw her, "I was afered of hire face" (I.10). Likewise, for Julian of Norwich, witnessing Christ's pallid face during the Passion leads to a glimpse of divine grace:

> I saw His swete face as it was drye and blodeles with pale deyeng, and sithen more pale, dede, langoring, and than turnid more dede into blew, and sithen more browne blew, as the flesh turnyd more depe dede. For His passion shewid to me most propirly in His blissid face, and namly in His lippis.[13]

For Julian, Christ's pale face enacts both the violence and the grace of his death, and Julian insists elsewhere that seeing his face during the Passion taught her that "we ought se of Him graciously, than arn we sterid by the same grace to sekyn with gret desire to se Him more blisfully" (356–57). In contrast to Exodus, in which God tells Moses, "You cannot see my face, for no one shall see me and live" (Ex. 33:20), the incarnate Christ offers a glimpse of the divine face and thus the possibility of accessing divine wisdom in earthly form. By extension, the face of a saint can also attest to divine knowledge, as, for example, the Legend of St. Stephen suggests. When Jews accuse Stephen of having blasphemed the law of Moses in his sermons, they send two false witnesses to "verify" their accusations.[14] But Christ turns Stephen's face into the face of an angel to be witnessed by all those gathered to judge the case: "And thanne all tho that weren in the iugement sawe the visage of hym as the visage of an aungell. And that was the victorie of the secounde batayle" (45). Similarly, when the fourteenth-century preacher's handbook, the *Fasciculus Morum*, quotes the Psalms in its discussion of false witness ("'You have thought unjustly that I should be like you; I will reprove you and set myself against your face'"), it warns sinners that divine justice will produce the truth before their faces, specifically rebuking false witnesses by asserting the divine face as the site of truth-telling and revelation (167). Faces can even be the site of divine knowledge for priests seeking to manage their unruly congregants. One poem included in the Vernon manuscript, for example, describes a story about a parish priest

---

13. *The Shewings of Julian of Norwich*, ed. Georgia Ronan Crampton (Kalamazoo, MI: Medieval Institute, 1993), 589–93.

14. Jacobus de Voraigne, *Gilte Legende*, vol. 1, ed. Richard Hamer, EETS 327 (Oxford: Oxford University Press, 2006), 44–55.

who, suspicious of two rowdy parishioners, prays "that he might know by the face" which is worthy to receive the sacrament of the altar. At the next Mass, as the priest looks out onto his congregation, he is astonished to see that some have red faces (the tyrants), some black (the lechers), some swollen (the backbiters) and some "pure and bright," which signify those who are clean of sin.[15]

But the medieval face does not always operate as a clear sign of divine wisdom; some texts present the face as a hermeneutic crux that must be unpacked. In *Pearl*, for example, the Maiden's "white face" seems at first to be a clear indication of her close relationship with God, and the Dreamer claims that her face stirs his desire for grace, much like Julian's encounter with Christ's face does: "The more I frayste hyr fayre face, / Her fygure fyn quen I had fonte, / Suche gladande glory con to me glace / As lyttel byfore þerto watz wonte."[16] Later, when the Dreamer is bold enough to ask the maiden who formed her "fair figure," he suggests that the beauty of her pale face exceeds human language: "Pymalyon paynted neuer þy vys, / Ne Arystotel nawþer by hys lettrure, / Of carped þe kynde þese propertez" (750–52). He thus suggests that her face, as an allegorical symbol of God's love, gestures to the possibility of revelation, a revelation that would exceed the confines of earthly language. However, as J. A. Jackson has pointed out, the Dreamer begins to become infatuated with the earthly beauty of her face, describing her ivory skin and gray eyes with courtly language. By indulging his earthly desire for the maiden and her beauty, the Dreamer disengages the Maiden's face from the possibility of divine revelation, insofar as her face "is not the face of the Maiden but the face of the Dreamer's own construction, an obstacle, ultimately, that he creates for himself."[17] In other words, as the Dreamer becomes increasingly enchanted by the Maiden's face and her beauty, he transforms her face into an object upon which he can map his own earthly desire, rather than recognizing it as a symbol that can render God's plan legible. Thus, as *Pearl* demonstrates, a pale face does not always signify Christian virtue or innocence; its signification can shift according to the desires of the observer.

15. "Septem Miracula de Corpore Cristi," in *The Minor Poems of the Vernon Manuscript Manuscript*, pt. 1, ed. Carl Horstmann, EETS 117 (London: Kegan Paul, Trench, Trubner, & Co., 1892), 206.
16. *Pearl*, in *The Poems of the Pearl Manuscript*, ed. Malcolm Andrew and Ronald Waldron (Exeter: University of Exeter Press, 2002), 169–72.
17. J. A. Jackson, "The Infinite Desire of *Pearl*," in *Levinas and Medieval Literature: The "Difficult Reading" of English and Rabbinic Texts*, ed. Ann W. Astell and J. A. Jackson (Pittsburgh, PA: Duquesne University Press, 2009), 161.

Similarly, when the Man of Law asks the Canterbury pilgrims to imagine the pale faces of fearful defendants as they head toward legal condemnation, he produces a hermeneutic crux that belies the ostensible simplicity of the image. Constance's pale face ought to convince both the crowd and the Canterbury pilgrims that divine truth can be made intelligible on the saintly body, particularly as torture and death loom.[18] Yet by linking Constance's face to the face of an anonymous, fearful defendant—one who, in the Man of Law's example, could be either innocent or guilty—the Man of Law emphasizes that her white face may not offer a transparent sign of innocence. Notably, such ambivalence about the pale face is reflected in medieval courtroom manuals, which suggested that a witness's pale face could reveal that he or she is hiding something. As William Durand warns lawyers in his *Speculum judiciale*: "Often, a face's paleness, redness, or stuttering made it so that less faith might be given, as in: Oh, how difficult it is not to show crime on one's face."[19] For Durand, the face functions as a bodily site of legal truth, but paleness did not necessarily indicate either innocence or honesty; in fact, a white face could point to the witness's guilt or even to perjury as easily as it could point to his or her innocence.

The Man of Law may want Constance's face to function as a symbol of God's grace as the legal system fails her, but her pale face does not immediately produce any divine intervention into the trial proceedings or into the false testimony that has condemned her. However, although Constance's pale face fails to function as the immediately legible signifier of innocence and divine revelation the Man of Law imagines, it serves a broader purpose in constructing the Canterbury pilgrims as witnesses to the injustices being perpetrated in Alla's court. By calling attention to Constance's face and departing from the narrative action to address the pilgrims, the Man of Law turns the image into an appeal for justice that contradicts the courtroom proceedings he is describing. In doing so, he asks the diegetic crowd and the pilgrims alike to empathize with Constance's plight at the hands of the false knight. He also encourages empathy for Alla, as both Constance and Alla are confined by the earthly systems of evidence and judgment to which they are subject, systems that fail to reveal Constance's innocence and thereby fail to enact divine justice.

18. For a discussion of Constance's depiction as a saint in the *Man of Law's Tale*, see V. A. Kolve, *Chaucer and the Imagery of Narrative* (Stanford, CA: Stanford University Press, 1984), 297–358. For a discussion of the saintly face in medieval imagery, see Michael Edward Moore, "Meditations on the Face in the Middle Ages (With Levinas and Pickard)," *Literature and Theology* 24.1 (2010): 19–37.

19. "Saepe pallor vultus, rubor & titubatio faciunt ut minus fidei alicui habeatur, iuxta illud: O quam difficile est crimen non prodere vultu" (I.iv.7).

For the Man of Law, then, Constance's face operates as a call to empathy through which the pilgrims can contemplate the way innocents who faithfully adhere to Christian ideals can be vulnerable to the fallibility of legal practices. Specifically, her face signals how such vulnerability sets the stage to transform the pagan Northumbrians who are witnessing the trial into a unified community that is drawn together through its common empathy for the Christian defendant. Accordingly, Constance's pale face functions, as Emmanuel Levinas would say, as an epiphanal sign that exposes the radical difference of the Other, wherein the encounter with the face of another produces the possibility of divine transcendence. As Levinas puts it, "The dimension of the divine opens forth from the human face."[20] For Levinas, the encounter with a radically different Other need not result in the violent sublimation described by a Hegelian dialectic (against which he explicitly argues).[21] Rather, an encounter with the face of another arrests that kind of violent revulsion, producing instead a charitable response to another human being. As James J. Paxson helpfully explains, the face is "the visage of one we meet and *must not* do violence against, the forward sign of the human body we must clothe, feed, and whose thirst we must slake."[22] With an empathetic and ethical response to the Other, Levinas claims, comes the possibility of divine connection:

> The dimension of the divine opens forth from the human face. A relation with the Transcendent free from all captivation by the Transcendent is a social relation. It is here that the Transcendent, infinitely other, solicits us and appeals to us. The proximity of the Other, the proximity of the neighbor, is in being an ineluctable moment of the revelation of an absolute presence (that is, disengaged from every relation), which expresses itself. His very epiphany consists in soliciting us by his destitution in the face of the Stranger, the widow, and the orphan. . . . God rises to his supreme and ultimate presence as correlative to the justice rendered unto men. (78)

Levinas argues here that the empathetic response to another's face not only opens the possibility of accessing the divine, it also produces a social relationship that calls for a charitable response to another rather than a violent

20. Emmanuel Levinas, *Totality and Infinity: An Essay on Exteriority*, trans. Alphonso Lingis (Pittsburgh, PA: Duquesne University Press, 1969), 78.
21. Bernard Waldenfels, "Levinas and the Face of the Other," in *The Cambridge Companion to Levinas*, ed. Simon Critchley and Robert Bernasconi (Cambridge: Cambridge University Press, 2002), 63–81.
22. James J. Paxson, "The Personificational Face: *Piers Plowman* Rethought through Levinas and Bronowski," in *Levinas and Medieval Literature*, 144.

one. Accordingly, the face can produce a sense of community, producing a mutually empathetic response among proximate people that unifies them via the common recognition of divine presence.

Read through a Levinasian sense of the empathetic encounter with the face of the Other, Constance's pale face signals two contradictory cruxes central to the *Man of Law's Tale*. First, as Dinshaw and Heng make clear, it clearly reveals the *Tale*'s racial and cultural politics, in which the white face of the innocent Christian transfixes and transforms the Muslims and pagans who witness it. In doing so, her face motivates a set of social relationships that establish a clear hierarchy between Christian and non-Christian, white and nonwhite, and, presumably, English and non-English. At the same time, however, it constructs Constance's pale face as the visage of another to whom the audience (both the Northumbrian crowd and the pilgrims) must respond with a sense of charity and empathy. These audiences must imagine a community that reframes the injustices about to take place in the trial with a new ideal of divine justice that emerges from the recognition of God's presence in Constance's face. By asking if they have seen a face like Constance's, fearful of the legal machinery of condemnation and human systems of evidence, the Man of Law positions both the crowd and the Canterbury pilgrims to attest to how these earthly legal proceedings fail to account for Constance's beatific innocence and to imagine her face as the locus of divine justice that will unify them through mutual empathy and conversion.

Thus, the Man of Law's momentary shift away from the narrative to call upon the pilgrims to imagine Constance's pale face turns them into witnesses who can attest to the possibility of Alla's sovereign power to convert and to unite a Christian "nacioun." Indeed, as Levinas goes on to explain, the encounter with another's face is always a both visual and juridical one, in which such an encounter requires one to bear witness to the vulnerability of the Other. Bearing witness, he says, "produces the commencement of intelligibility, initiality itself, principality, royal sovereignty, which commands unconditionally" (201). Because the face prefigures discursive categories such as veracity and deceit, it can circumvent the ambiguity of the true and the false to which all earthly justice is subject. Thus for Levinas the face attests to epiphanal possibilities and ethical requirements, rather than to the truth of a particular event. Yet Levinas also claims that bearing witness to another's face expresses the unconditional power of command at the heart of royal sovereignty. Its attachment both to empathetic response and to an unconditional royal sovereignty makes the face a crucial sign of benevolent sovereign power as well as of communal unity. As something that must be witnessed, Constance's face operates in the *Man of Law's Tale* as the primary site of both transcendental divine justice and sovereign Christian community. Accordingly, Constance functions outside the testimonial discourse of courtroom witnesses, which is always subject to varying degrees of truth-telling and deceit.

Nonetheless, Constance must stand trial, and the depiction of the trial focuses on other forms of testimonial authorization: in particular, the oath. When the trial begins, the knight who falsely accused Constance of murder confidently swears on a "Britoun book" and testifies to her guilt. The designation of the oath-text as a "Britoun book" is a peculiarly Chaucerian detail, and it emphasizes that this episode of false witness tries to expose how authentic witnessing can produce a specifically English community that coalesces around divine justice. Moreover, the knight's oath can be contextualized within fourteenth-century preoccupations with how false oaths can hasten the moral deterioration of the perjurer, unravel social fabrics, and destroy communities. According to *Handlyng Synne*, for example, taking a false oath turns God and the saints against the blasphemer and distances the blasphemer from his own internal moral compass:

ȝyf þou by god or our lady
Or ouþer seyntys þat þou sweryst by,
þou dost hym bere fals wytnes
Of þy lesyng þat soþ hyt ys.
How shulde þey þan helpe þe at þy nede
Whan þou hem draghst to þy falshede?
And þyn ynwyt, þyn owne skyle,
Aȝenseyþ þe þan & euermore wyle.[23]

To swear oaths thoughtlessly, as this wealthy man does, "dismembers" Christ.[24] Likewise, the *Fasciculus Morum* argues that perjury implicates God as a false witness and that the perjurer "burdens and hurts God by laying sin on him even more than that Jews did by killing Christ and laying punishment on him."[25] False oaths relive the trauma of Christ's torture by calling

23. Robert Mannyng of Brunne, *Handlyng Synne*, ed. Idelle Sullens (Binghamton, NY: Medieval and Renaissance Studies, 1983), 639–46.
24. The idea that false oaths tear at Christ's body was commonplace in Middle English didactic literature as well as in visual depictions of false swearers in church paintings. See Miriam Gill, "From Urban Myth to Didactic Image: the Warning to Swearers," in *The Hands of the Tongue: Essays on Deviant Speech*, ed. Edwin D. Craun (Kalamazoo, MI: Medieval Institute, 2007), 137–60.
25. "magis gravat Deum et ledit inponendo sibi malum culpe quam Iudei Christum occidendo et inponendo malum pene." *Fasciculus Morum,* ed. and trans. Siegfried Wenzel (Univer-

upon God, Christ, or the saints to act as accomplices in supporting the false testimony. Accordingly, for the *Fasciculus Morum,* false witnesses are worse than the devil, who "dares to commit every evil but does not dare to swear" (167).

Notably, in the second half of the fourteenth century, pastoral writing on false witness increasingly turned to legal exempla to expose the damaging effects of false oaths and lying, offering detailed taxonomies of the ways and reasons why legal actors might turn to perjury. For example, the *Speculum Vitae,* William of Nassington's versified translation of the *Somme le Roi* from around 1370, devotes some time to discussing false witness in its section on "sins of the tongue," which includes blasphemy, lying, and gossip.[26] In this section, Nassington describes perjurers as those who "do Godde mare skathe, / For ilk day þai do hym on rode, / And ilka day þay shede his blode / With sharp athes in body and hede" (14148–51). Here, false oaths are thought to function as violent weapons against the body of Christ, wounding the devotional community that coheres around his suffering body. The *Speculum* also pays considerable attention to perjury and suspicious legal practices in its discussion of avarice, listing the specifics of various legal officers' potential to bear false witness after listing the kinds of criminals who lie and steal for their own gain (such as common robbers and those who aid and abet thieves).[27] For example, Nassington states, "Fals Executours may bi skille / Be called Robbours for þai do ille; / þai suld thurgh Halykirke rede / Mynistre leely þe godes of þe dede / For thurgh athe þai er bunden þarto / And with þa dede godes leelly to do" (6521–26). After condemning false beadles, summoners, bailiffs, and sheriffs—all of whom use their legal status to bribe defendants and thus operate like common robbers—the *Speculum* turns its attention to those who "falshed vses agayne þe lawe": that is, false pleaders, plaintiffs, defendants, lawyers, and jurors. The false pleader is particularly insidious both because he does not see the sin in presenting false evidence and because he can make others blind to his falsehood. As Nassington puts it, "He charges noght his conscience / To shewe a fals euydence. / His falshed may men noght wele knawe, / For he can couer it with þe lawe. / þarefore in wrange he es mare balde; / A False Auoket he may be talde" (6673–78).

---

sity Park: Pennsylvania State University Press, 1989), 166–67.

26. *Speculum vitae,* ed. Ralph Hanna, EETS 331–32 (Oxford: Oxford University Press, 2008). For the dating of the poem, see Hanna's introduction, lx–lxiii.

27. For a discussion of the *Speculum*'s critique of legal officials, see Kathleen E. Kennedy, *Maintenance, Meed, and Marriage in Medieval English Literature* (New York: Palgrave, 2009), 90–92.

Like Nassington's false pleader, the false knight in the *Man of Law's Tale* uses the law to cover his treacherous perjury, and indeed it seems that his formulaic adherence to legal procedure and his confident oath-taking would substantiate his claims in the eyes of the court. But the Man of Law describes how, just as the false knight swears upon the book and utters his testimony, a disembodied hand abruptly surfaces and chops at his neck, causing him to fall down and his eyes to burst out of his face. The astonished crowd then hears a voice:

> A voys was herd in general audience,
> And seyde, "Thou has desclaundred, gilteless,
> The doughter of hooly chirche in heigh presence,
> Thus hastou doon, and yet hold I my pees!"
> Of this mervaille agast was al the prees;
> As mazed folk they stoden everichone,
> For drede of wreche, save Custance alone. (II.673–79)

The miracle of the disembodied hand convinces the crowd and Alla that Constance is a victim of false witness, verifying both her innocence and God's ability to make guilt and innocence visible on the human body. Once again, the face is the locus of divine justice, as the knight's face serves as the canvas upon which God enacts his punishment. Indeed, the fact that it is specifically his eyes that burst out of his face exposes the fallibility of the "eyewitness" testimony he offers the court.

Notably, Gower's version of the false knight's condemnation takes a slightly but significantly different path. After the knight swears an oath that his accusations are true, the voice of God emerges to articulate the legal truth of the matter:

> A vois was herd, whan that they felle,
> Which seide, "O dampned man to helle,
> Lo, thus hath God the sclaundre wroke
> That thou agein Constance hast spoke:
> Beknow the sothe er that thou dye."[28]

Although both Gower and Chaucer imagine God's voice emerging to explain why the legal proceedings cannot account for the "sclaundre" perpetrated by

---

28. John Gower, *Confessio Amantis*, vol. 2, ed. Russell A. Peck (Kalamazoo, MI: Medieval Institute, 2003), II.880–84.

the false knight, Gower omits the bodily "merveille" that spectacularly concludes Chaucer's version of the episode. For Gower, divine justice supports legal procedure; the voice of God insists that the knight confess his perjury, after which he abruptly but unceremoniously dies. Gower's depiction of the end of the scene of false witness thus highlights the way divine intervention can reaffirm legal process.

In contrast, Chaucer's version turns to the divine truth of the "merveille," a term that indicates wondrous response rather than legal or scientific analysis.[29] On one hand, Alla's use of an oath-text upon which the knight can verify his testimony (or expose his perjury) demonstrates Alla's judicial supremacy as both king and judge; indeed, unlike either Trevet's or Gower's versions of the story, Chaucer portrays Alla as interrogating the knight and deciding the case.[30] Yet on the other hand, as Lavezzo has pointed out, this scene depicts Alla's juridical authority as dangerously far from the divine justice that ultimately determines Constance's fate. Despite his careful inquiries of the knight, Alla is unable to prove the knight guilty of perjury and murder. Crucially, the marvelous intervention of divine justice into his own inadequate juridical system of assessment and judgment spurs him and many others in the crowd to convert to Christianity. Thus, Chaucer's version of this scene of false witness first establishes the boundaries of Alla's royal sovereignty and legal authority vis-à-vis the divine truth embodied by Constance's pale face. It then rejects the legal work of inquiry, testimony, and physical evidence in favor of the "merveille" that indisputably establishes Constance's innocence. The "merveille" of the disembodied hand of God that emerges to arrest and transform the legal proceedings taking place establishes the power of a Christian God and, by extension, the power of a Christian Constance, over and above the legal sovereignty embodied by Alla.

Crowds, *Clamor*, and the Marvel of Divine Justice

When the Man of Law turns away from legal analysis to divine marvel, he emphasizes that these happenings occur in front of a crowd ("prees") that witnesses the marvelous intervention on Constance's behalf. For the Man of Law, the crowd functions as a potential legal entity, a group of witnesses with

---

29. See Caroline Walker Bynum, *Metamorphosis and Identity* (New York: Zone, 2001), esp. chapter 1, "Wonder," 37–75; and L. O. Aranye Fradenburg, "Simply Marvelous," *SAC* 26 (2004): 1–27.

30. In the *Chroniques*, Alla merely punishes the knight, and in the *Confessio Amantis*, Alla later hears about the divine justice that decides the case. See Lavezzo, "Beyond Rome," 168.

the power to attest to the *judicium Dei* and thus to Constance's innocence. Moreover, the Man of Law envisions the crowd as a crucial synecdoche for the Christian "nacioun" he wants to imagine. His depiction of a witnessing "prees" draws on contemporary testimonial practice, since crowds had, in fact, assumed a new legal status in the second half of the fourteenth century. In particular, as Scase has shown, *clamor* came to imply widespread complaint or the collective probative voice of a community. *Clamor* surfaced as a legal principle at the beginning of the fourteenth century as a feature of inquisitional process. It signified a common complaint of the community, which could function as an accusatory voice. By the 1340s *clamor* could be used to produce notoriety or *publica fama*, which would initiate legal proceedings by claiming general communal knowledge of wrongdoing. *Publica fama* was recorded by the production of several bills or writs of complaint or, more informally, by the documentation of widespread complaint signaled by the formulaic phrase "the clamor of the people" (*clamour de poeple*) (Scase 55–56). In other words, fourteenth-century complaint procedure relied on bills that announced common knowledge of criminal activity, or *clamor*, to establish the grounds for having someone stand trial.

Toward the end of the fourteenth century, parliament mobilized *clamor*'s claims of communal representation to delimit the crown's juridical and political reach. In 1376 the "Good Parliament" impeached several royal counselors and ministers by drawing upon the probative phrases "clamor of the commons" or "clamor of the common people," and ten years later, the "Wonderful Parliament" impeached Michael de la Pole, the king's chief counselor, based on an "ancient law" that said a king could be deposed if he did not rule in accordance with good counsel (Scase 63–65). The following year, however, a panel of judges appointed by Richard decreed that parliament could not impeach a minister of the crown without the king's assent, and Michael de la Pole was released from prison. In response, the Appellant Lords lodged formal complaints of treason on behalf of the people against a number of government officials.[31]

Clamor was thus a legal linchpin in these complex negotiations between crown and commons toward the end of the century. Given its topical immediacy and legal importance, it makes sense that the Man of Law might gesture toward the evidentiary power of a crowd as he explores—even diminishes— Alla's legal power as king, inquisitor, and judge to determine the case against Constance. Chaucer himself was involved in parliamentary politics, as a

---

31. For a discussion of the political buildup to the Wonderful Parliament, see J. J. N. Palmer, "The Parliament of 1385 and the Constitutional Crisis of 1386," *Speculum* 46.3 (1971): 477–90.

controller of wool customs between 1374 and 1386, a clerk of the King's works, a deputy forester, and a diplomat to Spain, among other positions.[32] Given his work as a government bureaucrat, Chaucer was very familiar with royal and parliamentary systems of representation, and as Matthew Giancarlo shows, such bureaucratic and political knowledge undergirds his poetic exploration in the *Canterbury Tales* and elsewhere of how political communities formed and articulated themselves.[33] Moreover, as a sergeant-at-law, the Man of Law himself would have been a member of the Order of the Coif, whose members were considered the authorities on parliamentary law and who often acted as royal counsel.[34] He is thus not only in a position to recognize the legal role of a clamorous crowd in the Constance case, but he might also be inclined to see the voice of the people as an important control over the reach of sovereign rule. We might thus be tempted to read his emphasis on the "prees" watching Constance's trial as a counterweight to Alla's legal authority and the courtroom evidentiary procedures that will condemn Constance. Perhaps this "prees" attests to her legal innocence and moral rectitude, enacting the Christian unity Constance inspires.

However, despite the legal and literary interest in "common voice" at the end of the fourteenth century as well as Chaucer's particular dedication to conceptualizing how communities might collectively "speak," it is particularly notable that the Man of Law depicts this "prees" as silent. Without a clamorous voice of communal complaint, this crowd fails to perform its legal role as community of defendants which might try to protect the innocent Constance from a trial designed to put her to death for a crime she did not commit. We might thus instead read this crowd's silence as an indication of Chaucer's distrust of crowds as political and legal authorities. As Chaucer instructs his readers at the beginning of the *Balade de Bon Conseyl*,

---

32. See Matthew Giancarlo, "'Oure is the voys': Chaucer's Parliaments and the Mediation of Community," in *Parliament and Literature in Late Medieval England* (Cambridge: Cambridge University Press, 2007), 129–78, esp. 129–31.

33. At the beginning of his tale, the Man of Law says that the "commune voys of every man" spoke of Constance's goodness and beauty, and he takes this common voice to be so trustworthy that he hopes Constance herself will be made queen of all of Europe (II.154–61). Although Chaucer perhaps means us to understand that the "commune voys" stands in for God's, as used by a fourteenth-century lawyer such as the Man of Law, the phrase must also gesture to the relatively new practice of admitting public opinion and rumor as the probative testimony of a community. See David Weisberg, "Telling Stories about Constance: Framing and Narrative Strategy in the *Canterbury Tales*," *Chaucer Review* 27.1 (1992): 45–64.

34. Wallace describes the Man of Law's professional affiliations; see *Chaucerian Polity*, 183. For a longer explanation of the occupation of medieval sergeants-at-law, see J. H. Baker's introduction to *The Order of Serjeants at Law* (London: Selden Society, 1984).

> Flee fro the prees and dwelle with sothfastnesse;
> Suffyce unto thy thing, though it be smal,
> For hord hath hate, and climbing tikelnesse,
> Prees hath envye, and wele blent overal.
> Savour no more than thee bihove shal,
> Reule wel thyself that other folk canst rede,
> And trouthe thee shal delivere, it is no drede. (1–7)

In this poem, Chaucer contrasts "prees" and "sothfastnesse," ending with an exhortation to the reader to pursue a spiritual pilgrimage and look to God for "trouthe." Here, the "prees" is an obstacle to the recognition of truth, instead sowing envy and hate within itself and failing to produce the ethical "trouthe" that is the foundation of justice and community.

Yet the Man of Law's illustration of the "prees" in his *Tale* does not suffer such overt condemnation. Instead, the Man of Law seems to suggest that this crowd recognizes that divine justice has taken over for legal process. He thus positions it as a collective witness both to the hand of divine justice and to the false knight's perjury rather than registers it specifically as a legal entity that must offer courtroom evidence. Its silence specifically suggests that the "prees" can recognize God's law over and above the legal practices and standards of evidence that cannot save Constance. Instead of offering the kind of clamorous complaint that could either provide evidentiary public opinion or portend unruly dissent, the silence of this "prees" enacts the medieval commonplace *vox populi, vox dei,* testifying to the miracle that reconceptualizes authentic testimony as an attestation to divine justice rather than the kind of legal witnessing abused by the false knight in Alla's courtroom.

With the silence of the witnessing crowd in mind, we might also note that the Man of Law uses passive voice to describe the false knight's punishment. In doing so, he suggests that the *vox dei* emerges as the primary legal and moral authority in this episode. As the Man of Law puts it, the false knight "was slayn for his untrouthe / By juggement of Alla hastifly" (II.687–88). The syntax carefully positions Alla's sovereign power between his legal authority and the divine hand of God that has just very publicly killed the knight. The specific agent of the knight's physical punishment is left opaque by the use of passive voice (he "was slayn"), but the Man of Law also recognizes the power of Alla's judgment to rule that the knight committed perjury. Indeed, as we shall see, the Man of Law repeatedly uses passive structure when describing legal judgments and punishments throughout his *Tale,* always arguing on behalf of divine justice while also gingerly affirming the juridical power of the sovereign.

This scene of false witness densely collates multiple kinds of witnessing practices to assert the power of divine justice over and above the apparatuses and procedures of human law. Only the divine hand and explanatory voice of God can intervene in these perfectly standard legal proceedings to protect her against the false testimony that almost condemns her to death. Notably, the oath, a method designed to harness the word of God as testimony of legal truth, is the only part of the legal process that works in this episode. But it works, of course, contrary to the false knight's desires: rather than solidify his story in the eyes of the crowd and Alla, it calls upon God to intervene on Constance's behalf. In depicting the marvelous hand of the divine, this episode of false witness insists that Alla's sovereign power draw its legal authority from divine justice, transforming the pagan king into a Christian believer and, by extension, producing a new Christian community that emerges from and is structured by the beliefs and behavior of its newly converted sovereign. To pursue Alla's transformation from pagan ruler to Christian sovereign more fully, the Man of Law goes on to describe a very different kind of false witness, one that urgently puts Christian sovereignty and community in jeopardy.

Letter-Writing, Forgery, and Treasonous Mothers-in-Law

After witnessing his trial overtaken by divine "merveille," Alla is fully convinced of the power of divine justice, and he marries Constance with a newfound devotion to Christ. To emphasize Alla's conversion, when the Man of Law tells the pilgrims that Alla and Constance married after the trial, he explicitly marks Alla as a Christian subject, rather than a sovereign king: "And after this Jhesus, of his mercy, / Made Alla wedden ful solempnely / This hooly mayden, that is so bright and sheene; / And thus hath Crist ymaad Custance a queene" (II.690–93). With the matter of Alla's Christian conversion resolved and the authority of divine justice established, the *Man of Law's Tale* turns its attention to Alla's need to produce a genealogical line that will naturalize and extend his newfound Christian sovereignty. Again, false witness becomes the narrative impetus to imagine a unified "nacioun": now, episodes of false witness emphasize the importance of producing a Christian genealogy on behalf of Northumberland. Specifically, by threatening the sanctity of this inchoate Christian "nacioun," false witness provides the Man of Law the opportunity to express the importance of witnessing for bolstering the power of Christian sovereignty.

Soon after their wedding, while Alla leads his army into Scotland, Constance gives birth to their son, Mauricius, and the constable sends a letter that describes "this blisful tidyng" along with "othere tidynges spedeful for to seye" (II.726–27). But this message is intercepted by Alla's mother, Donegild, who remains unconverted. She is, not surprisingly, terrifically unhappy with her son's marriage to Constance and with his conversion. Constance's pagan mother-in-law, like the Muslim Sultaness, embodies the non-Christian origins of Alla's royal line, an origin that uncomfortably exists in the very recent past.[35] While Mauricius's right to the throne should be indisputable since he is Alla's first male child, Donegild strives to erase her grandson's existence from the realm along with Constance's and to restore Northumberland to its pre-Christian state of pagan sovereignty. She does so by manipulating the royal seal used to authenticate bureaucratic documents, a crime that in the fourteenth century was thought be a severe form of false witness, akin to treason.

When the Man of Law depicts Donegild's attempt to destroy Mauricius's claim to Alla's throne, he needles a particularly sore subject for Chaucer's audience. Succession to the throne was a major source of worry in the fourteenth century, particularly when the inheritance of the French throne came under dispute during the Hundred Years' War. In 1337, Edward III laid claim to the French throne through his mother, Isabelle, Phillip IV's daughter. In response, the French insisted that a woman could neither claim the throne for herself nor transmit the throne to her offspring.[36] The French response to Edward's claim to the throne inaugurated debates regarding whether women could transmit the royal patriline, and the English, encouraged by the possibility that they could take the French throne, emphasized the English rule that women could inherit and transmit royal bloodlines (Florschuetz 32). Yet the acceptance of female genealogical privilege in England was disputed later in the century, when Edward had to determine his own heir to the English throne. In a letter patent issued by Edward in 1376,

---

35. Sue Niebrzydowski, "Monstrous (M)othering: The Representation of the Sowdanesse in Chaucer's *Man of Law's Tale*," in *Consuming Narratives: Gender and Monstrous Appetite in the Middle Ages and the Renaissance*, ed. Liz Herbert McAvoy and Teresa Walters (Cardiff: University of Wales Press, 2002), 196–207.

36. For an outline of how these political developments influenced Chaucer's *Man of Law's Tale*, see Angela Florschuetz, "'A Mooder He Hath, but Fader Hath He Noon': Constructions of Genealogy in the *Clerk's Tale* and the *Man of Law's Tale*," *Chaucer Review* 44.1 (2009): 25–60. For a discussion of the territorial disputes that drove the Hundred Years' War, see Christopher Allmand, *The Hundred Years War: England and France at War c. 1300–1450* (Cambridge: Cambridge University Press, 1988).

in which he addressed concerns about his advancing age and the death of the Prince of Wales, the rightful heir to the throne, he reluctantly noted that the throne must go to the Prince's only surviving son, Richard, who was then only nine years old.[37] Richard's inheritance of the throne would pass over Roger Mortimer, the son of Phillippa of Clarence, Edward's granddaughter. Edward prioritized the nine-year-old Richard's inheritance because of his more direct—and specifically male—lineage through the Prince of Wales, and he thus suggested that royal patrilines ought to be authenticated through male genealogies.[38] Notably, however, in 1399 Henry of Bolingbroke claimed to be the true heir of the throne by tracing his genealogy to the elder brother of Edward I through his mother.

The complicated dynastic politics of the late fourteenth century turned on the problem of whether to accept women's participation in royal patriline. In the extended depiction of Donegild's attempts to thwart Constance's status as a new queen, Chaucer presents an extreme illustration of the ongoing crisis about the genealogical status of women, and he imagines Constance's mother-in-law as a monstrous example of the threats to community sanctity that can arise when women are considered royal genealogical agents. To offset the threat of a mother-in-law taking charge of the throne's inheritance, the Man of Law pronounces Constance's royal status as divinely sanctioned, baldly stating that "Crist ymaad Custance a queene" (II.693). Constance thus not only displaces Donegild as the reigning woman in the realm, she also draws her sovereign status from Christ. Indeed, the Man of Law explains Donegild's response to her son's marriage as her devastation that her son should marry "so strange a creature" (II.700), recapitulating the language Constance had used to describe Syria. As Angela Florschuetz succinctly puts it, Donegild's "hostility arises from a specifically dynastic concern, the potential for her son's mysterious wife to hijack his lineage by producing a child marked by her own strangeness" (49).

Donegild's strategy to disrupt Constance's genealogical privilege and Mauricius's inheritance is to falsify the bureaucratic devices designed to attest to the will of the sovereign in his absence. Her acts of false witness deliberately seek to dismantle the sovereign Christian community taking

---

37. Michael Bennett, "Edward III's Entail and the Succession to the Crown, 1376–1471," *English Historical Review* 113 (1998): 584.

38. As Bennett points out, the principle that a woman could pass a royal title to a son was well established in England, and Edward III himself had endorsed this principle when he laid claim to the French throne. With respect to Edward's transfer of power to Richard, Bennett states, "Given his advocacy, for over forty years, of the claims of the heir general against the claims of the heir male, the settlement of 1376 would appear a *volte-face* of some magnitude" (592).

shape through Alla's marriage to Constance and their production of a Christian heir. When the messenger encounters Donegild, he offers to include any letter she might want to send to her son in the packet of letters he is delivering; he takes care to show her that he holds official letters, marked with the royal seal: "'Lo, heere the lettres seled of this thyng, / That I moot bere with al the haste I may'" (II.736–37). The emphasis on the seal here alerts Donegild (and Chaucer's audience) that these letters are diplomatic missives from the queen to the king rather than personal communications between a wife and husband. Such an emphasis, in turn, frames Donegild's subsequent treachery as interference with the operations of the state, forecasted when the Man of Law describes her as "ful of tirannye" (II.696). Donegild tells the messenger she does not have any message to send her son at the moment, but later, she plies the messenger with ale. When he falls asleep, she steals his letters and writes another: "And countrefeted was ful subtilly / Another lettre, wroght ful synfully, / Unto the kyng direct of this mateere / Fro his constable, as ye shal after heere" (II.746–49). Alfred Hiatt has demonstrated that Chaucer's use of the term "countrefeten" here is one of the earliest instances in which the verb was applied to textual falsification, and it carries with it the specific negative connotations of the production of an imitation with the intent to deceive.[39] Chaucer further takes care to note Donegild's careful machinations by describing the forged letter as "wroght," a term he pejoratively attaches to magicians in the *Franklin's Tale*.

Counterfeiting royal letters in late medieval England was considered a serious crime, one that was, significantly, understood as a form of false witness. Glanvill includes forgery of documents under the rubric *crimen falsi*, which includes forging charters, royal seals, measurements, and coins.[40] A century later, Bracton specifically argues that the forgery of a lord's seal should be considered treason, a position upheld by the 1352 Statute, which lists forgery as one of seven kinds of treasonous false witness, including plotting the death of a king, aiding his enemies, or violating his wife or daughter.[41] Seals were critical authenticating apparatuses in England, either impressed in wax on the document itself or hung from a ribbon or strip of parchment. Clanchy has even described seals, particularly royal seals and those conveying the transfer of property, as "relics," arguing that they could be "seen and

---

39. Alfred Hiatt, *The Making of Medieval Forgeries: False Documents in Fifteenth-Century England* (Toronto: University of Toronto Press, 2004), 28.
40. Glanvill 176–77.
41. Bracton considers forgery of the royal seal a crime of lese-majesty, "a crime which surpasses all others" (2.334). His discussion of forgery occurs at 2.337.

touched in order to obtain from it that authentic view and feel of a donor's wishes which no writing could adequately convey."[42]

Indeed, royal seals could sometimes be understood as metonyms for the royal body, thought to be material signs of authenticity through which divine justice could emerge. For example, in one striking twelfth-century commentary on Psalm 4, which asks, "Let the light of your face shine on us, Lord," the German theologian Gerhoh of Reichersberg writes, "The Lord impressed his face like a royal seal on our faces, mirrored in our spirits, a true mirror when it is pure."[43] In fourteenth-century English law, the body and the seal were likewise understood as reflections of one another. To take one example, a case from 1328, which describes a man named John Le Gode being brought before the King's Bench on charges of forging the royal seal, includes the sheriff's assurances that he has both the body of the criminal and the counterfeit seal. As the sheriff claims, "I have attached his body and the counterfeit seal found on him."[44] Furthermore, the sheriff asks the king to allow him to pass "the body" onto the Oxford sheriff because he does not know the extent of John's criminal network:

> Therefore, more honourable lord, please allow me to bring the body through my bailiwick and through Berkshire as far as Oxford, for as far as there I dare undertake to bring the body safely so long as I am in my own district, and then let the sheriff of Oxford accept the body by your warrant and safely bring it to the next county, and so from one county to another until the body has come to you and, if it please you, my lord, send one of your serjeants to whom I can safely hand over the body at your order. (33)

John's body is paramount here, as the sheriff seems particularly worried that this counterfeiter will be able to slip away easily en route to trial. More striking, however, is the sheriff's abrupt turn from focusing on the criminal's body to authenticating the material evidence he has at hand: "My lord, I have in my possession the seal, sealed with the seal of the prior of Bradenstoke, and that seal I send you in a pouch, sealed with the seal of the prior and with my own seal, by Simond de Asshe, my chaplain, the bearer of this letter" (32). The almost absurd multiplication of seals illustrates both the need

---

42. Clanchy, *From Memory to Written Record*, 247.

43. "Sicut enim regale sigillum plumbo vel auro impressum format in eo vultum seu faciam regis ita tibi omnipotenti est possibile per impressionem tuae formae faciem meam faciei tuae conformare." Gerhoh of Reichersberg, *Commentarius Aureus in Psalmos et Cantica Ferialia*, PL 193: 1199D–1200A. Cited in Moore, "Meditations on the Face," 21.

44. "ieo ai attache son cors et le seal conterfait troue sur ly," in *Select Cases in the Court of King's Bench under Edward III*, vol. 5, ed. G. O. Sayles (London: Selden Society, 1958), 32.

to authenticate legal transactions with bureaucratic seals and the profound worry about distinguishing a counterfeit seal from a real one. In fact, forging the seal was seen as an attack on the king, as violent and treasonous as an attempt to injure him bodily. In the second half of the fourteenth century, claims of counterfeiting became more and more common, and these claims increasingly worry about forging the king's seal. For example, a few cases from 1367 describe a counterfeiting ring that had not only forged the great and privy seals of the king, the pope, archbishops, and bishops, but had created machines capable of reproducing these forgeries.[45] Fears arose about the easy reproducibility of the king's seal and the concomitant diminishment of the seal's power, so in 1371 a petition was put in front of parliament to make the forgery of private seals punishable by life imprisonment.[46]

For the Man of Law, the ongoing anxiety about documentary forgery and the authenticity of the royal word provides him the context through which he can argue that true sovereign authority must come from divine power rather than bureaucratic apparatus. Donegild's particular forgery tries to destroy Constance's royal authority as queen by turning Constance into a genealogical disruption and community threat. Donegild's forged letter tells Alla that Constance has given birth to a monster and even implies that Constance herself is not of this world:

> The letter spak the queene delivered was
> Of so horrible a feendly creature
> That in the castel noon so hardy was
> That any while dorste ther endure.
> The mooder was an elf, by aventure
> Ycomen, by charmes or by sorcerie,
> And every wight hateth hir compaignye. (II.750–56)

Alla responds undaunted, giving a letter to the messenger that welcomes Mauricius as a "sonde of Crist," and he implores Christ to keep both his child and wife safe until he can return home. The Man of Law again emphasizes the authenticating, metonymic work of the king's seal, not only emphasizing that it was written "of his owene hand" but also describing the moment Alla seals his letter and hands it over to the messenger (II.759, 768). Yet once again, Donegild intercepts the messenger, plies him with ale, and takes the

---

45. *Calendar of Patent Rolls, Edward III*, vol. 14 (London, 1913) mem. 23d, p. 51.
46. Nigel Ramsay, "Forgery and the Rise of the London Scriveners' Company," in *Fakes and Frauds: Varieties of Deception in Print and Manuscript*, ed. Robin Myers and Michael Harris (Winchester: St. Paul's Bibliographies, 1989), 100.

letter. The Man of Law condemns the messenger with an apostrophic aside that suggests he has become, unwittingly, a false witness of the king's will:

> O messager, fulfild of dronkenesse,
> Strong is thy breeth, thy lymes faltren ay,
> And thou biwreyest alle secreenesse.
> Thy mynde is lorn, thou janglest as a jay,
> Thy face is turned in a newe array. (II.771–75)

His claim that the messenger's face is "turned in a newe array" recalls the image of Constance's pale face from the earlier trial. Here, we can read in the messenger's face his inability to protect the king's words and deliver them unaltered. Once again, the face exposes the moral truth of the witness, and here that truth is contrasted with the bureaucratic documents the messenger carries. The Man of Law follows up this condemnation with a harsher excoriation of Donegild's actions: "O Donegild, I ne have noon Englissh digne / Unto thy malice and thy tirannye! / And therefore to the feend I thee resigne; / Lat hym enditen of thy traitorie!" (II.778–81). Demonstrating his familiarity with the statutory laws that consider counterfeiting royal seals a form of treasonous false witness, the Man of Law links the messenger's and Donegild's crimes against the state through his apostrophic condemnations.

Donegild's counterfeit letter purports to be a message from Alla to his constable, commanding him to ship Constance and Mauricius off in the same rudderless ship that brought her to the Northumbrian shores. Sorrowfully, the constable complies, with the entire community coming out to weep at the injustice. The restaging of Constance's cold ejection from Syria presents the non-Christian mothers-in-law, Donegild and the Sultaness, as doubly disruptive to the new "nacioun" shaped by Christian patrilineage. Not only do they exile Constance from their lands and away from their besotted sons, they attempt to shun Christian rule on behalf of their Muslim or pagan communities. Revisiting the critical image from the earlier scene of false witness, Constance here emerges from the crowd with a "deedly pale face," accepting her fate as Christ's will and reassuring the crowd by recalling the divine justice that had intervened earlier: "'He that me kept fro the false blame / While I was on the lond amonges yow, / He kan me kepe from harm and eek fro shame / In salte see, althogh I se noght how'" (II.827–30). She also amplifies her trust in divine justice by calling upon Mary as a witness to Christ's suffering, and by extension, to her own. "'Thy blisful eyen sawe al his torment; / Thanne is ther no comparison bitwene / Thy wo and any wo man may sustene. / Thow sawe thy child yslayn bifore thyne yen, / And yet now lyveth my litel child, parfay!'" (II.845–49). Constance links her own "sight"—she cannot "se" how Christ will keep her and Mauricius safe in the ocean—with Mary's eyewitnessing of her own child's torture.

Constance's response to finding herself shipped away in a rudderless boat for the second time, this time with an infant, is to return to her own body as the site of divine justice, which always triumphs over royal law and the bureaucratic devices that support it. Recalling that God had intervened before, Constance reminds herself (and the pilgrims) that her innocence and faith will protect her from the exile, torture, and death Donegild has in store for her. Likewise, when she recalls Mary's eyewitnessing of Christ's suffering, she reframes the earlier scene of false testimony as an opportunity to rehabilitate the truth-claims of the eyewitness. When the false knight's eyes burst from his face in a spectacular punishment for perjury, we were to understand that eyewitness accounts cannot always testify to the truth. In contrast, Mary operates as the ultimate eyewitness, and as such she rehabilitates the evidentiary claims of a courtroom eyewitness on behalf of the kind of divine justice that transcends the royal authority Donegild manipulates.

The third part of the *Man of Law's Tale* opens with Alla's return to Northumberland, where he discovers that his wife and child are missing. He asks the constable where they are, and in response, the constable "sheweth the kyng his seel and eek his lettre," explaining that he followed what he assumed were Alla's orders. The messenger is then tortured ("tormented") until he reveals that he had spent nights unaware that the letters were being stolen, forged, and replaced. "And thus," the Man of Law states, "by wit and sotil enquerynge, / Ymagined was by whom this harm gan sprynge" (II.888–89). James Landman notes that Alla's use of torture is unique to Chaucer's version of the story and argues that for the Man of Law, "it is a reminder of the fragility of the common-law institutions he represents, and of torture's alluring promise of certainty."[47] Indeed, by torturing the constable, the Man of Law seems consider the body as an infallible site of truth. But we must note the carefully passive syntax the Man of Law again deploys here: while Alla is posited as a legal authority who can inquire and torture in the service of garnering legal fact, the syntax suggests that the revelation of truth here emerges as much from a *judicium Dei* as it does from Alla's sovereign power to inquire and to torture. Significantly, now, as a Christian sovereign, Alla successfully used inquiry and legal procedure to expose the truth, whereas his attempts had failed when he was a pagan leader.

---

47. James H. Landman, "Proving Constant: Torture and the *Man of Law's Tale*," *SAC* 20 (1998): 2. Gower omits the depiction of torture, merely saying that the messenger was "sodeinliche opposed" (II.1257).

The third part of the *Tale* tracks a series of revelations, and through those revelations, the restoration of Christian sovereign authority and community. Alla recognizes the counterfeit letter's handwriting ("The hand was knowe that the lettre wroot"), and kills his mother. The Man of Law takes care to assert that Alla commits this act of violence as a king, rather than as an angry son: "His mooder slow—that may men pleynly rede— / For that she traitour was to hire ligeance, / Thus endeth olde Donegile, with meschance!" (II.894–96). Alla's recognition of his mother's treachery establishes royal legitimacy outside the documentary apparatus designed to support it. In other words, the tortured body of the messenger and Donegild's death anatomize Alla's sovereign power, and they trump the power of the royal seal to substitute for and protect Alla's status, given the ease with which the seal was counterfeited to serve treasonous purposes. Alla's return to Northumberland, the torture of his messenger, and the punishment of his mother collectively suggest that in the *Man of Law's Tale,* documents obscure sovereign power, while the body testifies to it.

With the threat of treason contained and Alla's sovereign power restored through his acts of authorized violence, the tale turns back to Constance, who has landed on the shores of "an hethen castel" (II.904). There, a thief threatens to rape Constance, but her struggles against him send him overboard and she and Mauricius sail safely on through the strait of Gibraltar. She meets a ship manned by a Roman senator whom her father has sent to Syria to enact revenge on those who killed the converted Syrians. Though he does not recognize her, the senator brings her home to Rome, where the senator and his wife, Constance's aunt, take her and Mauricius in. Meanwhile, Alla comes to Rome to receive penance for the death of his mother, whereupon Constance's father welcomes him with a feast, which Mauricius attends.

This extraordinary confluence of events emphasizes both the inevitability of Constance's return to Rome and the tight link between Rome and the newly Christian nation of Northumberland. Significantly, the Man of Law describes Alla's first encounter with Mauricius as a face-to-face meeting between sovereigns: "But sooth is this, that at his moodres heeste / Biforn Alla, durynge the metes space, / The child stood, lookynge in the kynges face" (II.1013–15). As Mauricius takes in Alla's face, Alla stands in wonder at the child's likeness to his mother:

Now was this child as lyk unto Custance
As possible is a creature to be.
This Alla hath the face in remembrance
Of dame Custance, and ther on mused he

> If that the childes mooder were aught she
> That is his wyf, and pryvely he sighte,
> And spedde hym fro the table that he myghte.
> "Parfay," thoghte he, "fantome is in myn heed!
> I oghte deme, of skilful juggement,
> That in the salte see my wyf is deed."
> And afterward he made his argument:
> "What woot I if that Crist have hyder ysent
> My wyf by see, as well as he hire sente
> To my contree fro thennes that she wente?" (II.1030–43)

Mauricius's face leads Alla to return to Constance's face in his memory, which in turn shifts the terms of Alla's powers of judgment. He claims that his knowledge of what happened in his realm ("juggement") should bring him to the conclusion ("deme") that his wife has died in the ocean, but Mauricius's face triggers the possibility of Christ's power to save Constance. Moreover, Mauricius's face inspires Alla's repentance. He weeps with joy when he sees Constance; Constance faints twice and then, with her characteristic saintliness, "hym excuseth pitously." In response, Alla announces his innocence and the return of his heir: "'Now God,' quod he, 'and his halwes brighte / So wisly on my soule as have mercy, / That of youre harm as giltelees am I / As is Maurice my sone, so lyk youre face; / Elles the feend me fecche out of this place!'" (II.1060–64).

The face thus reemerges at the end of the *Man of Law's Tale* as the site of truth and Christian sovereignty, as Mauricius's likeness to his mother solidifies the genealogical link between Northumberland and Rome and rehabilitates Alla as a righteous king of a Christian "nacioun." Accordingly, the end of the tale restores Christian belief as the foundation of Alla's sovereignty, and after Constance reunites with her father, the family returns to Northumberland. By this point in the *Tale*, "Northumberland" has turned into "Engelond," and Constance and Alla return the "righte way," suggesting that their conversion is complete, the promise of a Christian patriline is reinstated, and the sanctity of England's Christian unity is preserved (II.1130). Only a year later, the Man of Law tells us, Alla passed away and Constance returned to Rome, leaving Mauricius as the heir to the Roman throne and thus further ensuring the deep connection between Christian Northumberland/England and Rome.

For the Man of Law, false witness functions as a crucial backdrop against which claims of legal authority can be tested in the service of conceptualizing a coherent "Engelond" that expresses a harmonious Christian "nacioun."

The episodes of false witness at the center of the Constance story—and the Man of Law's particular versions of those episodes—present a central conflict between divine justice and human law as well as between Christian and non-Christian communities. The resolutions offered in these episodes demonstrate that witnessing is fundamental to shaping and protecting Christian community and sovereign law. Specifically, the multiple forms of witnessing the Man of Law features in his *Tale* demonstrate the importance of the body as a testimonial medium, one that can transcend the claims of bureaucratic documents and royal seals to affirm that divine justice will always triumph over earthly legal procedures. Likewise, as we shall see again and again the ensuing chapters, the episodes of false witness that surface repeatedly in fourteenth- and fifteenth-century pastoral, literary, and legal texts often pit the body and the document against one another as testimonial media that offer different kinds of testimony with different levels of authenticity. Yet the body does not always function as a reliable conduit of the divine Word. For some vernacular texts, such as the *Pistel of Swete Susan,* the body—particularly the mouth—can be the site of deceptive testimony, just as documents can be manipulated, as the Man of Law cautions.

t w o

Silence, Testimony, and the Case of Susanna

CHAUCER takes the Constance story as an opportunity to imagine a unified Christian "nacioun" which triumphs over the heathen communities that threaten it. In particular, the multiple scenes of false witness in the *Man of Law's Tale* demonstrate the necessity of witnessing to construct and affirm the cultural and ethical requirements of a community. Like the story of the saintly Constance, the story of saintly Susanna, a Scriptural tale that was enormously popular in England in the late fourteenth and fifteenth centuries, features scenes of false witness to test and affirm the integrity of a Christian community, one that coheres around the doctrinal prescription for female silence, chastity, and obedience. At the center of the story is a tale of false testimony, in which Susanna's steadfast faith directly contrasts with the legal corruption propagated by Church Elders in their own self-interests. It thus offers a lesson similar to the one illustrated in the *Man of Law's Tale* about the sanctity of divine justice and the corruptibility of earthly legal mechanisms. But unlike the story of Constance, the Susanna story also interrogates how true "witnessing" might be understood as a range of practices, including prayer and prophecy. In doing so, it expands the definition of witnessing to accommodate distinctly female modes of testimony.

The story of Susanna was familiar to medieval readers and congregants from the thirteenth chapter of the Book of Daniel, which describes an incident in which two Church Elders spy Susanna, the beatific wife of Joachim, as she bathes in a garden. They find themselves overwhelmed with desire: "ravished," as English versions of the text claim, by her beauty. They decide to approach and sexually proposition her. When she refuses their advances, the Elders take advantage of their juridical and moral authority, telling her that she must either submit or be accused of adultery, a charge she would be unable to deny credibly. After crying out with sorrow and outrage, Susanna silently stands trial for sexual transgressions she did not commit, unable to stand up against the social and legal standing of the Elders who falsely testify against her. Based on the testimony of the Elders, Susanna is convicted of adultery, only to be saved by Daniel, who uses legal inquiry to expose the Elders' falsehood and condemn them to death. The story was long read as a warning against false witness, an example of divine justice, and an exemplary tale of womanly chastity. Medieval commentators on the Book of Daniel persistently imagined Susanna as a saintly, silent victim in the face of almost certain social and legal condemnation, saved only by the last-minute intervention of divine justice, embodied by the child prophet Daniel. These commentators interpret Susanna's suffering silence as a sign of her steadfast faith. Like Constance, she is a woman at the mercy of legal officials but always protected by divine justice.

Significantly, however, Susanna's courtroom silence emerges as a site of protest in late fourteenth- and fifteenth-century English versions of the story, which seek to rehabilitate her silence as a kind of testimony itself, outside of Daniel's prophetic involvement in the case. As Lynn Staley has pointed out, "Susanna occupies a subtly different range of meanings in English texts, possibly because of the challenge to patriarchal control offered by heterodoxy and of the different English attitude toward law itself."[1] In particular, texts such as the *Pistel of Swete Susan* and the Lollard treatise "Of Prelates," a polemic against ecclesiastical corruption, carefully depict both how the silence of a condemned woman can be understood as testimony and how that silence might be "translated" into writing for a community of readers. Thus, rather than merely portray a silent woman performing her faith, these texts use Susanna's silence to expand what might be considered efficacious "witnessing," including private prayer, public testimony, and even, as this chapter argues, vernacular poetry. Moreover, as these English texts highlight the contrast between the false testimony offered by the communal protectors of the law and Susanna's silence, they suggest that at stake in this story of false witness is how different kinds of testimony, oral and written, signal their own

---

1. Lynn Staley, "Susanna's Voice," in *Sacred and Profane in Chaucer and Late Medieval Literature*, ed. Robert Epstein and William Robins (Toronto: University of Toronto Press, 2010), 48.

peculiar authenticity and shape multiple, even widely differing, Christian communities and authorities.

In fourteenth-century England, the story's investment in female silence and documentation emerged specifically as an exploration of the complex relationship among sexual transgression, female testimony, and silence. Traditionally, the medieval Church understood female silence as a sign of womanly obedience in marriage: as stated in the first letter to Timothy: "Let the woman learn in silence, with all subjection. But I suffer not a woman to teach, nor to use authority over the man: but to be in silence" (I Tim. 2:12–13). Likewise, Tertullian upbraids women for being both verbally and sexually promiscuous, while Jerome warns Eustochium not to "engage in adultery of the tongue."[2] Such anxieties and warnings were commonplace throughout the Middle Ages, and the long-term worry about female loquacity specifically dovetails with worries about sexual transgressions. Medieval commentators' strenuous attempts to link Susanna's chastity to silence—and to muffle the story's interest in testimony in favor of its assertion of female obedience—are thus based in hefty Scriptural and patristic precedent.

But at the end of the fourteenth century, the English *Pistel of Swete Susan* recuperates the story's emphasis on false witness rather than on female obedience, specifically concentrating on how Susanna's silence might speak to contemporary worries about the role of testimony in cases concerning sexual transgression. In doing so, the *Pistel* reformulates the patristic tradition it inherits by portraying silence as an efficacious model of female testimony. Such a portrayal poses complicated questions about various ways female testimony might be heard, recorded, and rendered vital to the coherence of Christian community. Indeed, unlike its patristic precursors, the *Pistel* envisions Susanna's silence not merely as the sign of an obedient wife but as an opportunity to experiment with the authoritative claims of oral testimony and documentary form. These experiments were, in turn, taken up in the fifteenth century by Lollard writers, who routinely cited the Susanna story in support of their own resistances against ecclesiastical control over written testimony.

By examining the *longue durée* of the Susanna story and focusing particularly on the late fourteenth-century *Pistel of Swete Susan* and fifteenth-century Lollard citations of Susanna, this chapter accounts both for the way female testimony emerges in various forms—prayer, legal document, vernacular poetry, even citation—and for the way late medieval English ideas about

---

2. *Letter to Eustochium*, in *The Principal Works of St. Jerome*, trans. W. H. Fremantle (Grand Rapids, MI: William B. Eerdmans, 1913), 22.29.

witness testimony and legal documentation reframe the stakes of this enduring story of false witness. Susanna's silence functions as a complex legal, doctrinal, and ideological touchstone for understanding multiple models of bearing witness in the later Middle Ages and for exploring how those models were used to formulate, challenge, and reshape the bonds of Christian community and authority.

Silence, Documents, and Susanna's Voice in Early Patristic Commentaries

The earliest extant form of the story of Susanna is in Greek (ca. 100 B.C.E.), and the story has been featured in stone carvings in third-century Roman catacombs, in patristic writing from the third and fourth centuries, and in Latin poetry from the twelfth and thirteenth centuries.[3] In England, the Susanna story was particularly popular in the fifteenth century, appearing in five miscellanies. The earliest English versions, in the Vernon manuscript and British Library Additional 22283, both date from around 1400, while the latest, Cotton Caligula A.ii, dates from around 1500.[4] The *Pistel of Swete Susan* circulated as a stand-alone text in the fifteenth-century manuscript owned by a nun named Matilde Hoyle.[5] In addition, medieval congregants heard the story of Susanna on the Saturday before the third Sunday in Lent, and a short citation of it is included in the Lollard tract *The Lantern of Light*. Beyond the Middle Ages, Susanna was written for the stage in Thomas Garter's 1578 *Commody of the moste virtuous and godlye Susanna*, in Lope de Vega's *Comedia de Santa Susana* (ca. 1600), and in Carlisle Floyd's 1947 opera, *Susanna*. In all of these versions, Susanna is depicted as a silent victim of false witness, a saintly figure who, like Constance, suffers at the hands of a corrupt legal system, only to be saved by divine intervention. In fact, the only point at which Susanna voices her protest is when the two Elders

---

3. For discussions of Susanna's appearance in antiquity, see Piero Boitani, "Susanna in Excelsis," and Betsy Halpern-Amaru, "The Journey of Susanna Among the Church Fathers," both in *The Judgment of Susanna: Authority and Witness*, ed. Ellen Spolsky (Atlanta, GA: Scholars Press, 1996). For an overview of the various patristic and medieval versions of Susanna, see Lynn Staley, "Susanna and English Communities," *Traditio* 62 (2007): 25–58. For the medieval Latin verse versions by Peter Riga, Alan of Melsa, and an anonymous author, see J. H. Mozley, "Susanna and the Elders: Three Medieval Poems," *Studi Medievali* n.s. 3 (1930): 27–52.

4. See the notes and commentary in *Susannah: An Alliterative Poem of the Fourteenth Century*, ed. Alice Miskimin (New Haven, CT: Yale University Press, 1969).

5. For a discussion of BL MS Additional 10596, which contains the stand-alone *Pistel*, see Mary C. Erler, *Women, Reading, and Piety in Late Medieval England* (Cambridge: Cambridge University Press, 2002), 4.

approach her in the garden, when she emits a cry, either aloud to signal to her handmaidens that she needs help or, as some versions have it, muted, to register her innocence only to God.

Indeed, Susanna's outcry is where various adaptations of and commentaries on the Susanna narrative take the opportunity to "silence" her. Such texts seek to emphasize her as the epitome of the chaste, obedient woman, rather than as a victim of false witness, and her voice is thus the central ideological pivot upon which commentators and translators shape the story to reflect their specific aims. The Vulgate Bible's Daniel 13 provides a "great voice" for Susanna, heard well beyond the garden walls: "Susanna cried out with a great voice, and the elders cried out against her, and one ran to the door of the orchard and opened it, and when the servants heard the clamor in the orchard they rushed through the back door to see what was going on."[6] Here, Susanna's voice extracts her from the seclusion of the garden, rendering her outrage (and the Elders' iniquity) public. This great shout comes after she carefully explains to the Elders that she feels stuck (*angustiae*) between two impossible choices: death or adultery. The Vulgate posits her cry against the cry of the Elders, a sound of truth versus one of treachery.

Likewise, Hippolytus's third-century commentary on the Book of Daniel juxtaposes Susanna's voice with that of the Elders, and it offers specific interpretive cues for understanding what her voice signifies. Hippolytus insists that Susanna shouted when the Elders approached her, emphasizing that despite the "large and spacious" size of the garden, her voice was heard and "understood."[7] Indeed, her shout renders the Elders' accusations "unbelievable": "See the proof in Susanna, whose education in God's Law since childhood and whose pure and prudent life, made the words spoken against her by the Elders seem unbelievable" (I.xxiv). Hippolytus emphasizes that the Elders' use of language must be read in contradistinction to Susanna's voice; the words that are specifically "pronounced" against Susanna cannot be believed because her cry signifies truth beyond the claims of their speech. Hippolytus thus understands Susanna's cry against the Elders' accusations as being a sound that registers as true because it emerges more directly from her body, unaltered by the machinations of discourse.

6. Daniel 13:24–26: "et exclamavit voce magna Susanna, exclamaverunt autem et senes adversus eam, et cucurrit unus et aperuit ostia pomarii, cum ergo audissent clamorem famuli domus in pomario inruerunt per posticum ut viderent quidnam esset."

7. "Voyez-en la preuve dans Suzanne qui, pour avoir été instruite dès l'enfance dans la Loi de Dieu, et avoir vécu pure et sage, a rendu incroyable la parole que les vieillards avaient prononcée contre elle." *Commentaire sur Daniel*, trans. Maurice Lefévre, Sources Chrétiennes 14 (Paris 1947), I.xxiii. My translation of Lefévre's French. Hereafter cited parenthetically by book and chapter.

Hippolytus's explanation and elevation of Susanna's vocal cry, however, is transformed when commentators begin to gloss the story to construct Susanna as an emblem of chastity. In his fifth-century *Commentary on Daniel*, Jerome silences Susanna's cry to portray her as an obedient woman who maintains her chastity in the face of an ostensibly insurmountable obstacle.

> "Her voice was great," he writes, "not because of the intense vibrations it sent through the air nor because of outcry that came from her lips, but because of the greatness of the chastity with which she called out to the Lord. And so for this reason Scripture did not attribute a great voice to the outcry of the elders, for the following statement is merely, 'The elders also cried out against her.'"[8]

Jerome reconstitutes the sound and audience of Susanna's outburst, translating her cry from a public, legal call for help into a silent prayer to God. In doing so, he reconstructs the Susanna narrative into an exemplary story about female virtue, signaled by womanly silence. Augustine takes up Jerome's muffling of Susanna's voice, citing her as a paragon of steadfast chastity and claiming, "Though her prayer was inaudible to human beings, it was heard by God."[9] He further claims that there are three kinds of life in the Church for a woman: married, widowed, and virginal, exemplified by Mary, Anna, and Susanna, respectively.[10] He takes care to note that each of these women "gives testimony" by living a chaste life. Thus, female testimony, understood as silent prayer and exemplary behavior, functions for these commentators as a way to express the Christian requirements of chastity and obedience.

Jerome and Augustine are the most influential commentators for the Middle Ages' reception of a silent Susanna, yet what it means for them to "silence" Susanna—and to what extent that is possible—is not always clear. For example, Augustine is careful to note that while Susanna's explanation and cry were not widely heard, they were documented: "Her words are recorded, which she spoke *in the paradise* (Dn. 13:7), that is her shrubbery; words no human being heard, apart from the two who were lying in wait to

---

8. *Commentary on Daniel*, trans. Gleason L. Archer (Grand Rapids, MI: Baker, 1958), 582. For the Latin text, see *Commentarii on Danielem*, ed. F. Glorie, CCSL 75 (Turnhout: Brepols, 1968).

9. Exposition of Psalm 34, *Exposition of the Psalms*, 33–50, vol. 10, trans. Maria Boulding (New York: New City, 2000), 5.

10. Notably, Constance seems to have internalized this triad. When she goes to trial for murder, she drops to her knees and prays: "'Immortal god, that savedest Susanne / Fro false blame, and thou, merciful Mayde, / Marie I meene, doghter to Seynte Anne, / Bifore whos child angeles synge Osanne, / If I be giltlees of this felonye, / My socour be, for ellis shal I dye!'" (II.639–44).

ensnare the modesty of another man's wife, and planning to give false evidence against her if she proved unwilling." He repeats again that only the two Elders heard that she feels compelled to choose death, lest she commit adultery for God to see. This claim is followed by a full citation of Susanna's complaint: "They were the only ones who heard what she said: *'I am trapped on every side. For if I do this thing, it means death for me, but if I do not do it, I shall not escape your hands. But it is better for me not to slip out of your hands than to sin in the sight of God.'*"[11] Although her complaint and her choice to rebuff the Elders, whatever the consequences, are meant only for the Elders' ears, Augustine ensures to "document" both, and accordingly, Susanna's words become evidence in support of her innocence. Moreover, in recording her complaint, Augustine assumes the authority to translate her muffled voice into a public document and thus into doctrinal instruction for a wide community of readers. The passive construction—"her words are recorded" (*conscripta sunt verba ejus*)—suggests that this translation from voice to text occurs organically, without authorial perspective or scribal intervention.

For Augustine, documenting her silent prayer can render it an illustration of female doctrinal obedience. By recording her words, words meant only for the Elders, Augustine extracts her from an isolating and damning silence and makes that silence efficacious for God and, crucially, for a community of Christian readers. Elsewhere, notably, Augustine argues in more general terms what he has enacted in his sermon about Susanna: that silence redresses the ephemerality of sound, making it so that voiced statements can be remembered. "Suppose that we hear a noise emitted by some material body," he suggests in his *Confessions*. "The sound begins and we continue to hear it. It goes on until finally it ceases. Then there is silence. The sound has passed and is no longer sound. Before it began it was future and could not be measured, because it did not yet exist. Now that it has ceased it cannot be measured, because it no longer exists."[12] Yet, he argues, "even when both the voice and the tongue are still, we review—in thought—poems and verses, and discourse of various kinds or various measures of motions, and

---

11. *Sermons* 343:1. Trans. Edmund Hill, in *The Works of St. Augustine: Sermons*, ed. John E. Rotelle (New York: New City, 1995). Italicized portions are Scriptural citations. For the Latin, see *PL* 39:1505. "Conscripta sunt verba ejus, quae habuit in paradiso, hoc est in viridario suo: quae verba nullus hominum audivit, nisi soli duo, qui pudori uxoris alienae insidiabantur, et reluctanti falsum testimonium meditabantur. Illi soli audierunt quod dictum est: Angustiae mihi undique. Si enim hoc fecero, mors mihi est; si autem non fecero, non effugiam manus vestras. Melius est autem mihi manus vestras non evadere, quam in conspectu Deo peccare" (Dan. XIII, 22).

12. *Confessions* 11.27. For a discussion of the relationship between sonority and embodiment in Augustine, see Bruce W. Holsinger, *Music, Body, and Desire in Medieval Culture: Hildegard of Bingen to Chaucer* (Stanford, CA: Stanford University Press, 2001), 296.

we specify their time spans—how long this is in relation to that—just as if we were speaking them aloud" (11.27). Augustine's formulations in the *Confessions* fuse silence and speaking, memory and voice: silence enables memory, and memory functions *as if* sound were emitted. With these formulations in mind, we can understand how Augustine's "documentation" of Susanna's unheard prayer provides him the opportunity to transform her ordeal and anguish into a text, imagining her silence as something that can be understood *as if* sound were emitted for others to hear. In doing so, he provides her a public voice and ensures that she becomes an enduring exemplar, chaste in the face of almost certain death, rather than merely a silent woman falsely accused.

After translating Susanna's outcry into a public text, Augustine praises Susanna for speaking her mind to the Elders: "Susanna too gave them something, and didn't send them away empty-handed, if they had been willing to take her advice about chastity. Not only, you see, did she not consent to them, but she did not, either, keep quiet about why she didn't consent."[13] Furthermore, in Augustine's version of the story, Susanna follows her muffled prayer and private statement to the Elders with a cry which was publicly heard and which inaugurated legal process: "The cry was raised, people came running, proceedings began."[14] Again, the passive construction here ("the cry was raised") omits a vocal agent, suggesting that the remaining story of Susanna's resolute chastity, as well as her participation in legal process, operates communally rather than through her individual complaint. In other words, Augustine focuses on the community responding to a cry and the legal process, rather than Susanna's personal outrage. Susanna's individual voice is thus a necessary condition for the possibility of other, legal enunciations on her behalf, which can turn her private prayer and immediate outcry into an opportunity for the community to witness divine intervention into a case of courtroom perjury.

In contrast, for Ambrose Susanna is completely silent, and her prayer is undocumented and left between Susanna and God. Indeed, her silence exemplifies God's precepts against idle talk. "If we must give an account for every idle word," he writes in his *De officiis*,

> we need to make sure that we do not find ourselves having to account for idle silence as well. For there is another kind of silence as well, one that is

---

13. *Sermons* 359:3.
14. *Sermons* 343:1.

characterized by activity. The silence of Susanna was an example of it. She achieved more by keeping silent than she would have done if she had spoken. In keeping silence before men, she spoke to God, and she devised no greater proof of her chastity than this silence. Her conscience spoke when her voice was not heard; she sought no judgment at the hands of men, for she had the Lord himself as her witness.[15]

Silence permits Susanna to converse solely with God, who trumps human judges in being able to hear true testimony even when the legal system cannot detect it. In this formulation, her silence offers the only possibility of transcending the probative claims of the two Elders' testimony in the courtroom, and it marks Susanna's turn away from courtroom practices to divine justice. Ambrose carefully notes various kinds of silences and testimonial voices: here, though Susanna remains quiet externally, she speaks in her conscience.

Similarly, the late fourth-century *De lapsu Susannae* (sometimes attributed to Ambrose) omits the words of Susanna's testimony altogether, instead taking Susanna's silence as a metaphor for the suffering of those who must witness the sinful actions of the lecherous and promiscuous go unpunished:

> Why are you so silent, my soul? Why are you troubled in your thoughts? Why don't you let your voice break forth and lay bare the ardent desire of your mind so that you might have some relief? This surely, this will be like a remedy for your trouble, if you would open up your mouth and set out to explain what the crime is. Similarly, lancing and draining a boil, however swollen it has been, offers relief from the festering.[16]

---

15. *De officiis*, vol. 1, ed. and trans. Ivor J. Davidson (Oxford: Oxford University Press, 2001), 123. For the Latin see *Sancti Ambrosii Mediolanensis, De officiis*, ed. Mauritius Testard, CCSL 15 (Turnhout: Brepols, 2000): "Deinde si pro verbo otioso reddimus rationem, videamus ne reddamus et pro otioso silentio. Est enim et negotiosum silentium ut erat Susannae quae plus egit tacendo quam si esset locuta. Tacendo enim apud homines, locuta est Deo; nec ullum maius indicium suae castitatis invenit quam silentium. Conscientia loquebatur ubi vox non audiebatur; nec quaerebat pro se hominum iudicium, quae habebat Domini testimonium" (I.III.9.2–9).

16. Maureen Tilley, "An Anonymous Letter to a Woman Named Susanna," in *Religions of Late Antiquity in Practice*, ed. Richard Valantasis (Princeton, NJ: Princeton University Press, 2000), 218. Hereafter cited parenthetically in the text. For the Latin, see *De lapsu Susannae*, ed. Ignatius Cazzaniga (Turin: G. B. Paraviae, 1948): "Quid taces, anima? Quid cogitationibus aestuas? Quid non erumpis in vocem et mentis tuae exponis ardorem ut aliquod solatium capias? Hoc plane, hoc erit quasi remedium aegritudinis tuae, si aperto ore conceptum digeras scelus. Nam et ulcus quamvis tumidum, cum fuerit apertum, evaporans praestat refrigerium passionis" (I.1).

The text navigates the various types of silences at the heart of the Susanna story. Here, the voice is imagined simultaneously as something heard and as an internal voice of conscience. Moreover, the speaker addresses his complaints to virgins near and far, imploring everyone to listen to his complaint: "Hear me now, you who are near, you who are far away," explaining that he wants to speak directly to lapsed virgins and adulterers (I.2, II.5). He thus imagines his objections both to be immediate and to endure beyond the moment of his speaking. Significantly, when he turns to Susanna as an example of chastity in the face of temptation, he takes up Susanna's voice as direct quotation: "But you say, 'I did not will this evil; I suffered violence.' That most brave Susanna, whose name you falsely wear, will answer you, 'Placed between two elders, there between two judges of the people, set there alone between the trees of the garden, I could not be conquered; because I did not will to be'" (III.12). For the author of *De lapsu Susannae*, then, the Susanna story is decidedly not about the injustices of evidentiary process or even about false witness. Instead, it functions as an exemplar for lapsed virgins to return to their prescribed chaste behavior. False witness is merely the narrative conceit by which this exemplary aim can be presented. Significantly, this version of the story permits the author to revoice Susanna, insofar as he uses Susanna's silence as an opportunity to put words in her mouth rather than simply quoting the Book of Daniel. Unlike the Susanna of *De officiis*, this Susanna speaks, but she addresses an audience far beyond the garden walls with a complaint about the behavior of virgins, not about the false accusation she suffers.

These various depictions of Susanna's voice illustrate patristic writers' ongoing struggles to shape the Susanna story to be about female chastity and silent obedience. Indeed, numerous versions of the story in the high Middle Ages obviously strain to explain away Susanna's *magna vox*. The *Glossa ordinaria*, for example, takes great care to muffle Susanna's voice, transforming her *magna vox* into "pure testimony," heard only by God.[17] Nicholas of Lyra makes a similar claim in his commentary on Daniel: "Her voice was great, not because of the beating of the air and cry from the throat, but because of the magnitude of its beauty, through which she called out to God."[18] He goes on to emphasize that her voice was heard not by men, but by God, because

---

17. Indeed, the *Glossa ordinaria* persistently suggests that voices require glosses. *Biblia Latina cum Glossa ordinaria*, vol. 3 (Turnhout: Brepols, 1992), 351.

18. *Supra Danielem XIII*, in *Commentariorum in Danielem, Libri III*, S. Hieronymi Presbyteri Opera, CCSL 75A (Brepols: Turnhout, 1964), 947. "Magna vox erat, non aeris percussione et clamore faucium sed pudicitiae magnitudine per quam clamabat ad Dominium." Hereafter cited parenthetically by page number.

of her purity of heart and mind.[19] Thus, the long hermeneutic history of Susanna's voice reveals that there are different kinds of silences that can be registered as "testimony," each with various social and doctrinal functions. Moreover, throughout the Middle Ages, Susanna's silence is described as a kind of "testimony" that reaches outside the problematic systems of human judgment and evidence to call upon divine justice.

The claim that her silence can be read as testimony is put to the test in the late fourteenth-century English alliterative version of the story, the *Pistel of Swete Susan*, which straddles the line between a vocal and a silent Susanna by describing her response to the Elders' accusations as a "careful cri."[20] The *Pistel*'s depiction of Susanna's cry challenges the patristic link between female silence and exemplary chastity. Specifically, it foregrounds Susanna's testimonial silence within the particular context of fourteenth-century changes in English common law that focused on how allegations of rape and sexual transgression could be made, which were required to conform to particular documentary forms of legal complaint. As it explores how Susanna's testimony might operate under these legal conditions, the *Pistel* suggests that the Elders' false testimony can be mitigated by Susanna's testimonial silence because her muffled voice can be witnessed, documented, and disseminated in vernacular poetry.

Accusation, False Testimony, and the Power of Silence in the *Pistel of Swete Susan*

The *Pistel* begins, like the Vulgate Book of Daniel, by emphasizing Susanna's literacy, particularly in "the maundement of Moises." Yet while the Vulgate merely states that her parents had dutifully instructed her in matters of faith,

---

19. "Cordis affectus et mentis pura confessio et bonum conscientiae, vocem eius fecerant clariorem; unde magna erat exclamatio eius Deo, quae ab hominibus non audiebatur." *Supra Danielem* 947.

20. Written after the *Pistel*, Christine de Pizan's *Book of the City of Ladies* notably restores Susanna's "magna vox": "Hearing their threats and knowing that women in such a case were customarily stoned, she said, 'I am completely overwhelmed with anguish, for if I do not do what these men require of me, I risk the death of my body, and if I do it, I will sin before my Creator. However, it is far better for me, in my innocence, to die than incur the wrath of my God because of my sin.' So Susanna cried out, and the servants came out of the house." Christine's ideal of Susanna imagines her as legally savvy, aware of the violent punishment of adulterers, and it gives her a voice that speaks with a certain kind of exemplary authority, distinct from the exemplary, silent obedience that Jerome, Augustine, and Ambrose attribute to Susanna. See *The Book of the City of Ladies* (New York: Norton, 1988), 156.

the *Pistel* insists that they "lerned hire lettrure of that langage."[21] This specific emphasis on her legal literacy sets up the law-focused expectations for the remainder of the text, which is saturated with legal references. These references both offer implicit instructions to read the *Pistel* as an illustration of the triumphant exoneration of a chaste and dutiful woman and remind us that this story can be understood as an exploration of multiple forms of witnessing, from silent prayer to legal documents and even, as the *Pistel* ultimately suggests, vernacular poetry.

As the *Pistel* describes the Elders' encounter with Susanna in the garden, their lecherous gazes are repeatedly articulated through legal vocabulary: "And whon thei seigh Susan, semelich of hewe, / Thei weor so set uppon hire, might they not sese" (44–45). The Middle English word "sese" ("cease") signals their inability to tear their eyes away, but it also gestures to two specific legal definitions, one meaning "to arrest and bind over to a session of court," the other signifying the term for land transfer.[22] The term "sese" thus emphasizes that the Elders' legal and social standing is at odds with their lustful gazes. In addition, as they watch Susanna play in the garden and devise an elaborate plan to "bewile that worly," the text describes their plotting as a legal test of her purity: "Every day bi day / In the pomeri thei play. / Whiles thei mihte Susan assay / To worchen hire wo" (62–65). By the middle of the fourteenth century, the verb "assaien" had accumulated a constellation of definitions. The verb often surfaced in romances and meant "to test": that is, to demonstrate one's knightly strength in combat. But it could also mean "to investigate" or "to inquire" by means of legal interrogation, as well as to have sexual intercourse.[23] Used here, the verb "assay" emphasizes the overlapping bodily, legal, and moral transgressions of rape, adultery, and false witness the *Pistel* will depict.

The Elders themselves make these overlaps clear when they approach Susanna and present her with the choice of having sex with them or being publicly accused of adultery. "'Wolt thu, ladi, for love on ure lay lerne,'" they ask lasciviously, "'And under this lorere ben ur lemmone?'" (135–36). To "learn their law" clearly means to submit to their advances, and the Elders suggest that she relinquish her body for her "love" of learning the law. Susanna responds with despair:

---

21. *Pistel of Swete Susan*, ed. Russell A. Peck, in *Heroic Women from the Old Testament in Middle English Verse* (Kalamazoo, MI: Medieval Institute, 1991), 18. All citations of the *Pistel* will be taken from Peck's text unless otherwise noted. Hereafter cited parenthetically by line number.

22. "sessen," *Middle English Dictionary* s.v. 1d.

23. "assaien," *Middle English Dictionary* s.v. 3, 4, 5.

Then Susan was serwful and seide in hire thought:
"I am with serwe biset on everiche syde.
Yif I assent to this sin that this segges have sought,
I be bretenet and brent in baret to byde;
And yif I nikke hem with nai hit helpeth me nought—
Such toret and teone taketh me this tyde!
Are I that worthlich wrech, that al this world wrought,
Betere is wemles weende of this world wyde." (144–51)

Her internal monologue is followed by noise: she emits a "careful cri," bringing her servants and valiant men into the garden. Susanna here follows the legal protocol for a complaint of rape, which required that a woman raise the "hue and cry," a procedure in which a victim of or witness to a crime was to shout in order to gather people from the community to help pursue the criminal. Specifically in cases of rape, an "open cry" must be made to register a claim of unwanted sexual activity.[24] Susanna's legal literacy suggests that she knows these procedures, and here she uses them appropriately.

However, Susanna's cry is more than a mere enactment of proper legal process. Rather, it illustrates and explores the complicated ways the female voice was deployed in fourteenth-century rape prosecutions. For most of the Middle Ages, rape complaints had to be registered orally with a cry. Only late in the fourteenth century did rape law catch up with the documentary procedures (including writs of complaint, petitions, and bills) already well in place for other legal accusations.[25] Specifically, in 1382 a new statute on rape and ravishment required that charges of sexual transgression be tried specifically "by inquisition of the country"; the statute did not offer the option to try the charge by battle, unlike in other kinds of criminal allegations.[26] Before

---

24. The requirement of the "open cry" (*nutesium levantum*) surfaces in the 1276 Office of the Coroner, assigned to 4 Edward I. See H. A. Kelly, "Statutes of Rapes and Alleged Ravishers of Wives," in *Inquisitions and Other Trial Procedures in the Medieval West* (Aldershot: Ashgate Variorum Series, 2001), IX.367.

25. Formal legal complaints, documented in writs or petitions, were used to pursue personal and communal accusations, and "plaints" were an important form of expressing grievances. For a discussion of the commonplace use of documentary complaints in the fourteenth century, see Sheila Lindenbaum, "London Texts and Literate Practice," *CHMEL* 284–309; and Wendy Scase, *Literature and Complaint in England, 1272–1553* (Oxford: Oxford University Press, 2007).

26. 6 Richard II, *Statutes of the Realm*, vol. 2, ed. A. Luders (London: Dawsons, 1810–28). There are numerous discussions of this statute, many of which focus on the term *raptus*, which likely signified kidnapping; *stuprum* often signifies rape in the modern sense of the word. Consent is at stake in both of these legal terms. See Kelly, "Statutes," and Christopher Cannon, "*Raptus* in the Chaumpaigne Release and a Newly Discovered Document Concerning the Life of Geoffrey Chaucer," *Speculum* 68 (1993): 74–94.

then, rape cases required material evidence to support, and sometimes even substitute for, the claim of the victim. In the twelfth century, for example, Glanvill claimed that a woman pursuing a plea of rape case should, "soon after the deed is done" (*mox dum recens fuerit maleficium*), go to the nearest vill to "show to trustworthy men the injury done to her, and any effusion of blood there may be and any tearing of her clothes."[27] She must then complain publicly to generate the *publica fama* necessary to begin legal proceedings.[28] For Glanvill, physical evidence and vocal complaint work in conjunction in the difficult process of proving a rape took place.

But by the fourteenth century, the requirement to provide immediate material evidence had dropped away: women were no longer required to expose a bloodied body or torn clothes to their community leaders. In addition, a woman could take up to 40 days to register a complaint of rape, and rape claims were to conform strictly to the documentary formulae of the writ.[29] The expectation of documentary iterability was paramount, insofar as the language used and details given in the original (oral) complaint to a family member, community authority, or sheriff had to match exactly with the claims made in the writ of complaint; any deviation, even of the most minor detail, could result in rendering the complaint legally null. Thus, the relationship between sexual transgression, vocal complaint, and documentary form was tightly controlled, such that legal procedure required a linear trajectory from bodily violation to vocal cry to oral testimony to legal text. Sexual violation must be "translated" into an "open cry" that would draw members of the community as judges and witnesses, and it should then be "translated" into a formal accusation and finally into a formulaic document in which the details of the event could be ossified and repeated. Adultery was even more difficult to track and prosecute than rape, since it was a transgression usually done in secret, without witnesses, and thus it could be difficult to generate the necessary *publica fama* to start proceedings. Nonetheless, it was subject to "multiple networks of informing, gossip, rumor, talebearing, and, on occasion, lies about neighbors' sex lives among community inhabitants, which brought such cases to the attention of officials and courts."[30] Like charges of rape, charges of adultery had to follow strict

27. Glanvill XLV.6.
28. For a discussion of inquisition and *publica fama*, see the introduction.
29. For a discussion of the documentary formulae and the requirement that details of the rape be repeated in all documents, see Barbara A. Hanawalt, "Whose Story Was This? Rape Narratives in Medieval English Courts," in *Of Good and Ill Repute: Gender and Social Control in Medieval England* (Oxford: Oxford University Press, 1998), 124–41.
30. L. R. Poos, "Sex, Lies, and the Church Courts of Pre-Reformation England," *Journal of Interdisciplinary History* 25.4 (1995): 585.

documentary formulae to move from gossip to formal complaint. For late medieval English writers, the systems designed to register allegations of rape and adultery were sufficiently new to the documentary practices of petitionary complaint that they offered them an opportunity to experiment with the relative probative efficacy of material evidence, oral testimony, and documentary form. The *Pistel*, as discussed below, conceptualizes the Susanna story as such an experiment. Specifically, Susanna's "careful cri" in the face of sexual and social transgression navigates the *Pistel*'s understanding of the relationship between body, voice, and document, particularly in terms of a woman's ability to announce her own chastity and pursue false charges of sexual transgression.

The *Pistel*'s interest in whether and how the written word can recuperate the testimonial voice of a silenced woman emerges early in the poem. Unlike either the Vulgate or the various commentaries on the Book of Daniel, the *Pistel* spends some time setting up the Elders' approach of Susanna. Predictably, when the two Elders are "ravished" by Susanna's beauty, they at first try to hide their lust from God and from one another:

> Heore wittes wel waiwordes thei wrethen awai
> And turned fro His teching that teeld is in trone;
> For siht of here soverayn, sothli to say,
> Heore hor hevedes fro hevene thei hid apon one.
> Thei caught for heor covetyse the cursyng of Kai,
> For rightwys jugement recordet thei none,
> They two. (55–61)

The description of their lust is commonplace in its depiction of "wayward wits" and self-oblivion, familiar from romance narratives in which a beautiful love-object transfixes the lover. But their desire to conceal their lust, formulated here as a refusal to "record" it, suggests that we ought to understand the Elders' ravishment in documentary terms. They seek to suppress, even erase, their lust by controlling whether it gets "written." For the Elders, recording their ravishment would potentially transform their inner feelings into external and visible testimony. By the time we hear Susanna's careful cry, then, we are primed to read it as a crystallization of the *Pistel*'s exploration of how a voice can be represented in text. Her careful cry stages the possibilities and limitations of oral and documentary testimony in terms of their ability to legibly register either female chastity or sexual transgression.

When Susanna's "careful cri" brings her servants to the garden, the Elders make good on their threat to accuse Susanna of adultery. In disbelief but unable to contradict the Elders' claims, the townspeople shackle Susanna and put her into a dungeon to await trial, while Joachim, "with al his affinité," rushes to the court.[31] To present their "playnt" to the judges, the Elders seal their accusation with an oath:

> Be this cause that we say,
> Heo wyled hir wenches away;
> This word we witnesse for ay,
> With tonge and with toth. (218–21)

The Elders' oath locates their authority and their truth-claims specifically in the mouth ("tonge and toth"), and in doing so, places special emphasis on their collective voice as public, legal, and evidentiary. Specifically, the Elders' oath sets up the terms by which we must read the *Pistel*'s description of Susanna's condemnation and eventual salvation: that is, as an investigation of the community-forming power of testimony within and beyond the courtroom, rather than a celebration of her innocence. Significantly, as the *Pistel* turns to Susanna's trial and Daniel's prophetic intervention, it repeatedly focuses on the mouths of both the Elders and Susanna, from which different kinds of testimony emerge to address different communities.

In a scene reminiscent of Constance's public trial, the crowd gathered to witness Susanna's trial reluctantly believes the Elders, given their social standing and solemn oath. As the Vulgate makes clear, "The multitude believed them as elders and judges of the people; and they condemned her to death."[32] The *Pistel* explains it slightly less overtly than the Vulgate: "Nou heo is dampned on deis; with deol thaugh hir deve, / And hir domesmen unduwe do hir be withdrawen" (235–36).[33] Notably, in one of the manuscripts of the *Pistel*, the multitude is particularly aural: in the version found in Cotton Caligula A.ii, the line reads, "with dyn they hyr deiue" ("they deafened her with din"). But in other versions of the *Pistel*, we are to understand that Susanna is deafened with grief ("deol"), rather than with the voice of the crowd. Alice Miskimin has tried to account for this discrepancy by suggesting that the *Pistel*-poet may have confused the Vulgate's *creditit* ("believed") with *crepi-*

---

31. Staley argues that the gesture to Joachim's "affinité" suggests the *Pistel*'s specific engagement with English models of justice. "Susanna and English Communities," 50.

32. "Creditit eis multitudo quasi senibus populi et iudicibus; et condemnaverunt eam ad mortem" (Dan. 13:41).

33. As both Miskimin and Peck note, these lines are particularly difficult to interpret. I follow Peck's translation: "Now she is damned on a dais; they deafened her with grief / And the unjust judges order her to be withdrawn."

tit ("roared").³⁴ But whether the translation is deliberate or accidental, the shift from the condemnatory rumble of the crowd to its grief (or, perhaps, Susanna's grief) suggests a link between the crowd's testimony and its emotional response to Susanna, rather than necessarily signaling their judgment of Susanna in the face of ostensibly incontrovertible legal evidence. Here, the crowd's noise signals both their inability to deny the Elders' testimony and their deep surprise and sadness that Susanna could be capable of such transgressions. Thus, unlike the "prees" that silently witnesses the "merveille" of the divine hand of justice in the *Man of Law's Tale,* this crowd functions as a legal and social entity that outwardly expresses its dismay at the legal trap in which Susanna finds herself. Yet significantly, the crowd cannot read her silence as testimony of her innocence; it can only hear the perjured testimony offered by the Elders.

Whereas the public din of the throng signals either its judgment of Susanna or, perhaps, its dismay at the condemnation of a woman it hopes is innocent, Susanna's voice of protest only comes when she withdraws from the crowd to await her fate alone in the dungeon. There,

> Heo asked merci with mouth in this mischeve;
> "I am sakeles of syn," heo seide in hir sawen,
> "Grete God of His grace yor gultus forgive
> That doth me derfliche be ded and don out of dawen
> With dere." (239–43)

Again, the *Pistel* emphasizes the mouth, suggesting that we are to read Susanna's prayer here against the false oath and testimony that had issued from the Elders' mouths. Certainly, the distinction between the Elders' mouths and Susanna's emphasizes the Elders' iniquity against Susanna's steadfast innocence, at least for readers of the *Pistel,* if not for the diegetic crowd. It also juxtaposes the Elders' public, authoritative (and false) testimony, offered in the courtroom, with the private (and true) testimony of a condemned woman. Thus, when Joachim visits Susanna in jail, she falls to the floor and kisses his hand, explaining, "'For I am dampned, I ne dar disparage thi mouth'" (253). She seeks to keep the perception of defilement away from Joachim, and to "disparage his mouth" would be to damage the power of his (male and public) word.

---

34. Miskimin 157. The manuscripts that contain the line "with deol they hyr deiue" are the Vernon manuscript, Huntington Library HM 114, and BM MS Additional 22283.

Given Susanna's courtroom silence, it might seem as though the *Pistel* corroborates a long-standing interpretation of the Susanna story that understands Susanna's testimony to be private, directed only toward God, while the Elders' voices are directed to the court and community. But there may be a different way to understand how the *Pistel* conceptualizes the different kinds of testimonies that emerge from Susanna and from the Elders, particularly if we read the *Pistel*'s repeated use of mouth imagery alongside another tale centrally about a silenced woman and the production of a public, evidentiary text: the story of Philomela.[35] Like Susanna, Philomela is ubiquitous throughout antiquity and the Middle Ages, taken up by Ovid, the *Ovide moralisé* author, Gower, Chaucer, and Christine de Pizan, to name just a few. The story describes Tereus's violent mutilation of Philomela, in which he rapes her and then, to keep her from accusing him of the crime, cuts out her tongue. Unable to speak, Philomela instead weaves her story into a textile for her sister, Procne. Chaucer's particular version of the Philomela story (roughly contemporaneous with the *Pistel*) strikingly suggests that the central issue is the role of a male author in a tale that details the textual expression of silenced women. When Tereus cuts out Philomela's tongue, Chaucer writes, "O sely Philomene, wo is thyn herte! / God wreke thee, and send the thy bone! / Now is it tyme I make an ende sone."[36] Leaving out the gruesome ending of the story in which Procne and Philomela kill Tereus's son and feed the child to him, Chaucer instead foregrounds his own sense of guilt for retelling a story that portrays the violent rape and silencing of an innocent woman. Indeed, he begins the tale with a self-conscious assertion of his own response to Philomela: "And, as to me, so grisely was his deed / That whan that I his foule storye rede, / Myne eyen wexe foule and sore also" (2238–40). Chaucer seems especially anxious to distance himself from the violence performed against Philomela, positioning himself as a sorrowful witness to the events. The ending reframes the story to ensure that Philomela be understood as a wholly innocent victim. More generally, the story depicts the possibility that silenced women can find alternative modes of public testimony, whether in a textile or in the vernacular poetry penned by a male author.

Like Chaucer's *Legend of Philomela*, the *Pistel* recognizes itself as a document that works to emphasize the legal and moral innocence of its protagonist. But rather than merely express sympathy as Chaucer does, the author classifies the *Pistel* as a kind of testifying document and the final word on

---

35. In addition, as Staley notes, the fact that the Elders' transgression occurs specifically under a laurel tree—a unique feature of the *Pistel*'s version of the story—contextualizes the *Pistel* with Daphne. "Susanna and English Communities," 47.

36. *The Legend of Good Women*, in *The Riverside Chaucer*, lines 2339–41.

the case of Susanna: "This ferlys bifel / In the days of Danyel, / the pistel witnesseth wel / Of that profete" (361–64). The particular form Susanna's text takes here is an epistle, which typically refers to a written letter, specifically one that takes its content from the apostolic letters of the New Testament, often read as part of the Mass. Indeed, the story of Susanna was read aloud during Lent, so the "pistel" here likely gestures toward its use in sermons and other doctrinal texts. But in the fourteenth century, "pistel" could also refer to an oral complaint or message, as when the old woman in Chaucer's *Wife of Bath's Tale* whispers a "pistel" in the ear of the knight, telling him what women really want.[37] Similarly, Hoccleve's *Jonathas* features a meeting between Jonathas and an anonymous prostitute on the street, in which "Shee thidir cam / and bothe foorth they wente, / And he a pistle rowned in hire ere: / Nat woot y what / for y ne cam nat there."[38] Both the *Wife of Bath's Tale* and *Jonathas* understand a "pistel" to be a whispered comment or complaint, specifically when female chastity is at stake. In these cases, the "pistel" remains unarticulated for the reader, heard only by the immediate recipient.

Given this range of meanings, its appearance at the end of the *Pistel of Swete Susan* signals the poem's interest in multiple testimonial forms and their gendered modes of authority and access. On one hand, the *Pistel* establishes itself as a documentary witness that can be accessed by readers who want to hear about the triumph of chastity and womanly obedience. On the other hand, however, this epistle could signify an oral witness that cannot immediately be heard, one that could potentially offer instruction in female sexual expression. As noted above, though official complaint petitions were open to women, forms of complaint about sexual transgression remained vexed even into the late fourteenth century, particularly in terms of encoding a woman's oral accusation into the iterable, written formulae acceptable in court. The *Pistel*'s final claim that such a "pistel" can "witnesseth wel" implicitly points out the complicated relationship between oral and written complaints made by and on behalf of women. By using the term "pistel," the poem asks whether "witnessing" is an oral activity or a documentary one, foregrounding the limitations and payoffs of voiced testimony and written witnesses. Oral testimony, it seems, can control its audience and determine who will hear it, while written testimony can claim iterability and legal force.

Of course, the relationship between speech and writing, and particularly their comparative claims to authenticity and truth, were debated long before the *Pistel*, and the poem's particular interest in oral and written testimony

---

37. *Middle English Dictionary*, "epistel," s.v. 5. *The Wife of Bath's Tale*, line 1021.
38. *Hoccleve's Works I: The Minor Poems*, ed. Frederick J. Furnivall, EETS e.s. 61 (London 1892), lines 166–68.

engages unexpectedly in this enduring philosophical discussion. Plato's *Phaedrus*, to take one foundational example, argues that writing encourages laziness and forgetfulness, while Isidore of Seville recognizes writing as a supplement to speech, in which letters are symbols of words that speak on behalf of the absent. Honing Isidore's formulation, John of Salisbury famously argued, "Fundamentally letters are shapes that indicate voices. Hence they represent things which they bring to mind through the windows of the eyes. Frequently they speak voicelessly the utterances of the absent."[39] In these formulations, writing is inextricably linked to voice, the originary site of cognition and articulation. More crucially, writing is a way for the silent (the "voiceless" or "absent") to speak, mimicking utterance.

Like Isidore, Hugh of St. Victor also imagines speech and writing to be intimate partners. For Hugh, the link between voice and writing enables the kind of authoritative commentary that muffles Susanna's voice:

> The word "gloss" is Greek, and it means tongue (*lingua*), because, in a way, it bespeaks (*loquitur*) the meaning of the word under it. Philosophers call this an *ad-verbum* (upon the word) because, with one single word, it explains that word concerning the meaning of which there is question, as, for example, when *consticescere* (to become silent) is explained by the word *tacere* (to be still).[40]

Hugh here follows William of Conches's commentary on the *Timaeus*, in which William asserts that a gloss must be as clear as if it were "the tongue of a doctor speaking."[41] Such emphasis on the clarity of commentators' glossing "tongues" surfaces in the *Pistel*'s recurring interest in men's mouths, particularly the "tonge and toth" that describes the Elders' false testimony against Susanna. The tongue is where theologians such as Hugh and William situate commentators' authority to gloss Scriptural texts, and the *Pistel*'s investment in male mouths reprises the link between doctors' tongues and Scriptural hermeneutics. But of course, the Elders' mouths are the site of false testimony, spoken under the auspices of ecclesiastical authority. The *Pistel* thus revises the link between authoritative glossing and tongues, experimenting with the metaphors that authorize male patristic authority—that is, the authority of

---

39. "Littere autem, id est figure, primo vocum indices sunt; deinde rerum, quas anime per oculorum fenestras opponunt, et frequenter absentium dicta sine voce loquuntur," I.13, *Metalogicon*, ed. C. C. J. Webb (Oxford: Oxford University Press, 1929).

40. *The "Didascalicon" of Hugh of Saint Victor*, trans. Jerome Taylor (New York: Columbia University Press, 1991), 119.

41. For William's commentary on the *Timaeus*, see *PL* 172: 250.

those who tell and retell Susanna's story—by disengaging the tongue from the page. Indeed, Hugh's description of silence to exemplify what he means by glossing uncannily anticipates the *Pistel*'s focus on Susanna's silence in the face of false accusations. For Hugh, silence can be rendered articulate by authoritative *lingua*, but the Elders take immoral, self-interested advantage of their ability to gloss Susanna's silence in the courtroom. However, although the Elders attempt to speak for Susanna, translating her silence into a story that transforms her into an adulteress and maintains their legal, doctrinal, and social status, their ultimate failure to testify convincingly via "tonge and toth" suggests the *Pistel*'s rejection of the authoritative-gloss-as-patristic-tongue metaphor.

Furthermore, the idea that silence is an enabling condition of writing—and voice a distraction from it—surfaces repeatedly in a wide range of fourteenth- and fifteenth-century vernacular poetry, when bureaucratic documentary production became increasingly central to the literary projects of several writers. To take one prominent example, Thomas Hoccleve elevates the bureaucratic work of a Privy Seal clerk to poetic production in the prologue to his early fifteenth-century *Regiment of Princes*. For Hoccleve, writing is linked to the ailing body but not to the voice: "A wryter moot thre thynges to him knytte, / And in tho may be no disseverance: / Mynde, ye, and hand—noon may from othir flitte, / But in hem moot be joynt continuance."[42] Claiming that writing tires the stomach, eyes, and back, Hoccleve goes on to argue that Privy Seal clerks must execute their jobs in silence, lest they be distracted by the talking and singing going on around them. Indeed, the need for silence distinguishes writers from manual workers, whom he calls "artificers":

> Thise artificers, see I day by day,
> In the hootteste of al hir bysynesse,
> Talken and synge and make game and play,
> And foorth hir labour passith with gladnesse;
> But we laboure in travaillous stilnesse;
> We stowpe and stare upon the sheepes skyn,
> And keepe moot our song and wordes yn. (1009–15)

Sarah Tolmie points out that Hoccleve actually fails to distinguish between the intellectual work of a writer and the physical work of a laborer, interested

---

42. *The Regiment of Princes*, ed. Charles R. Blyth (Kalamazoo, MI: Medieval Institute, 1999), lines 995–98.

as he is here and throughout the *Regiment* in his own bodily afflictions.[43] Moreover, Tolmie reminds us that the job of Privy Seal clerks was mimetic rather than inventive, and that they spent their time "directing their discrete wills to follow or co-produce the royal will embodied in the warrants issued by their office" (287). Thus, Hoccleve's call for silence might be read not so much as a writer's need for silence to concentrate but as a gesture to the radical absence of the author-scribe at the heart of the kind of bureaucratic production in which he was involved. Transcribing the utterances of others, Hoccleve-the-bureaucrat reconceptualizes Isidore's intimate relationship between voice and letter to imagine writing as representative of the authorial absence that renders bureaucratic production almost monastic in its focus and in its intense devotion to the state.[44]

Hoccleve exemplifies what might be seen as an increasing disengagement between voice and document in the later Middle Ages, a disengagement at the heart of the *Pistel*'s revision of the long-established philosophical and patristic link between tongue and text in the face of new kinds of legal and bureaucratic textual productions. For Hoccleve, silence can be deadening, a morose vision of John of Salisbury's voice-as-text under the tedious conditions of scribal labor. But if we examine another fifteenth-century Chaucerian, Robert Henryson, we might see yet another version of the relationship between voice and documentation, as he considers silence central to documentary production. Like the author of the *Pistel*, Henryson specifically explores the relationship between bureaucratic silence and female voice in his *Testament of Cresseid*, which revisits Cresseid after her affair with Diomede is over. She is condemned to a diseased life in a leper colony and given over to a parliament of gods to be judged. The *Testament* ends with a complaint and Cresseid's last will, which leaves most of her worldly possessions to her fellow lepers and cautions the "ladyis fair of Troy and Grece" to beware the vagaries of Fortune.[45] Significantly, what Cresseid laments most is the loss of her voice: "'My cleir voice and courtlie carrolling, / Quhair I was wont with ladyis for to sing, / Is rawk as ruik, full hiddeous, hoir and hace" (443–45). Nonetheless, she seems to imagine her writing as a way to ensure her testimony will endure, since, after concluding her complaint she begins

---

43. Sarah Tolmie, "The *Prive Scilence* of Thomas Hoccleve," *SAC* 22 (2000): 281–309.

44. For a discussion of late medieval bureaucratic and literary culture with particular emphasis on Hoccleve, see Ethan Knapp, *The Bureaucratic Muse: Thomas Hoccleve and the Literature of Late Medieval England* (University Park: Pennsylvania State University Press, 2001).

45. *The Testament of Cresseid*, in *The Poems of Robert Henryson*, ed. Robert L. Kindrick (Kalamazoo, MI: Medieval Institute, 1997), lines 452–55. Hereafter cited parenthetically by line number.

her last will and testament: "with paper scho sat doun / And on this maneir maid hir testament" (575–76).

The emphasis here on both the material paper and the "making" of her testament illustrates Cresseid's sense that for her testimony to be effective, it must be documentary, rather than oral; this written testament clearly substitutes for her absent raw voice.[46] In her document, Cresseid implores her readers to take heed of her experiences: "'Exempill mak of me in your memour,'" she writes. "'Quhilk of sic thingis wofull witnes beiris'" (465–66). Cresseid defines witnessing here as the documented accounts of her life, both the complaint she pens as well as Henryson's *Testament*. Thus, for Cresseid, "bearing witness" is fundamentally documentary, and as such, fundamentally iterable, accessible to a community of readers rather than listeners. Moreover, Cresseid conceptualizes her testament as a supplement to her deteriorating body and the loss of her "cleir voice," a way to mitigate the silence brought upon by her death.

But Henryson takes a more ambivalent stance with respect to the possibility that a written document produced by a male author can offer the kind of authentic testimony Cresseid might provide with her own voice and body. Indeed, like Chaucer, he seems to worry about taking over Cresseid's testimony once her voice is gone:

> Now, worthie wemen, in this ballet schort,
> Maid for your worschip and instructioun,
> Of cheritie, I monische and exhort,
> Ming not your lufe with fals deceptioun:
> Beir in your mynd this schort conclusioun
> Of fair Cresseid, as I have said befoir.
> Sen scho is deid I speik of hir no moir. (610–16)

The effect of Cresseid's death, he suggests, is to silence the author, though he carefully puts this silence in oral terms: "I *speik* of hir no moir." His overt refusal to "speak" on behalf of the dead Cresseid is supplanted by his textual production that claims to document Cresseid's voice. For both Cresseid and Henryson, then, the voice must be destroyed in order for the text to be efficacious; the absence of oral testimony provides the conditions by which a documentary witness can be written and, by extension, the conditions by

---

46. For a discussion about how literary complaints were invigorated and structured by legal forms of complaint (that is, a written bill that formalized a grievance for which legal remedy was sought), see Scase, *Literature and Complaint*.

which that document can imagine a community of present and future readers taking heed of its exemplary testimony.

Henryson's *Testament*, like Chaucer's *Legend of Philomela*, sets up a gendered system of witnessing: the loss of the female voice is the male author's opportunity to write (albeit with some anxiety). The end of the *Pistel* seems to participate in a similar system, since this witnessing "pistel" testifies on behalf of Daniel the prophet, not Susanna. To make a broad claim from these observations, we might suggest that testifying documents in the later Middle Ages tend to signal male authorship, or at least masculine authority. If this is the case, the Elders' legal downfall would not celebrate Susanna so much as it would elevate Daniel, and the *Pistel of Swete Susan* would attest to the transfer of religious authority from the perjurous Elders to a young prophet. But the use of the term "pistel," rather than "compleinte," suggests perhaps that the *Pistel* wants to posit an alternative. Even if we are to recognize that this poem documents the divinely sanctioned, authoritative power of Daniel's prophetic voice, we must also consider the possibility that there is an oral testimony, a "pistel" whispered so that it cannot be immediately accessed by readers. Perhaps this "pistel" is Susanna's testimony, a female voice that subtends the documentation of Daniel's judgment.

Citation, Notaries, and Documentary Presence in the Case of Susanna

Thus far, this chapter has tracked various patristic interventions into the Susanna story, demonstrating that Susanna's silenced voice was key to the influential and enduring transformation of the story from a warning against false witness into an exemplary tale of female obedience. The previous section argued that the late fourteenth-century *Pistel of Swete Susan* rehabilitated the story's interest in false witness, restaging the evidentiary possibilities in female silence and written documents, particularly when examined both through fourteenth-century complaint procedures regarding sexual transgressions and through other fourteenth- and fifteenth-century vernacular texts that explore the complicated relationship between female silence, official document, and male-authored vernacular poetry. This section turns to late medieval citations of the Susanna story (rather than adaptations of or commentaries on it) to examine how fourteenth- and fifteenth-century writers used the story's complex negotiations between vocal and documentary witnessing to reconsider the communal unity promised by the exemplary

Susanna.[47] For some vernacular writers at the turn of the fifteenth century, Susanna's stoic silence offered a model of resistance against corrupt ecclesiastical or legal hierarchies, rather than a tale of false witness that could reaffirm orthodox doctrine. These texts envisioned the Susanna story as a way to challenge the authority of the Church to assert an alternative heterodox Christian community.

Significantly, many of the texts that cite the story of Susanna understand it in legal terms, emphasizing its investment in how legal testimony might be registered. For example, when Chaucer's Parson cites Susanna, he insists the Susanna story is of particular importance for jurors and notaries: "Ware yow, questemongeres and notaries! Certes, for fals witnessyng was Susanna in ful gret sorwe and peyne, and many another mo" (X.796). Notaries, discussed more fully in chapter 4, were the legal scribes charged with documenting the oral testimonies of courtroom witnesses, and they represented a fairly new scribal occupation in the fourteenth century, one that was already flourishing in Italy but only beginning to emerge on the English legal scene. Notaries were not required to write down testimony word for word, but rather to construct testimony as a coherent narrative. Because they were afforded a significant amount of inventional leeway but also considered arbiters of legal truths, they were often the subject of suspicion and satire in the late fourteenth and fifteenth centuries. The Parson not only understands the Susanna story as fundamentally about false witness rather than about female obedience and chastity, he imagines bureaucratic scribes as the pertinent audience for it, rather than wives or virgins. Accordingly, he inserts the Susanna narrative into a contemporary legal context, worrying particularly that what the narrative exposes—that is, the potential fallibility inherent in transcribing oral testimony into a legal document, particularly when that testimony is silent—might happen under the relatively new conditions of notarial practice.

Similarly, the Wycliffite treatise "Of Prelates" views the Susanna story as a warning for notaries to watch out for false witnesses and as a caution for them to pay attention to how they document testimony. The treatise particularly worries about the negotiation between voice, silence, and document. It claims that when corrupt ecclesiastical officials want to condemn an innocent man, they

---

47. Here, I draw on another meaning of "witness": that is, "to cite." "witnessen," *Middle English Dictionary* s.v. 5 a–d.

> brynge many false witnesses & notaries in his absence, & in presence speke no word, & þei feynen þis false lawe, ȝif þre or four false witnesses hirid bi money seye sich a þing aȝenst a trewe man, þan he schal not be herd, þouȝ he wolde proue þe contrarie bi two hundrid or þre; & þes false men seye in here doynge þat crist was lafully don to þe deþ, & susanne also, for bi sich witnessis þei weren dampnyd, but cristene men bileue techiþ þe contrarie.[48]

The treatise's vocabulary takes up the dense connotations of "witness": that is, to provide oral testimony to an event, as the Elders (falsely) do, and to document that testimony, as notaries were supposed to do. "Of Prelates" is particularly anxious about the work legal documentation is designed to perform, insofar as it worries that while prelates might be silent in the face of the "trewe man," a false accusation might nonetheless enter into the legal record. In such a scenario, notarial writing might supplement silence in order to support and ossify the claims of a false witness, particularly since, as the Susanna story shows, silence offers corrupt Church authorities the opportunity to falsify the legal record. Moreover, the treatise presents such documentary manipulation as an exploitation of the principles of presence and absence: the testimonial silence that occurs in the presence of the "trewe man" results in lies and slander written in his absence.

Indeed, Wycliffite texts repeatedly worry about false witnesses' exploitation of official modes of documenting testimony, citing Susanna as an example of ecclesiastical authority gone wrong. For example, William Thorpe uses Susanna as a way to authorize his refusal to submit to Archbishop Arundel's demand that he abjure his Lollard practice of preaching without Church permission:

> And I heerynge þese wordis þouȝte in myn herte þat þis was an vnleeful askynge, and I demed mysilf cursid of God if I consented herto; and I þouȝte how Susanne seide "Angwysschis ben to me on euery side," and forþi þat I stoode stille musynge and spak not.[49]

Throughout his *Testimony*, as discussed in chapter 5, Thorpe maintains his silence to the frustration of Arundel and his henchmen. That he draws upon Susanna as a foundational text in support of this strategy suggests that he understands the Susanna story to be about managing the relation-

---

48. *The English Works of John Wyclif*, ed. F. D. Matthew, EETS 74 (London: Kegan Paul, Trench and Trubner, 1880; repr. 1902), 74–55.

49. *The Examination of William Thorpe*, in *Two Wycliffite Texts*, ed. Anne Hudson, EETS 301 (Oxford: Oxford University Press, 1993), lines 365–68.

ship between testimonial silence and textual production, particularly when the legal and doctrinal record is at stake.[50] The layers of citation here are multiple and complicated: Thorpe documents—but does not utter—something Susanna purportedly said, either to the Elders, to herself, to God, or to her readers. Thus, rather than merely use Susanna as a model for faithful silence—that is, silence that, as prayer, can result in divine intervention—Thorpe puts pressure on the story's complex negotiations between voice and document and, by extension, between presence and absence. Thorpe's silence frustrates Arundel's attempts to turn his testimony into a self-accusing document, but Thorpe can also imagine his own silence turning into text that will reach beyond Arundel to a sympathetic audience. By using Susanna to negotiate his own silence with various kinds of documentation (the legal transcript Arundel seeks to produce as well as the extralegal autobiography Thorpe wants to provide a Lollard audience), Thorpe transforms the Susanna story into an iterable text that supports his resistance against ecclesiastical and legal corruption.[51]

The Wycliffite championing of Susanna centers on larger questions about divine mediation and presence, discussed more fully in chapter 5. In the case of "Of Prelates," the treatise worries in particular about the work of a notary, who operates as a kind of intermediary between the defendant and the court and, as Thorpe points out, between oral testimony and documented transcript. In "Of Prelates," Susanna represents an exemplar of truth unadulterated by corrupt clergy or legal officials.[52] Likewise, Thorpe sees Susanna as a way to argue on behalf of his own righteousness without the interference of the legal officials who want to shape him into a legal and moral heretic. We might fruitfully understand these complex citations of Susanna in terms of Derrida's discussion of spectrality, which operates according to the same

50. Another Lollard tract, the fifteenth-century *Lanterne of Liȝt*, also cites Susanna as a warning against false witness, but it emphasizes God's intervention into a seemingly intractable situation. *Lanterne of Liȝt*, ed. Lilian M. Swinburn, EETS 151 (London: Kegan Paul, Trench, Trubner & Co., 1917), XII.10–19.

51. For an argument that the *Pistel* itself has Lollard leanings, see David Lyle Jeffrey, "Victimization and Legal Abuse: The Wycliffite Retelling of the Story of Susannah," in *Retelling Tales: Essays in Honor of Russell Peck*, ed. Thomas Hahn and Alan Lupack (Cambridge: D. S. Brewer, 1997), 161–78.

52. Debates about clerical mediation between individual and God are, of course, an enormous and complex issue for Wycliffism and Lollardy. Although I discuss these debates more in chapter 5, I cannot pursue their details fully in this book. For a more in-depth discussion of mediation and presence in Wycliffite studies, see J. Patrick Hornbeck II, *What Is a Lollard?: Dissent and Belief in Late Medieval England* (Oxford: Oxford University Press, 2010), and Anne Hudson, *The Premature Reformation: Wycliffite Texts and Lollard History* (Oxford: Oxford University Press, 1988) as well as studies by Hudson, Fiona Somerset, and Andrew Cole cited in chapter 5.

logic as iterability: the spectral word, like the iterable word, can be detached from its immediate context, bubbling up in unexpected places and with unintended results.[53] Derrida defines spectrality as the inevitable return, what he calls the "frequenting," of a dead or absent authority, such that even the excoriation or rejection of that authority retains its residual presence. Spectrality thus operates via citational logic, which works according to a principle of reflection, "reproducing in a mirror the logic of the adversary at the moment of the retort, piling it on there where one accuses the other of abusing language" (157). In other words, spectrality denotes not merely a ghostly haunting in which something dead or absent unexpectedly returns, but a persistent, dialectical reproduction, in which the rhetorical techniques of an adversary are learned and mimicked so as to destroy the adversary.[54] Thorpe's citation of Susanna reflects and assumes Archbishop Arundel's ecclesiastical power to quote Scripture, and in doing so, Thorpe asserts the power to produce his own legal document, beyond the ecclesiastical arm of the Archbishop. That he does so with a citation of Susanna suggests that he envisions her silence as a particularly powerful model of spectrality, from which he can counter Arundel's efforts to indict him as a heretic.

Moreover, when Derrida explains that spectrality connotes repetition and frequency, insofar as the specter returns to haunt the present, he uncannily returns us to the *Pistel*. As Derrida explains, the specter haunts repeatedly:

> Visit upon visit, since it returns to see us and since *visitare*, the frequentative of *visere* (to see, examine, contemplate) translates well the recurrence or returning, the frequency of a visitation. The latter does not always mark the moment of a generous apparition or a friendly vision; it can signify strict inspection or violent search, consequent persecution, implacable *concatenation*. The social mode of haunting, its original style could also be called, taking into account this repetition, *frequentation*. (126)

Strikingly, when the *Pistel* describes the Elders lurking around the garden walls, gazing upon Susanna, it describes them as specters:

> Iwis, ther haunted til her hous, hende, ye may here,
> Two domes of that lawe that dredde were that day,

---

53. Jacques Derrida, *Specters of Marx: The State of Debt, the Work of Mourning, and the New International*, trans. Peggy Kamuf (New York: Routledge, 1994).

54. For a discussion of spectrality, medieval rhetoric, and intellectual practice, see Rita Copeland, "Sophistic, Spectrality, Iconoclasm," in *Images, Idolatry, and Iconoclasm in Late Medieval England*, ed. Jeremy Dimmick, James Simpson, and Nicolette Zeeman (Oxford: Oxford University Press, 2002), 112–30.

Preostes and presidens preised als peere;
Of whom ur soverein Lord sawes gan say,
And tolde
How heor wikkednes comes
Of the wrongwys domes
That thei have gyve to gomes,
This juges of olde. (31–39)

The *Pistel* follows the Wycliffite Bible's use of the Middle English verb "hauntiden" as a translation of the Vulgate's *frequentabunt*.[55] Though the Elders do not repeatedly visit the garden, they "haunt" the text insofar as they signal the return to a moment of transgression, to the violation of Susanna. In other words, when the Elders "haunt" the garden, they do not merely lurk and gaze upon Susanna; they perform the historical and textual work of the specter, loitering in the space between presence and absence, between the transitory quality of the utterance and the iterability of the written word. Read with Derridean spectrality in mind, the *Pistel*'s use of the word "hauntiden" here indicates that the Elders' moral transgression can be understood as something that returns again and again, first as their proposition to Susanna and then as false witness. In other words, their lascivious gazes and their perjury mirror one another, violating Susanna in the eyes of her husband, the community, and the court.

In explaining the frequenting quality of the specter, Derrida also recognizes the intimate relationship between seeing and spectrality. This "visor effect," as he calls it, describes the feeling of being seen without being able to gaze back, of being haunted without knowing from where or by whom. How, he asks, do we respond to something we cannot see but somehow know is there? For Derrida, the only way to respond is to hear the specter: "Since we do not see the one who sees us," he writes, "we must fall back on its voice" (7). Notably, the *Pistel* specifically depicts the Elders' lecherous gazes—gazes the unwitting Susanna cannot return—as an aural moment for the reader, injecting "hende, ye may here" to direct the reader to *listen* to this moment in the story. This narratorial intrusion is unique to the *Pistel*'s version of the Susanna story. Reading it through Derrida, we might conceptualize this directive as a suggestion that the readers of the *Pistel* pay attention to the multiple ways voice can surface in a text. Accordingly, Susanna's "careful cri" exists between utterance and documentation, a silence that can be "heard" by readers despite the Elders' attempts to muffle it.

---

55. Daniel 13:4–6. See Peck's notes to this stanza.

By considering spectrality as a framework for thinking about how the *Pistel* understands Susanna's cry in the garden and, more broadly, about how late medieval texts take up the Susanna story as a call to resist ecclesiastical manipulation of the written record, we can recognize that fourteenth- and fifteenth-century adaptations and citations of the Susanna story foreground the complexities of textual iterability and authority, particularly when it comes to female testimony. Moreover, the long history of the Susanna story illustrates the way vocal and written testimony can be used to construct the requirements of Christian obedience, particularly for women. However, whereas early commentators translate Susanna's silence into a model for women to bear witness to their steadfast faith in Christian doctrine and divine justice, later English versions reconceptualize female silence as a model of resistance. By extension, these English versions of the story use Susanna's silence to imagine communities of Christian believers that could bear witness to the iniquities of some Church authorities and assert obedience to "true" Church doctrine that operated outside ecclesiastical hierarchy.

Thus, like the *Man of Law's Tale,* the story of Susanna provides opportunities to imagine a unified Christian community; the threat of false testimony is the impetus to articulate and shore up the Scriptural requirement to bear witness to one's faith, even in the face of legal manipulation. But whereas the *Man of Law's Tale* depicts a "nacioun" that emerges unified and triumphant out of false witnesses' threats against Alla's Christian authority, the Susanna story depicts the authorities themselves as the threats to Christian community. Moreover, as late medieval adaptations of the Susanna story reveal, the tensions at the heart of this story of false witness occur between the multiple forms of witnessing. The various kinds of testimony featured in this story—from private prayer to public testimony, from whispered epistles to vernacular poetry—lay claim to different models of legal and moral authority. The portrayal of different witnessing forms is most fulfilled in the *Pistel of Swete Susan,* and later citations of the Susanna story take up the *Pistel*'s exploration of different kinds of witnessing to critique ecclesiastical authority and to imagine alternative Christian communities.

These explorations of various forms of witnessing demonstrate the complex ways witnessing can produce different, even competing, devotional communities, in which Church authorities might be the target of critique. Indeed, even though the Susanna story functioned for patristic writers as a foundational example of female obedience and chastity, it comes to operate as a challenge to orthodox forms of community-unification and -discipline. The next chapter shows how witnessing was fundamental to a particularly important and vexed discourse of community-formation in the later Middle

Ages: neighborliness. The witness and the neighbor were unexpected but crucial reflections of one another in a wide range of late medieval discourses about community, from pastoral treatises to legal statutes to outlaw poetry. Those texts, like the *Pistel*, depict witnessing as a fundamental but flexible mode of constructing a community and show that determining who is one's neighbor is a more complicated task than it first seems. In addition, as we shall see in the final two chapters of this book, the competing authoritative claims that could be made by oral and documentary testimony were crucial to late medieval writers who sought to stretch the boundaries of Christian community to include those marginalized by ecclesiastical restrictions and discipline. The medium of witnessing—whether the body, the voice, or the document—was an important consideration for writers exploring how testimony is defined and how the requirement to bear witness could be used to reconfigure Christian obedience, community, and authority.

three

Neighbors, Witnesses, and Outlaws in the Fourteenth and Fifteenth Centuries

IN A SERMON preached to a Norfolk community sometime around 1365, John Waldeby, an Augustinian friar and Yorkshire preacher, condemned a congregation for failing to testify about a murder in the area. Waldeby argues that the congregation's reticence unfortunately placed the burden of guilt on God, with disastrous effects for the community:

> People today are like those who live in a certain region of England, who, because of a particular murder that had been committed, were unwilling to pass sentence on any one of their neighbors, but instead claimed that God had killed the man. And after they had conducted legal proceedings, they outlawed God. And from this arose an opinion that neither God, nor any of his saints, either lived, or wanted to live, in that part of the country.[1]

This exemplum is part of Waldeby's *Novum opus dominicale*, a collection of Sunday sermons he compiled as a guide for preachers wanting to instruct

---

1. "Similes sunt homines iam hominibus cuiudam patrie in Anglia qui, propter homicidium quoddam perpetratum, noluerunt aliquem vicinum suum iudicare, sed dixerunt quod Deus ipsum occidit, et, facto processu, vtlagauerunt Deum. Et inde surrexit opinio / quod in ista patria existit nec morari voluit Deus nec aliquis sanctus." MS Laud misc. 77, fol. 37r–v. Cited and translated by H. Leith Spencer, in *English Preaching in the Late Middle Ages* (Oxford: Oxford University Press, 1993), 96, 403 note 70.

congregants in the divine commandments. In it, Waldeby takes a community's failure to report a crime and refusal to testify about it as an opportunity to preach about the consequences of false witness and silence for the sanctity of Christian community. The congregation's refusal to provide witnesses to this crime, he suggests, profoundly misunderstands the neighborly loyalty it seeks to protect, and he pushes the point further by asserting that their silence has "outlawed" God from their community. Like Chaucer and the author of the *Pistel,* Waldeby here demonstrates that witnessing is crucial to shaping and protecting the integrity of devotional and legal communities. Indeed, Waldeby's exemplum suggests that this community's reticence functions much like the episodes of false witness featured in the *Man of Law's Tale* and the *Pistel of Swete Susan,* insofar as its refusal to bear witness threatens the bonds of Christian community as much as perjury and counterfeiting can.

For Waldeby, the most important form Christian community takes—and what is most threatened by false witness—is neighborliness. Significantly, in a wide range of late medieval texts, from pastoral manuals to legal statutes to outlaw literature, ideals of neighborliness were often imagined and tested in scenes of false witness. These scenes depict the Scriptural and legal requirements of bearing witness being violated, show divine justice being meted out, and demonstrate that the integrity of Christian communities is ultimately protected by God. Accordingly, what constituted true neighborly conduct was assessed and expressed in such episodes. Yet the depictions of what constituted neighborly behavior in these texts are remarkably varied: some suggest that neighborliness requires demonstrating one's loyalty to a local community, even if that means resisting testifying about a crime, while others suggest that neighborly conduct means testifying against others in the service of legal order and royal authority. In parsing Waldeby's claim that failing to bear witness may weaken the neighborly bonds of this community and even "outlaw" God, this chapter examines the multiple registers of neighborliness Waldeby draws upon in this exemplum, tracking how this term variously emerges in pastoral, legal, and literary discussions about witnessing and justice in the thirteenth, fourteenth, and fifteenth centuries. In particular, it argues that Waldeby's exemplum unexpectedly draws on thirteenth- and fourteenth-century statute law as much as on Scriptural ideals of neighborliness and witnessing, and in doing so, the exemplum opens itself to various readings, both in support of ecclesiastical and royal authorities and resistant to them.

More broadly, then, analyzing this exemplum offers insight into the later Middle Ages' ubiquitous worry about multiple and sometimes competing definitions of neighborliness, a worry that surfaces particularly as English law sought to streamline its practices under the centralized authority of the crown in the thirteenth and fourteenth centuries. The medieval neighbor was at the center of debates regarding the vexed relationship between local customary practices and royal legal and bureaucratic operations. As scholars such as Robert Palmer, Susan Reynolds, Richard Firth Green, and Anthony Musson have shown, the expansion of royal jurisdiction in the thirteenth and fourteenth centuries produced new relationships within and between local communities, such that "neighbors" could be understood as mutual crown subjects or, at times, as partners in resistance to the king's law.[2] Indeed, L. O. Aranye Fradenburg has suggested that in the later Middle Ages, we can see what she calls an "apotheosis of the neighbor," when multiple allegiances—to God, to country, to lord—were entangled to varying degrees of success.[3] She shows that new horizontal affiliations and loyalties (among, for example, guild members) both accommodated and resisted older hierarchical relationships (between, for example, laborer and lord, or subject and king). These competing zones of fidelity produced multiple definitions of neighborly behavior that did not necessarily complement one another. Neighborly fidelity to local members of the same community—whether understood as a vill, a parish, or even class—sometimes worked against the kind of "neighborly" fidelity the crown expected subjects to express on its behalf.

The conflicting arenas in which neighborly witnessing was debated can be demonstrated in some early ecclesiastical attempts to define and discipline false witness as a crime. At the Council of Oxford in 1222, Archbishop Stephen Langton declared excommunication for anyone maliciously imput-

---

2. Robert Palmer, *English Law in the Age of the Black Death, 1328–1381: A Transformation of Governance and Law* (Chapel Hill: University of North Carolina Press, 1993); Susan Reynolds, *Kingdoms and Communities in Western Europe, 900–1300* (Oxford: Oxford University Press, 1997); Green, *Crisis of Truth*; and Anthony Musson, *Medieval Law in Context: The Growth of Legal Consciousness from Magna Carta to the Peasants' Revolt* (Manchester: Manchester University Press, 2001).

3. L. O. Aranye Fradenburg, "Pro Patria Mori," in *Imagining a Medieval English Nation*, ed. Kathy Lavezzo (Minneapolis: University of Minnesota Press, 2003), 30. The idea and function of the neighbor (and neighbor-love) is perhaps most familiar from Freudian and Lacanian psychoanalysis, in which the neighbor (*nebenmensch*) symbolizes the double pull between desire and sacrifice that structures subject-formation. This psychoanalytic framework has been central to investigations of neighborliness in the Middle Ages and is best exemplified by Fradenburg's *Sacrifice Your Love: Psychoanalysis, Historicism, Chaucer* (Minneapolis: University of Minnesota Press, 2002). For discussions of the relationship between psychoanalytic and political constructions of neighborliness, see the essays by Slavoj Žižek, Eric L. Santner, and Kenneth Reinhard in *The Neighbor: Three Inquiries in Political Theology* (Chicago: University of Chicago Press, 2005).

ing a crime to someone "who is not of ill fame."[4] This is the beginning of an English law of defamation, but it is not clear from the records whether slander, perjury, and other kinds of false witness were considered spiritual crimes, to be adjudicated by canon law, or secular ones, left to the state. It seems that private defamation between individuals, including slander, was to be considered under secular jurisdiction: in fact, in the local court systems operating in the shires, defamation could be considered a form of trespass, akin to stealing property. But blasphemy, including false oaths, was to be handled by Church courts, since it violated the sanctified relationship between God and person. Likewise, perjury was thought to be a spiritual crime, even when committed in a secular court. Oddly enough, despite the new legal designation of defamation as a crime, royal courts seemed largely unconcerned with it; it was treated as a local infraction, whether secular or spiritual. These negotiations about defamation prosecution illustrate that while it could be considered a local, secular problem—as a crime that damages the relationships between individuals—it was also sometimes more broadly considered a spiritual threat to a Christian community, particularly when bad oaths were involved. Defamation laws were one way to manage the relationships between neighbors, but even in these legal discussions it is not always immediately apparent whether a neighbor signified someone who lived in one's local community or whether it indicated someone who participated in a larger Christian community.[5]

For the later Middle Ages, "neighbor" was an analytic category deployed by an astonishing range of texts and communities, from local sheriffs to crown representatives to the Church. This chapter follows the logic of Waldeby's exemplum to trace the intimate but complicated relationship between witnessing and neighborliness. The first section examines how pastoral treatises and didactic literature understand how witnessing can construct neighborly communities (and, by extension, how false witnessing and refusing to bear witness can weaken neighborly bonds). The next section demonstrates the centrality of neighborliness in the development of English common law, particularly in its attempts to centralize legal authority around the crown, rather than around the customary practices of local legal communities.

    4. "Excommunicamus omnes illos qui gratia odii, lucri, vel favoris, vel alia quacunque de causa malitiose crimen imponunt alicui, cum infamatus non sit apud bonos et graves, ut sic saltem ei purgatio indicatur vel alio modo gravetur." *Councils and Synods with Other Documents relating to the English Church II: 1205-1313*, ed. F. M. Powicke and C. R. Cheney (Oxford: Clarendon, 1964), 107.
    5. For a discussion of the status of defamation in Church courts, local courts, and royal courts, see Richard Helmholz's introduction to *Select Cases of Defamation to 1600*, ed. R. H. Helmholz (London: Selden Society, 1985).

Together, these two sections show that Waldeby works within these didactic and legal contexts to formulate his insistence that neighborliness requires people to come forward when witnesses are needed.

Moreover, when Waldeby warns that this community has turned God into an outlaw, he suggests that outlaws, like false witnesses, threaten the bonds of neighborly, Christian community. Although Waldeby's suggestion that God can be imagined as an outlaw may seem startling, depictions of outlawry in the later Middle Ages—particularly depictions featured in popular literature such as Robin Hood ballads—built upon the legal and didactic thinking about witnessing and neighborliness. But those depictions do not cohere into a single, unified picture of how neighborliness ought to be defined. Some outlaw texts resist the legal ideal of neighbors bearing witness against one another by conceptualizing communities of outlaws as neighbors working on behalf of a kind of extralegal ethical justice. Other texts imagine outlaws as "neighbors" to the king who act in support of the royal jurisdiction of the crown to construct and manage legal authority. The range of portrayals of neighborliness in the poems and ballads that feature outlaws reveals that distinctions between legal official and criminal (and the communities they represent) can be difficult to discern. Accordingly, these texts remind us that what it means to be truly "neighborly" may require resisting the institutions and systems that claim to shape and produce neighborly relationships and communities. Thus, the final section of this chapter shows that outlaw literature provides a surprising but important context for Waldeby's exemplum, since it illustrates that the neighbor and the outlaw can (and perhaps should) be considered extensions of one another. Reading Waldeby's exemplum through these diverse contexts suggests that Waldeby's sense of Christian neighborliness may be more capacious or resistant than it first appears, and it demonstrates just how complex it was to be a good neighbor in the Middle Ages.

False Witnesses, Good Neighbors, and Corrupt Lawyers in Late Medieval Pastoralia

Despite his oblique reference to a local murder, Waldeby addresses his exemplum to a general audience (*homines*), so his call to bear witness might be read as a general warning to all Christians about the requirements of building unity among neighbors.[6] As Waldeby's exemplum makes clear, medieval

---

6. MS Laud 77 includes a marginal note, "Nortifelchia," next to this exemplum, perhaps indicating that Waldeby or one of his readers thought the exemplum might have particular

ideals of neighborliness and neighborly behavior are inextricably linked to the act of witnessing, insofar as bearing witness unites communities through common belief and neighborly trust. As Zechariah formulates it, "Speak the truth, everyone to his neighbor" (8:16). Indeed, the idealized relationship between neighborliness and witnessing emerges most profoundly out of the many Scriptural warnings that bearing false witness will destroy neighborly relationships. For example, Exodus cautions, "You shall not bear false witness against your neighbor" (20:16), while Proverbs claims, "A man who bears false witness against his neighbor is like a dart and a sword and a sharp arrow" (25:18).[7] Furthermore, failing or refusing to bear witness is considered equivalent to bearing false witness, as Leviticus asserts: "If anyone sins and hears the voice of one swearing and is a witness either because he himself has seen or because he is conscious of it: if he does not utter it, he will bear his iniquity" (5:1).[8] Following these Scriptural injunctions, the *Somme le Roi* lists keeping quiet as the last of the twenty-four sins of the tongue. Waldeby follows these Scriptural and pastoral injunctions against testimonial reticence, and he likewise argues that failing to bear witness destroys the neighborly bonds that are crucial to Christian unity.

Notably, pastoral and didactic discussions of witnessing often center on assessing the potential damage to neighborly bonds, suggesting that neighborliness was becoming a central category through which to articulate the importance of bearing witness. As outlined in the first chapter, didactic treatises of the period often focus on false oaths and perjury as particularly dangerous to Christian fidelity and doctrinal knowledge. Such treatises tend to identify these forms of false witness as insidious expressions of envy that destroy neighborly relationships by rejecting Christian *caritas* in favor of base or material desires.[9] The *Fasciculus Morum*, for example, discusses a

resonance in Norfolk. Notably, Norfolk was a growing center for criminal activity in the thirteenth and fourteenth centuries, especially homicide. In the thirteenth century, Norfolk boasted higher-than-average murder rates, and in the fourteenth century, cases from Norfolk were often used to illustrate legal principles in statute collections detailing coroners' duties. For example, in one collection from the second half of the fourteenth century, the guidelines for coroners' duties regarding pleas of the crown are accompanied by three case examples, all of which happened "apud C. in Norffolk." See Huntington Library, HM 906, folios 83r–v. James Buchanan Given calculates Norfolk's overall homicide rate (based on eyre rolls between 1250 and 1269) as around 15/100,000 per annum, with Bedford topping the list with 18.9/100,000 per annum in 1276 and Kent boasting the lowest rate with 6.8/100,000. See *Society and Homicide in Thirteenth-Century England* (Stanford, CA: Stanford University Press, 1977), 36–37.

    7. For other warnings specifically about bearing false witness against one's neighbors, see Deuteronomy 5:20, 19:16–21, and Proverbs 24:28.

    8. See also Proverbs 29:24.

    9. For a list of preachers' handbooks that include extended discussions of false swearing, see G. W. Owst, *Literature and Pulpit in Medieval England* (Cambridge: Cambridge University Press, 1933), 414–24.

parable of a simple man (*simplex*) whose property is coveted by a more powerful neighbor:

> If the lower-class citizen does not want to sell or make over his property, what I pray will his more powerful neighbor do? Will he not go to the bailiffs or the hundred-court and accuse him of being a thief or murderer or traitor to his town or the realm? This way he will come injustly to the land or have that lower-class citizen hanged, just as such a tyrant once said to the peasant for the sake of the latter's land: "I swear to God," he said, "you will either give, sell, or swap that land with me, or else 'grin at the moon,'" that is to say, you will at once be hung by your neck. (153)

Here, class distinctions and the legal influence that accompanies them are exploited, supported with a false oath that works to satisfy the envious desires of the powerful, wealthy neighbor. The abuse of status position, this example suggests, leads to violence and tyranny, and the envy supported by a false oath destroys the charitable relations that should structure any Christian community. Indeed, false oaths not only permit the wealthier citizen to take property from his neighbor; they provide the opportunity for the helpless neighbor to be treated like a traitor to his community. Thus, false oath-taking problematically allows the wealthier neighbor to determine who belongs within his circle of neighbors and who does not. Similarly, Robert Mannyng's worries about taking false oaths (described in the first chapter) divides communities of people into distinct classes rather than unites them around Christian *caritas*. Mannyng particularly chastises "gentyl men" who think of oath-taking merely as an act of courtesy rather than an assertion of truth-telling (669–70). For Mannyng, communities based around performances of empty courtesy fail to nurture the doctrinal unity that should supersede class consciousness and fidelity. As he puts it, "þys gentylmen, þys gettours, / þey beyn but goddys turmentours," further explaining that "So euery man vnto oþer / þe pore to þe ryche ys broper / Yn oþys and yn wykkydhede" (761–62; 771–73). The author of *Ayenbite of Inwit* (ca. 1340) similarly argues that perjury leads to chiding, strife, slander, reproach, and threats, linguistic and social crimes the author specifically likens to "war with neighbors and those close to us."[10]

Repeatedly throughout the fourteenth and fifteenth centuries, didactic texts incorporate demonstrative episodes of legal strife to portray how any

---

10. *Dan Michel's Ayenbite of Inwit*, ed. Richard Morris, EETS 23 (London: Trubner & Co., 1866), 64.

friction between Christian neighbors could be amplified by abuse of legal process. These episodes often specifically depict common law as supportive of a general culture of false witness that damages Christian neighborliness and unity. Langland's Clergie, for example, complains that Religion (which Langland associates particularly with the monastic life) has become too closely affiliated with legal administration, and in doing so, he has left "the commune" behind while he wanders aimlessly: "'Ac now is Religion a rydere, / a romere by stretes, / A ledere of lovedayes and a lond buggere, / A prikere [up]on a palfrey fro manere to manere, / An heep of houndes at his ers as he a lord were.'"[11] Similarly, in *Jack Upland*, a fifteenth-century complaint against corrupt friars and other ecclesiastical officials, the narrator criticizes the widespread unraveling of neighborliness among the "comoun peple" as a result of the troublesome affiliations between ecclesiastical authorities and secular administrators:

> To þe comoun peple haþ Anticrist ȝouun leue to leue her trewe laboure and bicome idil men ful of disceitis to bigile eche oþere, as summe bicome men of crafte & marchauntis proffessid to falsnes, and summe men of lawe to distroye Goddis lawe & loue amonge neiȝboris.[12]

Here, lawyers are accused of destroying both God's law and neighborly love, due in part to the rampant backbiting that has grown among the "comoun peple." *Jack Upland* worries specifically about the detachment of legal officials from those they are supposed to serve, imagining a gap between the "commons" and the law as it is administered on earth. Together, *Piers Plowman* and *Jack Upland* illustrate that the worry about the ways false witness might dissolve neighborly relationships extends to various kinds of didactic texts that depicted a range of Christian communities. For Langland's Clergie, an advocate for Latin learning and Church hierarchy, as for Jack Upland, an iconoclastic critic of ecclesiastical officials, neighborliness is the backbone of doctrinal community, and it suffers when legal authorities forget to serve the community they have been charged with protecting.

Like *Piers Plowman* and *Jack Upland*, *Dives and Pauper* argues that abuses of the law can disrupt neighborly trust, and it articulates the eighth commandment, against bearing false witness, in specifically legal terms. Pauper

---

11. All citations from *Piers*, unless otherwise noted, will be from the B-text from *The Vision of Piers Plowman*, 2nd ed., ed. A. V. C. Schmidt (London: Everyman, 1995), X.305–8. Hereafter cited parenthetically by passus and line number.

12. "Jack Upland," in *Jack Upland, Friar Daw's Reply, and Upland's Rejoinder*, ed. P. L. Heyworth (Oxford: Oxford University Press, 1968), 40–44.

first takes the time to explain in detail the way courtroom testimony ought to proceed and the necessity of ensuring that testimony be true and objective. Despite his turn to legal example, however, Pauper insists that bearing witness is a function of neighborly justice in the service of a truth that exceeds the legal requirements of the courtroom:

> And ȝif a man see þat hys neyebore schulde fallyn in hys trewþe & lesyn his ryȝt for defaute of witnesse, ȝif he knowe þe trewþe & mon beryn witnesse in þe cause, but he bere witnesse & seye þe trewþe for sauacioun of his neyebore ellys hy synnyth greuously þou he be nout brout to beryn witnese. (VIII.x.10–14)

Pauper argues that if any neighbor knows the truth and hears another neighbor falsifying a story, he must come forward "for the salvation of his neighbor," whether or not he is summoned to court. Notably, however, Pauper's emphasis on the relationship between true testimony and neighborly community makes exceptions for ecclesiastical officials. Claims against priests or bishops require extra witnesses, he says,

> For þer schulde no man ben in dignete neyþer spirituel ne temporel but trewe folc to wose trewþe men schuldyn ȝeuyn mor credence þan to þe speche of simple folc whyche knowyn nout wel what is trewþe ne what is fals, what is profytable to þe comounte ne what is noyous to þe comounte, and oftyn wol lytil dredyn God. (VIII.x.38–43)

This formulation is different from the example of the wealthy, devious false witness offered in the *Fasciculus Morum*. In the *Fasciculus Morum* the privileged few could manipulate the law in the service of their own material gain and at the expense of those who live more simply. Here, priests are figured as "trewe folc" whose reputations may be damaged as a result of the speech of "simple folc," who cannot tell the difference between what is true and what is false. Their inability to distinguish between true and false, moreover, is linked to an inability (or indifference) to act on behalf of the communal good. Thus, for Pauper, the neighborly fidelity that characterizes Christian community must be monitored by ecclesiastical officials, who must always maintain truth and communal integrity.

These few examples show that pastoral and didactic treatments of neighborliness in the later Middle Ages reveal a number of fissures in the ideal of community sanctity that "neighborliness" ostensibly performs. Repeatedly, pastoral and didactic texts depict suspicion of the legal authorities that attempt to determine the truth or falsity of a witness's claims, instead claiming that true neighborliness can only be expressed by attesting to the moral and ethical ties of a community. Similarly, Waldeby's exemplum insists that Christian neighborliness must be articulated and strengthened by bearing witness against any threat to the community. Indeed, his exemplum sounds much like the one included in *Dives and Pauper,* which advocates for the morality of the requirement to bear witness for the salvation of one's neighbor. But unlike many of the treatises discussed above, Waldeby's exemplum does not seem to register any suspicion of the law or legal administrators. In fact, it seems to argue that the community he addresses has failed to adhere to the legal requirement to testify about a crime as much as to the moral obligation to bear witness. The exemplum thus suggests that the legal and the moral ought not to be distinguished so easily. Indeed, the next section argues that Waldeby is as invested in legal definitions and models of neighborly behavior as he is in pastoral definitions and models. Crucially, this legal context opens up new and unexpected possibilities for understanding what kind of neighbor Waldeby might have imagined in his exemplum as well as the multiple ways one might enact the ideal of neighborliness.

Neighbors, *Vicini,* and Witnesses of the Realm in English Common Law

As discussed in the previous section, Waldeby's exemplum illustrates a concern with neighborly behavior, a concern shared by several fourteenth- and fifteenth-century pastoral and didactic texts. But the peculiar vocabulary Waldeby uses in his exemplum suggests that it ought to be contextualized within the discussions about legal neighborliness ongoing in the thirteenth and fourteenth centuries. In particular, it must be understood through what jurists called "vicinage": that is, the requirement that jurors be drawn from the local village or town because of their knowledge of the case and the accused. As if signaling this exemplum's investment in the common law's definition of neighborly witnessing, Waldeby uses the legalistic term *vicinum,* rather than *proximum,* which is much more common in sermons, sermon collections, and *ars praedicandi* manuals. *Proximum* is also the term used in the Vulgate and Rheims-Douai versions of the Good Samaritan parable and in other Scriptural discussions of neighborliness, such as Matthew. By using *vicinum* rather than *proximum,* Waldeby calls attention to his awareness of and interest in legal models of neighborliness, and his use of this term complicates any simple understanding of what he might be preaching to his congregation about witnessing and neighborliness.

Vicinage requirements stretch back to early Anglo-Saxon and Anglo-Norman legal codes, in which groups of *vicini,* or neighbors, were asked to give testimony on local facts and crimes. Vicinage was based on the idea that neighborly knowledge of the accused's reputation and of community custom was evidentiary and that neighbors were the best source of judgment, since they could accurately attest to community beliefs and suspicions as well as to the facts in dispute.[13] The principles of vicinage engineered much of early English legal process, when local custom structured legal and ethical standards and when juridical administrators were drawn directly from the local community. Systems of frankpledge, for example, relied on local knowledge as the foundation of justice and discipline. Used in the counties and manorial courts, frankpledge operated through units of ten men, called tithings, and each member of the tithing vowed to serve the tithing faithfully and to suppress crime and disorder within the community.[14] To do so, the tithing primarily relied on the hue and cry, in which a shout, a horn blow, or a ringing bell alerted community members to suspicious activity and summoned the neighbors within earshot to pursue the criminal.[15] The hue and cry meant that the jurisdiction of the tithing and the neighbors within that jurisdiction were understood as those within earshot. Under such a system, the term "neighbor" signaled spatial proximity, and neighbors functioned as disciplinary watchdogs for the community.

The operations of frankpledge endured in manorial courts into the thirteenth century and even beyond in some areas, but beginning in the twelfth century, English law slowly began to transfer its procedures away from local customary justice to centralized royal legal systems. Significantly, such shifts in operations produced new conceptualizations of the neighborly witness, particularly in terms of local legal knowledge and loyalty to the community. In 1166, Henry II declared in the Assize of Clarendon that 12 of every 100 men must report suspicious behavior in their neighborhood royal sheriffs.

---

13. Mike MacNair, "Vicinage and the Antecedents of the Jury," *Law and History Review* 17.3 (1999): 537–90. See also responses in the same volume by Charles Donohue, Jr., "Biology and the Origins of the Jury" (591–96) and Patrick Wormald, "Neighbors, Courts, and Kings: Reflections on Michael MacNair's *Vicini*" (597–602), as well as MacNair's response to Donohue and Wormald (603–8). Much of my explanation of the development of neighbor-witnesses is drawn from this discussion.

14. William A. Morris, *The Frankpledge System* (London: Longman, Green, & Co., 1910).

15. Musson, *Medieval Law,* 90–91.

These 12 men, called *vicini*, were the kind of neighbor-witnesses familiar from frankpledge, who could attest to the accused's reputation or community standing. They also, significantly, took on an accusatory function on behalf of the realm. Accordingly, these 12 men operated as early forms of juries, insofar as the group was asked to tender a verdict on a case to a judge, who would then take the jury verdict as one piece of evidence as he made his decision.[16] To explain and defend the dual function of the *vicini*, Glanvill states that jurors must be neighbors in order to judge both the facts and the circumstances of the case. Indeed, Glanvill considers groups of neighbors to be particularly foolproof in meting out justice, given their familiarity with the events at hand and their dedication to communal discipline.

Vicini were thought to be especially useful in land transfer and inheritance cases. For example, Glanvill insists that family members must be the primary witnesses to testify to the terms of an inheritance, but he adds that if there is insufficient or inconsistent testimony among the family, "recourse must be had to the neighborhood (*ad visnetum*) whose testimony, if it confirms that of blood relatives, shall be conclusive" (II.6). Glanvill thus treats the neighborhood as a legal supplement for or extension of the family, important if the bonds of kinship were to break down in the face of legal dispute. Notably, Glanvill argues these neighbor-jurors might be familiar with the case in a range of ways: "The knowledge required from jurors is that they shall know about the matter from what they have personally seen and heard, or from statements which their fathers made to them in such circumstances that they are bound to believe them as if they had seen or heard for themselves" (II.6). Such a claim—that to be an eyewitness could be considered equivalent to hearing something from "their fathers"—is striking in its elision of distinctions between types of probative knowledge, insofar as firsthand knowledge and hearsay are thought to be the same. This elision also expresses the ways both familial and neighborly ties were thought to be bonds that can be trusted, both within a community and in a courtroom.

This is not to say, however, that neighbor-witnesses were *always* fully trusted, nor that they always offered honest testimony and sound judgments. For example, one case from around 1155 laments that the system of vicinage allows neighbors to take advantage of their legal authority. The case

---

16. Wormald argues that the accusatory function of the *vicini* was "emphatically a feature of Henry's inheritance," rather than a sea change ushered in by the Assize of Clarendon. Likewise, Hyams argues that "the Assize of Clarendon sought to institutionalize in twelve-man juries that concept of neighborhood reputation used in England since at least the eleventh century." *Rancor and Reconciliation*, 159. See 158–60 for an explanation of how early English juries worked.

describes how the Abbot Robert of St. Albans lost the rights to his land to a lay brother of the Order of the Hospitallers based on the manipulated testimony of neighbors:

> It was finally decided by judgment of the king's court to have the problem settled by the oath of the men of the town of Luton. Some people, swayed by the gifts of the aforesaid man H. and corrupted by numerous promises, produced mendacious witnesses who were ready to prove by oath that the said land belonged in no way to the said church of Luton, and although their wickedness was patent to all, their testimony, because such was the custom of the land, was admitted and confirmed by oath. And thus that land henceforward was possessed by the aforesaid H., but he did not get away with it unpunished, for he was immediately seized by a horrible and sudden indisposition and died miserably.[17]

The "custom of the land" is here recognized as the acceptance of the testimony offered by its own community members, even when it is clear that the witnesses are not truthful. Furthermore, it illustrates the way such corrupt legal operations were perceived to be subject to divine justice. The custom of relying on neighbors as witnesses, particularly about property rights, falls flat as these neighbors' fidelity to the lay brother trumps the courtroom expectation that they give truthful testimony. But the intervention of God in the form of a terrible disease reassuringly submits all human witnessing to the ultimate testimony and judgment of divine justice. Accordingly, this document suggests that the legal call to neighborly witnessing is always subject to divine law, especially when the sense of neighborly community that coheres in bearing witness fails in the face of greed or corruption.

In the thirteenth century, the vicinage requirements of testifying witnesses and courtroom judges were replaced by the rule of venue, which required that a trial take place at the site from which the alleged facts issue. The rule of venue assembled juries from the injured region, rather than gathered accusatory and judging people who knew the accused, his family, and his circumstances. Under the rule of venue, a trial could take place at Westminster as well as anywhere else, since jurors needed only to be informed of the facts and did not need to be familiar with the life of the accused. The status of the legal neighbor-witness (and the neighbor-juror) thus stretched and changed as English common law sought to construct a system of justice

---

17. *English Lawsuits from William I to Richard I*, vol. 2, ed. R. C. Van Caenegem (London: Selden Society, 1990–91), 468.

under the authority of the king, a system that would come to contend with, if not fully supplant, the customary laws governing the counties and shires.

Yet royal documents from the thirteenth century do not always reveal a hard distinction between the king's justice on one hand and neighborly, localized justice on the other, attempting instead to conceptualize a kind of neighborly justice that could accommodate both local customary practice and royal law. For example, "The Proclamation of 1258," issued in Latin, French, and English, explains the newly centralized system of juridical administration to suggest a certain amount of involvement on the part of local communities. The text claims that royal administrators

> beoþ ichosen þur3 us and þur3 þaet loandes folk on vre kuneriche, habbeþ idon and shullen don in þe worþnesse of Gode and on vre treowþe, for þe freme of þe loande þur3 þ3 besi3te of þan tofrensiseide redesmen.[18]

The proclamation links the royal administration ("us") to the people of a particular community ("that land's folk"), using vocabulary that suggests the law's dedication to neighborly unity and local culture. Ralph Hanna has shown that the demands of this Proclamation are rooted in an Oxford committee's insistence that the king follow their counsel, as commanded in Magna Carta; after three drafts, the Proclamation was "grudgingly" adopted as royal policy in 1263.[19] The production and dissemination of the text itself, as Hanna shows, emerges out of debates regarding the reach of royal jurisdiction, the role of customary justice, and the need for voices of representatives from the shires and elsewhere. The vocabulary of the Proclamation carefully works to subsume the shires beneath the king's jurisdiction, stressing in particular the neighborly commitment that might structure the shires' relationship to the king.[20] That these juridical officials will work on behalf of "vre treowþe," for example, suggests a desire to emphasize their ethical motivations on behalf of a local community. As Green has outlined, the term "trouthe" often signaled binding integrity and community fidelity. By deploying the term "treowþe," this Proclamation tries to depict a working relationship between royal officials and the local communities they police, taking up the rhetoric of local community and neighborly fidelity to construct royal administrators work-

---

18. *English Historical Documents, 1189-1327*, ed. Harry Rothwell (London: Eyre and Spottiswode, 1975), 367. Hereafter abbreviated as EHD.

19. Ralph Hanna, *London Literature, 1300–1380* (Cambridge: Cambridge University Press, 2005), 45.

20. Hanna notes that government pronouncements such as the Proclamation of 1258 "were routinely promulgated and archived in the shires" (52). See also George E. Woodbine, "The Language of English Law," *Speculum* 18.4 (1943): 395–436.

ing in the outer counties as members of those communities. Yet the Proclamation also carefully insists that the administrators are agents of the crown, not of the counties.

Indeed, in the second half of the thirteenth century, statute law and royal documents redefine legal neighbors as crown subjects, rather than as those linked through their knowledge of and adherence to local custom. The 1267 Statute of Marlborough, for example, chastises the residents of the town for failing to adhere to proper royal procedure in prosecuting crimes. In this statute, neighborly relations are explicitly managed by royal courts. In fact, these "neighbors" are treated almost as children having a spat that requires intervention by a calm, disinterested authority:

> Whereas at the time of a Commotion late stirred up within this Realm, and also sithence, many great Men, and divers other, (refusing to be justified) by the King and his Court, like as they ought and were wont in Time of the King's noble Progenitors, and also in his Time; but took great Revenges and Distresses of their Neighbours, and of other, until they had Amends and Fines at their own Pleasure; and further, some of them (would not be justified) by the King's Officers, nor (would) suffer them to make Delivery of such Distresses as they had taken of their own Authority; It is Provided, agreed, and granted, that all Persons, as well of high as of low estate, shall receive Justice in the King's Court; and none from henceforth shall take any such Revenge or Distress of his own Authority, without Award of (our) Court, though he have Damage or Injury, whereby he would have amends of his Neighbour either higher or lower.[21]

The statute not only excoriates the justice meted out by neighbors of the community; it repeatedly insists that everyone in the community, whether of high or low estate, must submit to royal systems of justice. In this statute, then, the term "neighbors" signifies those working in contradistinction to royal precept, and the way it is used here flattens out any class differences that might exist within the community itself, class differences that could critically structure internal neighbor-relations, as illustrated in some of the didactic treatises discussed in the previous section.

One consequence of this shift in neighborly relations and juridical authority is that legal infractions were measured as injury to the crown, rather than as local injuries between people who knew each other. In fact, the 1275 Statute of Westminster explicitly defines false witness as treason:

---

21. 52 Hen. III. *Statutum de Marleberge*, in *Statutes of the Realm*, vol. 1, page 19.

> Forasmuch as there have been oftentimes found in the Country (Devisors) of Tales, whereby discord (or occasion) of discord, hath many time arisen between the King and his People, or Great Men of this Realm; for the Damage that hath and may thereof ensue; It is commanded, That from henceforth none be so hardy to tell or publish any false News or Tales, whereby discord, or (occasion) of discord or slander may grow between the King and his People, or the Great Men of the Realm; and he that doth so, shall be taken and kept in Prison, until he hath brought him into the Court.[22]

Not surprisingly, this statute imagines bearing false witness in administrative and legal terms, rather than (or at least as much as) in moral terms. Crucially, the statute attempts to envision the act of bearing witness as supportive of royal authority, suggesting that false witness destabilizes not so much the peer relationships between neighbors as the hierarchical bonds between people and king (or people and magnate). According to this statute, then, the king must be understood as everyone's neighbor, who both inspires and polices the witnessing practices of a community structured by its fidelity to the crown. Indeed, the Westminster Statute seems very worried about the possibility that some people might refuse to recognize royal authority and instead believe false witnesses:

> Forasmuch as certain People of this Realm doubt very little to make a false Oath (which they ought not to do,) whereby much People are disherited, and lose their Right; It is Provided, That the King, of his Office, shall from henceforth grant Attaints upon Enquests in Plea of Land, or of Freehold, or of any thing touching Freehold, when it shall seem to him necessary.[23]

The Statute suggests that because false oaths are standard practice among "certain People of this Realm," the king must step in to supervise inheritance and land transfer rather than rely on the testimony of neighbors, as was the custom a century back. The Statute thus establishes the king as an authority who can root out and deflate the power of false witnesses to ensure the integrity of the legal community he is meant to structure. However, we must nonetheless note that despite the turn toward centralized, royal legal administration in the latter half of the thirteenth century, the conceptual importance of neighborliness in attesting to local community beliefs and customs remains important. For example, William Durand's 1271 *Speculum*

22. 3. Edw I. c. 34. *The Statutes of the Realm*, vol. 1, page 35.
23. 3. Edw I. c. 38, page 36.

juris insists, "We are presumed to know the deeds of our neighbors,"[24] and as mentioned above, frankpledge still operated as an important mode of juridical administration in the counties throughout the thirteenth century. On one hand, then, the thirteenth-century neighbor could testify on behalf of a local community, and his or her fidelity was anchored in the neighbor-bonds produced by local custom, reputation, and belief. But on the other hand, a neighbor could be understood as someone bound to royal law, rather than—or at least as much as—to local community custom.

In the fourteenth century, England saw significant administrative and legal upheavals regarding definitions and procedures that were centered on neighborly justice. Public disorder was a major social and political issue from the turn of the century into the 1330s, and the crown repeatedly tried to shore up its influence over local juridical administrators by experimenting with several kinds of administrative agencies, to varying degrees of success. In 1305, for example, Edward I instituted the commission of trailbaston, an itinerant group of royal justices who were to patrol the counties and shires and report any suspicious activity to the king's court. Widely upbraided for corruption and ineffectiveness, trailbaston officials were seen as strangers who infiltrated local communities to upstage local administrators. Yet at the same time, the number of tithing groups dwindled in the fourteenth century, suggesting that royal justice was overtaking the localized mechanisms of manorial courts.[25]

Three particular parliamentary moments help illustrate the tug of war between local and royal jurisdictional power in the fourteenth century. In 1341, several counties issued petitionary requests that parliament withdraw itinerant justice commissions and instead appoint men with knowledge of local conditions to police the counties. Apparently dissatisfied with parliament's response, other petitioners asked for the same thing in 1348, declaring firmly that the best method of keeping the peace throughout the counties would be to elect six men to hear and determine cases, since "residents are best suited to deal with local needs."[26] Yet in 1361, just a few years before Waldeby recorded his exemplum, parliament felt the need to enact a statute

---

24. "vicinorum facta praesumimur scire," *Decretum Gratiani Universi Iuris Canonici* (Venice, 1567), C. 23, q. 1, page 84. Discussed by MacNair, "Vicinage."

25. Phillip R. Schofield, "The Late Medieval View of Frankpledge and the Tithing System: An Essex Case Study," in *Medieval Society and the Manor Court*, ed. Zvi Razi and Richard Smith (Oxford: Clarendon, 1996), 408–49.

26. *Rotuli parliamentorum; ut et petitiones, et placita in parliamento*, vol. 2, ed. J. Strachey (London, 1767–77), 161. See Bertha Haven Putnam, "The Transformation of Keepers of the Peace into the Justices of the Peace, 1327–1380," *Transactions of the Royal Historical Society*, 4th ser., vol. 12 (1929): 19–48.

that specifically condemned bribing jurors and allowing members of judicial commissions to be nominated by interested parties. That statute suggests that the local residents charged with keeping the peace were working for material gain. It also officially acknowledges the (widely ignored) sense that local keepers of the peace were attentive only to the needs of the magnates and gentry class, rather than to the overall needs of everyone who lived within their jurisdiction, regardless of status.[27]

In addition, the complex relationships between royal and local jurists and administrators were drastically affected by the Black Death, which ravaged up to a third of the population in the first outbreak between 1348 and 1350. As has been widely discussed, the loss of so many people restructured relationships between worker and lord, particularly as workers moved from place to place in search of good wages.[28] The demographic devastation also produced profound changes in English legal practices, particularly in terms of centralizing legal control around the king and taking it away from local courts. As Robert C. Palmer puts it, "Governance after the Black Death was qualitatively different, exhibiting a government intent on using the law to control society, to preserve as far as possible the status quo" (5). Indicative of such royal control was the 1349 Ordinance of Laborers (reinforced two years later by the Statute of Laborers), which required all able-bodied people under the age of 60 to work at pre-plague rates. The enforcement of the statute exacerbated the friction between royal and local juridical administrators: local keepers of the peace were required to search out violators of the statute, and king's justices were charged with ensuring that the local officials remained uncorrupted by their loyalty to their neighbors.[29] But between 1352 and 1359, local keepers of the peace were no longer charged with enforcing the labor statute, a task that was left solely to royal bureaucrats.[30] These rapid changes in legal administration in the second half of the fourteenth century profoundly affected neighbor-relations and the witnessing procedures designed to uphold them. In part, the problem centered on determining whom to consider a "neighbor" in the eyes of both local and

27. W. M. Ormrod, *The Reign of Edward III: Crown and Political Society in England* (New Haven, CT: Yale University Press, 1991).

28. See, for example, Palmer, *English Law*, 3–4. See also John Hatcher, "England in the Aftermath of the Black Death," *Past and Present* 144.1 (1994): 3–35.

29. Bertha Haven Putnam, *The Enforcement of the Statute of Laborers during the First Decade after the Black Death, 1439–1359* (New York: Columbia University Press, 1908). See also Palmer, *English Law*, 21.

30. Musson and Ormrod point out that justices of laborers and keepers of the peace were often the same persons, so even if the law theoretically distinguished between royal and local administrators, it rarely did so in practice. *The Evolution of English Justice: Law, Politics, and Society in the Fourteenth Century* (Hampshire: Macmillan, 1999), 52–53.

royal jurisdictions. James H. Landman summarizes the dual fidelities of the neighbor-jurist succinctly: "Called upon to bring their local knowledge to bear on the case and yet to remain above the influence of local, partial interests, the jurors occupy an ambiguous space, of the locality yet sworn to apply their understanding of the facts to the fulfillment of the king's law; supposedly impartial yet feared subject to subornation."[31]

As this outline of English law's understanding of the neighbor-witness suggests, neighborliness was a crucial but elastic concept in the production of royal juridical authority and the administrative offices that supported it. As both a Scriptural and legal figure, the witnessing neighbor operated as a sign of community unity, but it is difficult to tell whether that community was construed via geography, class, royal fidelity, or Church doctrine. Waldeby's exemplum marshals the overlapping jurisdictions of the late medieval neighbor and its elasticity to present his reticent congregation as stuck in the crossfire between, on one hand, the requirement to witness in the service of Christian *caritas* and the increasingly coercive demands to bear witness on behalf of the state on the other. Indeed, once we take into account the complicated legal underpinnings of Waldeby's directive to this group of *vicini*, it becomes less easy to read the exemplum as simply asserting that these neighbors ought to come forward about a local murder. In addition, as we shall see in the next section, Waldeby's surprising admonition that this community has "outlawed" God initially registers as the dire consequences of its inability to choose between local neighbors and "neighborly" fidelity to the crown. But read within late medieval literary depictions of outlaws, this outrageous condemnation might be transformed into a rehabilitative gesture toward this community. It is possible, given the multiple models of neighborliness Waldeby draws upon, that his claim that these neighbors have turned God into an outlaw may actually salvage their silence as an act of doctrinal fidelity rather than condemn it as a rejection of spiritual and legal neighborliness.

Neighbors, Criminals, and Royal Sovereignty in Late Medieval Outlaw Literature

What does it mean to imagine God as an outlaw? Outlawry was the secular equivalent of excommunication, and it was typically used as the punishment

---

31. James H. Landman, "'The Doom of Resoun': Accommodating Lay Interpretation in Late Medieval England," in *Medieval Crime and Social Control*, ed. Barbara A. Hanawalt and David Wallace (Minneapolis: University of Minnesota Press, 1999), 98.

for failure to appear in court to respond to a summons. The community Waldeby addresses could certainly be outlawed for failing to testify, but such punishment was rarely meted out and was not taken seriously.[32] Rather, the consequences of an outlawed God would register in rhetorical and imaginative, rather than strictly legal or social, terms. Indeed, in the fourteenth and fifteenth centuries, the outlaw was as much a powerful literary and imaginative figure as a legal one, and it often functioned as a counter to the neighbor. To take one important example, in his idiosyncratic version of the Good Samaritan parable—in which Jesus responds to the lawyer's question "Who is my neighbor?"—Langland inserts an outlaw, suggesting that for him, the outlaw was critical to exploring how Christian community could be united by ethical calls to charitable neighborliness. As the Good Samaritan explains to Langland's dreamer, Faith and Hope must find the blood of a child born from a virgin to heal the wounded man they have encountered on the road. The Christ child will also, presumably, heal the social wounds that have ravaged Christian communities, wounds that have been propagated by Outlawe:

"For Outlawe is in the wode and under bank lotieth,
And may ech man see and good mark take
Who is bihynde and who before and who ben on horse—
For he halt hym hardier on horse than he that is a foote." (XVII.104–7)

For Langland, the outlaw is Luciferian, lurking in the woods and awaiting unsuspecting travelers, and he disrupts Christian communal bonds by all but destroying Faith and Hope. The idea of the lurking outlaw who disturbs the sanctity of law-abiding Christian communities was common in late medieval literature. Yet the outlaw, like the neighbor, is not so easily defined. Some medieval texts envision the outlaw working on behalf of neighborly justice in heroic defiance of corrupt royal rule, while others imagine the outlaw to be easily reabsorbed into the social systems that outlaws only temporarily disrupt. Indeed, the medieval outlaw exemplifies what Jeffrey Jerome Cohen has called a "difficult middle": one who defies easy categorization, since the outlaw is suspended between criminal and moral savior, between lawless transgressor and royal bureaucrat.[33]

Strikingly, the exploration of the principles of outlaw justice is often verbalized as "neighborliness," and, moreover, such explorations concern them-

---

32. Edward Powell, *Kingship, Law, and Society: Criminal Justice in the Reign of Henry V* (Oxford: Clarendon, 1989), 74–76.

33. Jeffrey Jerome Cohen, *Medieval Identity Machines: Hybridity, Identity, and Monstrosity in Medieval England* (Minneapolis: University of Minnesota Press, 2003).

selves specifically with false witness as test cases for outlaw ethical principles. For example, in *The Outlaw's Song of Trailbaston*, an Anglo-Norman poem written soon after Edward I's 1305 institution of trailbaston commissions, the narrator curses a commission's intrusion into what he feels are personal matters, such as disciplining one's children. He also sneers at its willingness to accept bribes and complains that he has been unfairly accused of theft and "other misdeeds." In response, the narrator takes to the woods, where "there is no deceit nor any bad law" ("La n'y a faucété ne nulle male lay").[34] Green reads the poem as a general critique of royal law and the operating systems that support it, and it is true that trailbaston was a particularly sore subject for communities in the shires, because it focused exclusively on "trespass against the king's peace."[35] Indeed, complaints of "trespass against the king's peace" were lobbied at an astonishing rate in the fourteenth century, ostensibly either by the gentry trying to align itself with the monarchy or even by the king himself against unpopular officials, so much so that those living on the outskirts of London and Westminster protested that such focus on trespass took resources away from local justices charged with rooting out and disciplining real crime.[36]

As an administrative body, trailbaston emphasized the gap between those who asserted fidelity to the sovereign and those who remained locally loyal. In the *Outlaw's Song*, the narrator is particularly outraged at his perceived mistreatment, since, he claims, he has spent much of his life serving the king. His retreat into the woods offers an alternative to the "common law," which he claims is "too uncertain" ("trop est doteuse," 56). Beyond an indictment of the new commission of trailbaston, this poem explores the conceptual role of the legal neighbor, using it to imagine alternative communities on the margins of official operations of law. The narrator blames "ill-favored people" ("le male desynes") for turning him in to the commissioners, such that he must shun his "friends" ("mes amis") lest they be assumed guilty by association. As his frustration with both his community and the commissioners grows, he begins to provide hypothetical questions to express his doubts about the new system:

If I am a good guy and can draw a bow
My neighbor will say, "He is of that company

---

34. The poem is included in Isabel Aspin, *Anglo-Norman Political Songs* (Oxford: Anglo-Norman Text Society, 1953), 67–78; this citation on 69, line 18. Hereafter cited by line number.
35. Green, *Crisis of Truth*, 171. Green's translation.
36. Alan Harding, *The Law Courts of Medieval England* (London: Allen & Unwin, 1973), 86.

That goes poaching in the woods and does other mischief.
If he wants to live, he will live like swine."³⁷

The narrator's designation of himself as a "compagnoun" is positioned in contradistinction to his neighbor, "mon veisyn." When he calls himself a "compagnoun," he signals his membership in a *compagnie*, a loaded term in both Anglo-Norman and Middle English. As David Wallace has explained, in fourteenth-century England, the term *compagnie* signaled a community based on a kind of consensus model, "where the right to exist as a group is simply assumed from within rather than conferred from without."³⁸ For the *Outlaw Song*'s narrator, a *compagnie* offers a safe community that exists in the forest, just outside the community that seeks to criminalize him for a life he feels neither corrupts royal law nor hinders others' ability to live as they please. His neighbor, on the other hand, is not a part of that loyal band, operating under the distasteful sense of fidelity to the commission and, by extension, the king. The neighbor in this poem exemplifies a rigid boundary between those who live within the confines of royal law and those who retreat to the forests to exist outside of them.

Yet in other texts that depict outlaw culture, the "neighbor" and the "outlaw" can be difficult to tell apart, and outlaw communities are not necessarily totally divorced from the operations of the crown. The intimate—or, perhaps more accurately, extimate³⁹—relationship between royal sovereignty and outlaw justice emerges particularly in *Fouke le Fitz Waryn*, an outlaw text written in Old French prose and dated around 1330.⁴⁰ Fouke, the son of the Norman king, is absorbed into King Henry's household when his father dies, becoming an almost-brother to Henry's four sons. He moves to the royal forests after an inheritance dispute with Henry's son John, who was crowned King of England after the death of his brother, Richard. The royal forest is a crucial setting for many late medieval outlaw texts, and it was envisioned as

---

37. Si je sei compagnoun e sache de archerye / Mon veisyn irra disaunt: "Cesti est de compagnie / De aler bercer a bois e fere autre folie. / Que ore vueille vivre come pork merra sa vye." Aspin, *Anglo-Norman Political Songs*, lines 85–88.

38. Wallace, *Chaucerian Polity*, 66–104.

39. Here, I draw on Cohen's definition of extimacy, which he draws from Lacan's *extimité*. The idea of "intimate alterity" suggests the inextricability of another from the identity of oneself, indicating "an abjected realm outside but entwined within, the 'normal,' the unambiguous, the culturally central." *Of Giants: Sex, Monsters, and the Middle Ages* (Minneapolis: University of Minnesota Press, 1999), xiii–xvi.

40. For a discussion of the poem's date, see the introduction to *Fouke le Fitz Waryn*, in *Robin Hood and Other Outlaw Tales*, ed. Stephen Knight and Thomas H. Ohlgren (Kalamazoo, MI: Medieval Institute, 1997).

a site in which such outlaw systems of justice might flourish. Indeed, forests are often discussed as the site of adventure precisely because of their proximity to, but crucial distance from, the court. However, if we broaden our view of the literary forest to include legal discussions of land ownership and use, we can contextualize the forest as a space in which royal officials and local residents jockeyed for juridical authority.[41] In the thirteenth and fourteenth centuries, forests were legally liminal, at once the jurisdictional space of the king and of local communities, and they were often under dispute in terms of ownership and use. Under Henry III, the 1217 Charter of the Forest established an official system of patrolling forests, noting that while forests were royal land, commoners were allowed to use them (EHD 337). In 1225 the Charter was specifically addressed to "all bailiffs and faithful subjects who shall look at the present charter," suggesting that Henry was successful in developing a system to adjudicate forest lands on behalf of both the crown and local residents (EHD 337). Indeed, thirteenth- and fourteenth-century forest law records show a fairly symbiotic relationship between king and those living near his forest. The king often permitted locals to water their animals or even cultivate small parcels of land under the legal rubric of ancient demesne, which afforded the tenants of lands particular rights of use, even though the land belonged to the royal household. These tenants could not be treated as villeins or serfs, and so they enjoyed certain legal privileges with respect to the land.

But forests were also where strangers could loiter and commit unexpected violence against the communities around them. For example, in 1255, when Richard of Grafham, a canon of Huntingdon, was found wandering through the forest, he was suspected of being a vagabond (*venit per patriam quasi vagus, suspectus*), and he was required to testify that he was not an "evil doer in the forest" (*malefactor in foresta*) before the forest justices.[42] And in the late thirteenth century, the crown widened highways so that "there may be no ditch, underwood or bushes where one could hide with evil intent within two hundred feet of the road on one side or the other."[43] Despite this statutory precaution, however, local communities and royal foresters had

---

41. Though many of the extant Robin Hood and outlaw tales are from the late fourteenth and fifteenth centuries, Maurice Keen dates the circulation of Robin stories to around 1265, so the early thirteenth-century forestry laws could provide some important context for considering how these tales regard the forest as a space to experiment with the interaction between royal sovereign authority and outlaw justice. *The Outlaws of Medieval Legend* (New York: Routledge, 1961), 128–207.

42. *Select Pleas of the Forest*, ed. G. J. Turner. Selden Society 13 (London: Bernard Quaritch, 1901), 11.

43. *Statute of Winchester*, in *English Historical Documents*, 461.

to remain vigilant. A case from Oxfordshire in 1338 details the testimony of a jury ("twelve good and free men dwelling within the aforesaid forest & adjoining the same") that accuses a few members of their community of entering the forest of Stowood with "seven unknown men" who attacked the foresters with great force. The roll emphasizes that the foresters raised the hue and cry and caught the strangers, who "took nothing of the Lord King's deer."[44] In this case, a great number of foresters and other judicial officials worked with the free tenants of the surrounding areas to monitor the entry and egress of unknown strangers in the forest. Forests may have had the romantic allure of courtly adventure, but they were also troubled spaces in which jurisdictions—royal and outlaw, legal and ethical—could be confused.

Given the jurisdictional liminality of the forest, fourteenth- and fifteenth-century outlaw texts such as *Fouke le Fitz Waryn* often used it as a setting in which to imagine the formation of communities with juridical and ethical structures that are just out of reach of the king's law. Once banished from any genealogical claim on Henry's royal household, Fouke quickly establishes himself as the leader of a forest-dwelling company of outlaws. Indeed, Fouke's status as a member of the royal household yet not a blood relation to the king establishes him as the perfect outlaw: proximate to but not of the royal patriline, a member of the gentry class who has been let down by royal systems of ownership and inheritance. But Fouke does not construct a totally alternative society, completely apart from the aristocratic organization that has marginalized him. Instead, he heads a community that maintains similar hierarchical social and governmental structures. For example, while hiding in the forests adjacent to the king's lands, Fouke and his company come across a group of merchants carrying expensive goods for the king:

> Fouke took them in to the forest, where they told him that they were the King's merchants. When Fouke heard this he was delighted, and said, "Sir merchants, if you lose this property, on whom will the loss fall? Tell me the truth." "Sir," they said, "if we lost it through our cowardice, or by our own carelessness, we ourselves are responsible; but if we lost it otherwise, by danger of the sea, or by force, the loss will fall upon the King."[45]

Fouke responds by taking the merchants' cloth and furs, cutting them with his lance, and dividing them among his retinue "according to his degree."

---

44. *Oxfordshire Forests, 1246–1609*, ed. Beryl Schumer (Oxfordshire: Oxfordshire Record Company, 2004), 139.
45. *Fouke le Fitz Waryn*, trans. Thomas E. Kelly, in *Robin Hood and Other Outlaw Tales*, 696–97.

Here, even as these outlaws deliberately take the property to injure the crown, they are invested in ranking systems ("degree"), belying the fantasy of a horizontally affiliated, purely egalitarian society that challenges the entrenched hierarchies of royal systems of power.[46]

The *Tale of Gamelyn*, a rhyming Middle English poem from around the mid-fourteenth century, features a strikingly similar premise, focusing on the neighbor and the witness to explore how outlaw justice both resists and reflects orthodox forms of legal community. Like *Fouke le Fitz Waryn*, the *Tale of Gamelyn* opens with a dispute over inheritance. Gamelyn, the youngest son of a powerful lord, receives no property from a trusted knight, who is charged with distributing the ailing lord's land and goods. The lord, upset at this transgression, addresses his executors:

> Than saide the knight, "By Saint Martin,
> For all that ye have y-doon, yit is the lond min.
> For Goddes love, neihebours, stondeth alle stille,
> And I will dele my lond after my wille."[47]

The oath "by Saint Martin" is significant, as Martin of Tours is the Roman soldier who cut his own cloak to share with a beggar. The lord's citation of Martin gestures toward the kind of charitable neighbor-love he chastises his knights for lacking, as does the plea "for Goddes love." Gamelyn's older brother, however, is not happy with his father's desire to bequeath Gamelyn some property, so he plots to leave Gamelyn with nothing while dissembling with a false oath: "That shalt you have, Gamelyn," he promises, "I swere by Christes ore! / All that thy fader thee biquath, though thou woldest have more" (159–60). *Gamelyn* thus juxtaposes the lord's call to neighborly unity and righteous inheritance supported with a genuine oath on one hand and his son's false vow on the other. This juxtaposition asserts both neighborliness and witnessing as fundamental to determining the workings of royal households and the transmission of aristocratic power and goods; here, a false oath can destroy the neighborly unity required for the proper genealogical transfer of power.

---

46. Green notes that outlaws deployed fraternal language to articulate their sense of egalitarian loyalty to one another, rather than hierarchical loyalty to the king: terms such as *societas, compagnie, fellowship*, and even *frers* were used to claim outlaw confederacy. While it is clear that outlaw writing deployed such vocabulary of affiliation, here I want to nuance Green's claim by showing that outlaws were just as often depicted as deploying hierarchical vocabulary to describe outlaw communities. See *Crisis of Truth* 189–90.

47. *Gamelyn*, in *Middle English Verse Romances*, ed. Donald B. Sands (New York: Holt, Rinehart and Winston, 1966), lines 53–56.

When the text turns to depicting outlawry, it illustrates how the manipulation of witnessing practices might actually authorize the outlaw communities royal households were supposed to suppress. Gamelyn discovers his brother's falsity and finds he has, in fact, been left with nothing, so he flees to the forest to live as an outlaw. There, Gamelyn assumes the status of quasi-sovereign, referred to both as a "maister outlawe" and as "her king" as he commits theft and trespass to support his forest community (688). The dramatic confrontation between royal officials and outlaws takes place in a courtroom, where Gamelyn and his gang are put on trial for treasonous activity. Based on the false testimony of several jurors, the judge finds them guilty of treason. But just before the judge sentences the outlaws, Gamelyn announces to the judge, "'Now is thy power y-don; thou most nedes arise; / Thou hast yeven domes that been ivel dight; / I will sitten in thy sete and dressen hem aright'" (846–48). The substitution of Gamelyn for the judge—"I will sitten in thy sete"—is accomplished first by violence, when Gamelyn and his company beat the judge, sheriff, and corrupt jurors, and then by sovereign decree, when the king makes Gamelyn the chief justice of the forest. His status as "king of the outlaws" is thus rendered official, and Gamelyn is reabsorbed into the juridical community ruled by royal law. Likewise, "Adam Bell," a fifteenth-century rhyming ballad, depicts a band of outlaws' rescue of William Cloudesley, who had been arrested and jailed for trespass and for stealing deer from royal forests. At the end of the tale, though the king is outraged that William has been liberated from prison by other outlaws, he recognizes William's prowess in archery, telling him, "'And over all the north countre / I make the chyfe rydere.'"[48]

Like the *Tale of Gamelyn* and "Adam Bell," "Robin Hood and the Monk," a fifteenth-century ballad, illustrates the entrenched hierarchical structure of outlaw societies and their proximity to the royal communities they ostensibly oppose. When Robin Hood is jailed for treason, Little John finds a way to engineer his escape. In gratitude for Little John's loyalty and in recognition of his bravery, Robin Hood tells Little John that he is now his master. But Little John shuns his new status: "'Nay, be my trouth,' seid Litull John, / 'So shalle hit never be; / But lat me be a felow,' seid Litull John, 'No noder kepe I be.'"[49] Little John's response carefully navigates the pair's outlaw bond and their difference in rank. Robin Hood's suggestion that Little John could become his master offers an egalitarian ethos that imagines a society that dissolves the distinction between sovereign and subject, a society that constructs one

---

48. "Adam Bell, Clim of the Clough, and William of Cloudesly," in *Rymes of Robyn Hood*, ed. R. B. Dobson and J. Taylor (Pittsburgh, PA: Sutton, 1976), 272, verse 163.

49. "Robin Hood and the Monk," in *Rymes*, 121, verse 80.

another as "fellows." But Little John's refusal to assume the master role powerfully reinforces Robin's status as *capitalis de societate,* a kingly role that is reflected in the writing produced by actual bands of outlaws. As both E. L. G. Stones and Barbara A. Hanawalt have pointed out, threatening letters from outlaws to kings or parsons often adopted a royal style of address, as though one authority were writing to another.[50] Such letters show that outlaws themselves sometimes envisioned and articulated themselves via available, royal modes of justice and authority, resistant but close to the systems of sovereignty they sought to disrupt.[51]

Given the plasticity of the figure of the outlaw as a representative of local ethics, a royal bureaucrat-in-training, or a marauder who unravels the fabric of society, Waldeby's claim that his reticent community has "outlawed" God might be read in any number of ways. We can certainly understand the image conservatively: false witness (and particularly false oath-taking) was considered a crime against God, and the community's perpetration of this crime goes against not only doctrinal precept but also the legal requirement to accuse one another's neighbors on behalf of royal justice. As such, we might understand Waldeby as tying together the requirements to bear witness found in Church doctrine and in common law, thereby supporting the divine power of the king. On the other hand, however, we might read the exemplum more experimentally: that is, as a suggestion that this community envisions God, *rather than* the king, as their juridical and ethical authority. In this interpretation, God would operate as a kind of *capitalis de societate,* an authority that envisions outlaw ethics as a corrective to royal corruption. Perhaps, for Waldeby, to be a good neighbor is to consider the margins of royal, ecclesiastical, or doctrinal law as necessary to the operations of that law. In this reading, the final line of Waldeby's exemplum—"And from this arose an opinion that neither God, nor any of his saints, either lived, or wanted to live, in that part of the country"—could be understood as a reproach of those who misunderstand or misrepresent the refusal to bear witness as merely a rejection of the king's authority. It might, in other words, seek to protect this community as a group of loyal neighbors who refuse to

---

50. E. L. G. Stones, "The Folvilles of Ashby-Folville, Leicestershire, and Their Associates in Crime, 1326–1347," *Transactions of the Royal Historical Society* 5th ser., no. 7 (1957): 134–35; and Barbara A. Hanawalt, "Ballads and Bandits: Fourteenth-Century Outlaws and the Robin Hood Poems," in *Chaucer's England: Literature in Historical Context,* ed. Barbara A. Hanawalt (Minneapolis: University of Minnesota Press, 1992), 161.

51. For an argument that fifteenth-century Robin Hood ballads confront the way sociojuridical authority was exercised in both local and national arenas, see Christine Chism, "Robin Hood: Thinking Globally, Acting Locally," in *The Letter of the Law,* ed. Emily Steiner and Candace Barrington (Ithaca, NY: Cornell University Press, 2002), 12–39.

participate in the witnessing strategies that support the king's law over local custom.

This chapter has sought to contextualize Waldeby's exemplum within a capacious cultural framework, arguing that its worry about neighborly unity and false witness emerges out of several overlapping (and sometimes competing) institutional attempts to shape and express the requirements of doctrinal and legal communities. Indeed, doctrinal and legal communities in late medieval England relied on complicated triangulations of neighbor, witness, and outlaw that circulated in a wide range of texts, from pastoral treatises to statute records to vernacular ballads. The neighbor, the witness, and the outlaw were deployed in support of Scriptural precept and royal jurisdictional control alike, and yet they were also mobilized by communities determined to recreate a kind of localized, customary sense of justice, one we might think of as "ethical" rather than purely "juridical." Attending to the range of contexts for and possible readings of Waldeby's exemplum makes it clear that while witnessing is a crucial mode of expressing neighborly community, what it means to attest to one's neighborliness was a point of serious contention for late medieval preachers, jurists, and vernacular writers.

In addition, given its flexibility to shape and articulate a wide range of ideologies and communities, neighborliness might be a useful conceptual device to respond to the persistent challenge that faces scholars of the Middle Ages: that is, to think through our own relationship to a distant past. Perhaps we can envision the various overlaps and fissures between "neighbor" and "outlaw" as a potential theoretical model for thinking about the Middle Ages themselves as both our temporal neighbor (something to which we, as scholars, offer our empathetic loyalty) and as a kind of outlaw (a tantalizing but suspicious Other).[52] Indeed, recognizing the cultural centrality of neighborliness in the later Middle Ages might help us construct a relationship to the past that refuses either complete assimilation or differentiation. If we can conceive of the Middle Ages as a neighbor to the present, then, like Waldeby's congregation, we are asked to bear witness to it, to act, perhaps, with both a charitable love of the past and a neighborly suspicion of it.

These first three chapters have demonstrated that narratives of false witness were crucial for late medieval jurists and writers to explore how the

---

52. Cohen has urged us to study the Middle Ages by acknowledging "the impossibility of choosing alterity or continuity." See "Midcolonial," in *The Postcolonial Middle Ages*, ed. Jeffrey Jerome Cohen (New York: Palgrave, 2001), 5–6. Maura Nolan has similarly warned against "controlling literary meaning by building an edifice of historical causation or theoretical analysis designed to erase difference." See "Historicism after Historicism," in *The Post-Historical Middle Ages*, ed. Elizabeth Scala and Sylvia Federico (New York: Palgrave, 2009), 84.

boundaries of community were formed, transgressed, and reshaped. Vernacular texts such as Chaucer's *Man of Law's Tale* and the *Pistel of Swete Susan* animate the legal and Scriptural precepts against false witness, and in doing so, they expose how witnessing mediated between divine justice, earthly law, and the ethical ties that solidified communal relationships. At the same time, we see in Waldeby's exemplum how even those texts charged with defining and emphasizing the importance of witnessing to Christian community-formation could potentially speak to multiple, even competing, communities that were defining their boundaries by distinguishing themselves from certain kinds of legal authorities. The next two chapters focus on how various witnessing media—that is, the body, the voice, and the document—were used to assert the integrity of different authorities and communities. As we saw with the *Pistel of Swete Susan,* the medium through which one expresses testimony can make all the difference in asserting the authority to act as a witness on behalf of a Christian community. The final two chapters argue specifically that William Langland and William Thorpe exploit the authoritative rhetoric of different witnessing media to critique and challenge the ecclesiastical hierarchies that attempt to construct sharp divisions between those who can access divine knowledge directly and those who should require an official intermediary. These chapters demonstrate that while devotional and legal witnessing practices are central to constructing and articulating doctrinal and legal communities, they are also practices that could be used to critique those communities and the authorities that police them. Accordingly, witnessing practices could be used to construct alternative devotional or legal communities that operated beyond the reach of ecclesiastical or royal officials.

f o u r

Piers Plowman, Book, and the Testimonial Body

CHAUCER'S Wife of Bath begins her prologue by asserting that she can easily expound upon the trials and woes of marriage, since she has had five husbands and is in search of a sixth. She establishes the foundation of her expertise immediately: "'Experience, though noon auctoritee / Were in this world, is right ynogh for me / To speke of wo that is in mariage'" (III.1–3). According to the Wife, her experience in her many marriages has taught her as well as any book could, giving her license to argue against the misogynist claims of such patristic authorities as Jerome and Valerian. For the Wife, experience provides a counterdiscourse to any masculine (and misogynist) "auctoritee," and the *Prologue* constructs a critical gap between what one knows personally and what can be read in books.

The complex relationship between personal experience and book-knowledge animated in the Wife's prologue nourished much of the thinking about lay piety and devotional knowledge in the second half of the fourteenth century. The most sustained exploration of the relationship between lay piety and devotional knowledge is William Langland's magisterial *Piers Plowman*, which portrays the dreamer's search for spiritual understanding through repeated negotiations of "experience" and "auctoritee." When the dreamer first meets Holy Church, for example, he falls to his knees, crying out for grace: "Thanne I courbed on my knees and cried hire of grace, / And preide hire pitously to preye for my synnes, / And also kenne me kyndely on Crist to bileve / That I myghte werchen His wille that wroghte me to manne" (I.79–82). The dreamer desperately searches for what Langland repeatedly calls "kynde knowyng"—that is, wisdom derived from grace and love, rather than theory or books[1]—but in his search for such knowledge, he encounters an incredible range of texts that could fall under the rubric of "auctoritee": Scriptural citations, canon law axioms, charter formulae, snippets of patristic commentary. Indeed, the entire poem could be described as the dreamer's search for "kynde knowyng" through a labyrinth of texts, and Langland most forcefully foregrounds the relationship between the dreamer's visionary experiences and textual knowledge in passus 18, when the poem accelerates toward the Harrowing of Hell and Judgment Day. As James Simpson has argued, passus 18 overtly juxtaposes two kinds of narration that are throughout the poem understood as distinct and exclusive: one that "authenticates itself by reference to the narrator's experience," and the other that derives its authority from texts.[2]

Significantly, passus 18 is also when Langland inserts his peculiar witnessing personification, Book, who surfaces briefly to testify to Christ's birth and Passion and to promise his certain resurrection. As an eyewitness to Christ's birth and death as well as an—even *the*—authoritative text around which Christian devotion can cohere, Langland offers Book as an example of how "experience" and textual "auctoritee" might work together in the service of Christian eschatology. In some ways, Book is the perfect figure through which Langland can imagine the grace of "kynde knowyng" and the clerkly knowledge of many of the dreamer's interlocutors as mutually supportive, since Book is "a unifying figure who introduces a kind of transcendent harmony" into the poem.[3] Certainly, Book personifies the incarnational hypostasis of the divine Word; he is at once a Bible with a body, an authoritative text, and an eyewitness to the Passion. But as a personified text with a body and a voice, Book poses challenging questions about the testimonial possibilities of the body, material texts, and the divine Word. What does it mean to treat the Bible as a personification? Specifically, why does Langland depict Book as a witness who can testify, like the apostles, to Christ's birth and death? This chapter uses Book's speech as a touchstone to track Langland's use of testifying witnesses throughout *Piers Plowman*,

---

1. Mary Clemente Davlin, "Kynde Knowyng as a Major Theme in *Piers Plowman* B," *Review of English Studies* n.s. 22 (1971): 1–19.

2. James Simpson, "Desire and the Scriptural Text: Will as Reader in *Piers Plowman*," in *Criticism and Dissent in the Middle Ages*, ed. Rita Copeland (Cambridge: Cambridge University Press, 1996), 216.

3. George Shuffleton, "*Piers Plowman* and the Case of the Missing Book," *YLS* 18 (2004): 70.

arguing that Langland imagines an intimate relationship between salvific knowledge and personification through depictions of witnessing.

Langland's fullest investigations into this relationship are his repeated discussions of the oath, which permit him to conceptualize the way contractual language can harness the power of the divine Word to verify a promise, whether legal or eschatological. Significantly, however, Langland inserts oaths into the mouths of personifications that most stretch the connection between their bodily signifiers and the abstractions they signify.[4] By inserting oaths into personifications in which the links between material body and abstract signification are contested and fragmented, Langland exploits the perlocutionary power of an oath. Langland's oath-takers disengage the certainty of the link between a witness's speech and the events to which he or she testifies, and this disengagement has enormous consequences for oaths such as Book's, which promises an eschatological future. Langland thus uses oaths to consider how language and the body might both access and obscure the divine Word.

Moreover, Langland's complicated experiments in personification and witnessing surface in the fifteenth- and sixteenth-century texts that envision *Piers Plowman* as a call to doctrinal and political reform. The chapter closes by exploring how the post-Langlandian witness provided the resources for diverse audiences to claim doctrinal and political authority. *Mum and the Sothsegger* offers a case study in the legacy of the Langlandian witness in the fifteenth century, when Langland's experiments in testimony informed vernacular poetry's engagement with turbulent Henrician politics. In the sixteenth century, "Piers Plowman" shows up as a witness who can testify on behalf of Reformation polemics in a number of texts, including vernacular pamphlets and the editorial prologues appended to the earliest printed editions of Langland's poem. In these texts, witnessing functions as the autho-

---

4. For a discussion of Langland's peculiar personification poetics with respect to Gluttony and Anima, see Helen Cooper, "Gender and Personification in *Piers Plowman*," YLS 5 (1991): 31–48; James J. Paxson, "Gender Personified, Personification Gendered, and the Body Figuralized in *Piers Plowman*," YLS 12 (1998): 65–96; Larry Scanlon, "Personification and Penance," YLS 22 (2008): 1–29; and Masha Raskolnikov, "Promising the Female, Delivering the Male: Transformations of Gender in *Piers Plowman*," in *Body Against Soul: Gender and "Sowlehele" in Middle English Allegory* (Columbus: The Ohio State University Press, 2009), 168–96. For discussions of Langland's personification poetics more generally, see Lawrence M. Clopper, "Langland and Allegory: A Proposition," YLS 15 (2001): 32–45; Ann W. Astell, "Response to 'Langland and Allegory: A Proposition,'" YLS 15 (2001): 43–46; James J. Paxson, *The Poetics of Personification* (Cambridge: Cambridge University Press, 1994); Mary Carruthers, "Allegory without the Teeth: Reflections on Figural Language in *Piers Plowman*," YLS 19 (2005): 27–44; and Elizabeth Fowler, *Literary Character: The Human Figure in Early English Writing* (Ithaca, NY: Cornell University Press, 2003).

rizing principle for the reformist projects that envision *Piers Plowman* at the center of vexed doctrinal and ideological debates about the status of lay spiritual authority and ecclesiastical hierarchy.

Lady Mede, Gluttony, Anima, and Empty Oaths

Langland establishes his interest in oaths and promissory language prominently in the first vision, during the marriage negotiations for Lady Mede. In this scene, Langland posits oath-taking as a kind of speech-act used by sinful personifications such as Liar, Guile, and Gluttony, and he imagines oaths in conjunction with other kinds of untrustworthy speech, including false witnessing and backbiting. When the marriage ceremony of Mede to False is first pronounced by Liar, he produces a charter for Simony and Civil Law to read "'Lo! here a chartre / That Gile with his grete othes gaf hem togidere,' / And preide Cyvylle to see and Symonye to rede it" (2.69–71). The charter begins formulaically, calling everyone present to "witeth and witnesseth" that Mede's marriage will be based merely on material gain. It goes on to claim that "Favel with his fikel speche feffeth by this chartre / To be princes in Pride, and poverte to despise / To bakbite and to bosten and bere fals witnesse, / To scorne and to scolde and sclaundre to make, / Unbuxome and bolde to breke the ten hestes" (2.79–83). Cataloguing all of Mede's "property" (that is, the deadly sins), the charter distributes the "erldom of Envy and Wrathe" as well as the "countee of Coveitise" and the "lordshipe of Leccerie" to the marital parties. In this catalogue, Gluttony is notably described as a tavern-goer with a drinking buddy, Great Oaths, a pair Langland reunites in the next vision: "Glotonye he gaf hem ek and grete othes togidere, / And al day to drynken at diverse tavernes, / And there to jangle and jape and jugge hir evencristen" (2.93–95). After Theology objects to the marriage, Mede and her retinue (made up of a number of legal administrators, including assizers, bailiffs, and sheriffs) go to Westminster, where the King offers Conscience as an appropriate husband, one who might finally translate Mede's promiscuous gift-giving into acts of spiritual support and exchange.

Oaths were used for multiple purposes in medieval England. In the county court system, for example, oaths were taken when a male turned twelve and was officially inducted into the tithing, the legal unit in charge of keeping the peace, and oaths of fealty were made to English kings up to and beyond Richard's reign.[5] Oaths could register and solidify a public

---

5. See Green, *Crisis of Truth*, 231–32.

reputation, particularly when compurgatory oath-helpers were called upon; oaths could also verify the truth of a legal document, such as when witnesses took an oath that a last will and testament accurately reflected the deceased's wishes. Langland's depiction of oaths here—as language used by devious, sinful people—spurs his investigation of the status of "meed" as an indefinite term that signifies both God's gifts and the corrupting monies that keep justice tied to earthly gain rather than to spiritual truth. Lady Mede floats flirtatiously and dangerously among justices and government administrators, and repeated attempts to marry her off signal repeated attempts to affix her meaning to a moral code. As Simpson explains, "At the heart of the action of these passus, then, is an ambiguity, a word which refuses to be tied down in any fixed way, and which can provoke exclusive and opposed definitions from two figures of apparently unimpeachable authority, Holy Church and Theology."[6] Even when spoken correctly, Langland suggests, oaths might not always have the kind of perlocutionary power they ought to have, depending from whose mouth an oath is issued.

Conscience refuses the position as Mede's husband, insulting her at length and predicting that when Reason reigns again and unites the world through "love and lowenesse and leautee," Mede will lose her status. When he cites Scripture to prove his point, Mede counters with a quotation from Proverbs that supports her gift-giving practices as spiritually and socially sound, and she proudly cites it in Latin. Conscience acknowledges that her Latin is correct, but admonishes her for failing to turn the page of her book to find the "true" text:

> "Ac thow art lik a lady that radde a lesson ones,
> Was *omnia probate* and that plesed hire herte—
> For that lyne was no lenger at the leves ende.
> Hadde she loked that other half and the leef torned,
> She shold have founde fel[l]e wordes folwynge therafter:
> *Quod bonum est tenete*—Truthe that texte made." (3.338–43)

After the King puts an end to their squabbling, he turns his attention to a petition Peace has issued against Wrong for a number of crimes, including trespass and theft. Mede offers Peace gifts to make amends for Wrong, which Peace accepts. Yet the King refuses to release Wrong from jail, upbraiding Mede for corrupting the law and disrupting rational government: "'Mede

---

6. James Simpson, Piers Plowman: *An Introduction* (Exeter: University of Exeter Press, 2007), 44.

shal noght maynprise yow, by the Marie of hevene!'" he proclaims. "'I wole have leaute in lawe, and lete be al youre janglyng, / And as moost folk witnesseth wel, Wrong shal be demed'" (4.179–81).

Here, the king effectively fixes the meaning of "meed" as unlawful bribes and gift-giving ("maynprise").[7] He also verifies this definition and solidifies his authority to condemn Wrong by calling upon the testimony of "moost folk." In doing so, the king points out a critical paradox at the heart of the trial of Peace and Wrong, a paradox that emerges throughout the Mede passus and that typifies Langland's investigation of witnessing as a mode of establishing legal, ethical, and moral truths. As Andrew Galloway points out, Peace acts both as an individual complainant—that is, as a private individual—and as an embodiment of the "king's peace"—that is, as a representative of the public good.[8] When Mede offers Peace gifts, she treats him as an individual complainant against an individual defendant. When the king rejects the amends, he treats Wrong as a transgressor against the communal good. His call upon "moost folk" to attest that Wrong will be judged by the standard of the king's requirement to have "leaute in law" registers witnessing as a communal act on behalf of the king's peace and treats Peace as a representative of the communal good. Thus, the king argues that these testifying "folk" act as witnesses on behalf of royal law as well as on behalf of justice, understood as a kind of ethical obedience to royal law. Whereas the first vision began with all sorts of suspect contractual language and documents, including oaths and charters, it ends with the promise of a social contract that will enact a government run by "leaute" rather than bribes, and one that elevates the community over the individual. It does so by rejecting the individuated testimony of Wrong in favor of the communal testimony of Peace and "moost folk."

The Mede passus are crucial pretext for understanding Langland's interest in witnessing and oath-taking throughout *Piers Plowman*. Progressing from Guile's charter to Conscience's codicological argument to the testifying role of "moost folk," the vision's attempts to affix Mede's significatory elasticity to legal and moral justice dramatize Langland's skepticism that contractual language, whether oath, charter, or royal decree, can reveal God's will. Instead, communal testimony can unite "moost folk" through ethical loyalty to the king's law. In the second vision, Langland moves inward to examine how oaths work in the context of penitential discourse. Waking up after the

---

7. For an explanation of the systems of mainprise and maintenance in these passus, see Kathleen E. Kennedy, "Retaining a Court of Chancery," *YLS* 17 (2003): 175–89.

8. Andrew Galloway, *The Penn Commentary on "Piers Plowman,"* vol. 1 (Philadelphia: University of Pennsylvania Press, 2006), 374–86.

King's excoriation of Mede and Wrong at the end of passus 4, the dreamer falls asleep again and sees the seven deadly sins dawdling as they make their way to church. Here, we get an extended portrait of Gluttony. Lured into a tavern on his way to church, Gluttony proceeds to befriend his fellow tavern-goers and consume over a gallon's worth of ale. The description of Gluttony is particularly dedicated to "sins of the tongue," which include body-based sins such as overeating and -drinking and language-based sins such as lying, rumormongering, blaspheming, and, as described in chapters 1 and 2, bearing false witness.[9] In addition, as Larry Scanlon points out, the mouth, Gluttony's site of transgression, "crosses the fundamental divide between sins of the spirit, like pride and envy, and sins of the body" (20). More than any of the other seven deadly sins, Gluttony sits at the intersection of the material and the discursive, and his bodily excesses and his words are tightly knit together. While his most obvious sins and misbehaviors include drinking too much and urinating in public, Gluttony is also, notably, prone to swearing false oaths. In fact, when Gluttony chooses to enter the tavern rather than go to church, he is followed by a shadow figure, Great Oaths: "Thanne goth Gloton in, and grete othes after" (5.307). Later, after his bender, Gluttony promises to mend his ways and go to church, confessing a litany of bad behavior—including repeatedly taking false oaths—to Repentance.

Gluttony's oath-bound confession offers a fantasy of certainty, a promise that he can and will mend his ways and find repentance. But Gluttony's confession enacts a paradox: if Gluttony were to confess his sins to Repentance, he would erase those gluttonous sins, and in the process, he himself would disappear.[10] The confession could thus potentially redeem Gluttony out of existence, though the implication, of course, is that it may save his soul. In addition, Gluttony's confession is strikingly recursive: he takes an oath in order to verify the truth of his confession, then confesses that he has repeatedly taken false oaths: "'I, Gloton,'" quod the gome, 'gilty me yelde— / Of that I have trespased with my tonge, I kan noght telle how ofte / Sworen Goddes soule and his sydes! and So helpe me God and halidome!'" (5.368–70)[11] The

---

9. Scanlon discusses the enduring link between gluttony and other "sins of the tongue," beginning with Peter Cantor's twelfth-century *Verbum abbreviatum* and turning to William Peraldus's *Summae virtutum ac vitiorum* and Laurent de Bois's *Somme le roi*. See "Personification and Penance."

10. See Scanlon's argument about Langland's portraits of confessing sins, "Personification and Penance," 26. For a discussion of the paradox of confessing sins, see Lee Patterson, "Chaucerian Confession: Penitential Literature and the Pardoner," *Medievalia et humanistica* n.s. 7 (1976): 153–73.

11. For a discussion of Langland's peculiar portrayals of auricular confession, see Katherine C. Little, *Confession and Resistance* (Notre Dame, IN: University of Notre Dame Press, 2006), 25–29.

logic of Gluttony's confession is decidedly circular: to take an oath to verify that he has repeatedly taken false oaths leaves no anchor of certainty, nothing to prove that this particular confessional oath is genuine and that it will effectively perform the sacrament that is necessary for salvation.

Thus, Gluttony's oaths are both the agents of his demise (as they might verify his confession and redemption) and examples of the kind of language that enables his existence as Gluttony, an abuser of words and food. In both the first and second visions, then, the figures who use oaths are personifications whose significatory existence is shaky—either because they animate an ambiguous term, as in the case of Mede, or because they exist on the brink of self-effacement, as in the case of Gluttony. The next time Langland turns his focus to oath-taking is in the fifth vision, when the dreamer wakes to wonder whether he would ever "kyndely knowe what was Dowel," then promptly falls asleep again (15.2). In his dream, the dreamer encounters Anima, who chastises him for searching in the first place, since "'it were ayeins kynde'" to know everything that God does (15.52). Predictably, the dreamer wants to know who this creature is, and asks her name. Described as someone "withouten tonge and teeth," Anima cites Isidore to offer a long list of Latin and vernacular signifiers: while "quykke the corps," she is *Anima*, but the faculty that wishes and wills is called *Animus*; she might also go by *Mens, Memoria, Ratio,* Resoun, *Sensus, Amor,* lele Love, or *Spiritus*. Significantly and surprisingly, she is called "Conscience" when acting as "Goddis clerke and his notarie" (15.32).

In claiming that she can "notarize" God's authority as Conscience, Anima internalizes and transforms the bureaucratic office that was charged with, among other tasks, transcribing the oral testimony of witnesses into the documentary formulae of public record.[12] Widely used in Italian juridical and bureaucratic circles, medieval notaries were a much smaller part of English legal operations. Nonetheless, they were part of a growing population of trained bureaucratic clerks in fourteenth-century England, primarily serving the ecclesiastical and Chancery Courts, and their functions expanded in the later Middle Ages to include paralegal work such as authenticating wills and offering legal advice.[13] When notaries transcribed the oral testimony

---

12. For a discussion of notaries as transcribers of witness testimony, see chapter 2.
13. Common law courts did sometimes use notaries, but they had a separate documentary system of writs and petitionary complaints. See C. R. Cheney, *Notaries Public in England in the Thirteenth and Fourteenth Centuries* (Oxford: Clarendon, 1972); Nigel Ramsay, "Scriveners and Notaries as Legal Intermediaries in Later Medieval England," in *Enterprise and Individuals in Fifteenth-Century England*, ed. Jennifer Kermode (Gloucester: Alan Sutton, 1991), 118–31; and *Medieval Notaries and Their Acts: The 1327–1328 Register of Jean Holanie*, ed. and trans. Kathryn Reyerson and Debra A. Salata (Kalamazoo, MI: Medieval Institute, 2004).

and authenticated it with their seal (an act performed in front of several witnesses), they produced documents that rendered courtroom testimony dispositive. Judges could use these documents to determine cases or award damages. So when Anima (as Conscience) assumes the office of "notarie," she takes the clerkly, specialized labor of the notary out of legal and ecclesiastical circles and instead reclaims the notarial procedures of authentication to offer extrajudicial authority to anyone with a conscience, particularly the "lewed."

In addition, Anima's mutilated mouth emphasizes that her work as God's notary relies on a different economy of authority than those operating within the clerkly world of the law. As described in the second chapter, in the *Pistel of Swete Susan*, the Elders promise the veracity of their false accusation against Susanna by witnessing "with tonge and toth," evoking an enduring patristic tradition that locates commentators' authority in their mouths and tongues. Anima's lack of a tongue and teeth challenges this tradition in pointedly bodily terms. She cannot take such an oath as the Elders do: that is, she cannot guarantee her speech "with tonge and toth." Her open face thus not only indicates the speechlessness of the soul—that is, as something beyond the human constraints of language—but also positions Anima outside the clerkly *auctoritas* of a patristic hermeneutic tradition.[14] The portrait of Anima thus suggests that she works to open spiritual authority to those not specifically schooled in *clergie,* and more specifically, that she does so by appropriating and reimagining the bureaucratic office that translated witness testimony into official documents.

When Anima takes her oath, she does so specifically to condemn "freres and fele othere maistres" who preach to "lewed men." Her oath establishes the truth of her condemnation, and it locates her authority both in authoritative texts and in her own body:

"Gooth to the glose of the vers, ye grete clerkes;
If I lye on yow to my lewed wit, ledeth me to brennyng!
For as it semeth ye forsaketh no mannes almesse—
Of usurers, of hoores, of avarouse chapmen—
And louten to thise lordes that mowen lene yow nobles
Ayein youre rule and religion. I take record at Jesus,
That seide to hise disciples, '*Ne sitis acceptores personarum.*'
Of this matere I myghte make a muche bible;

---

14. For discussions of what Anima's disfigured face might signify, see Paxson, "The Personificational Face," 154; and Raskolnikov, "Promising the Female, Delivering the Male," 98.

> Ac of curatours over Cristen peple, as clerkes bereth witnesse,
> I shal tellen it for truthe sake—take hede whoso liketh!" (15.82–91)

Anima promises to burn herself should her accusations prove false, and in doing so, she follows both customary and canon law, which require that accusers be punished if they cannot prove their cases. She also offers her own body in exchange for a false gloss and then translates her bodily guarantee into a citational promise by "taking record at Jesus." Her oath constructs an intimate relationship between body and document, conceptualizing both as witnessing media through which she can voice her critiques of ecclesiastical officials who let their spiritual obligations to the laity fall by the wayside.

Repeatedly in *Piers Plowman,* oaths emerge from the mouths of personifications who foreground the complex relationship between their body and the word they represent. The link between oath-taking and such vexed personifications suggests that Langland wants to explore the way witnessing discourse relies upon a perlocutionary certainty that might not be so available when it comes to salvation and the search for divine wisdom. His exploration of witnessing discourse centers on how the "lewed" might be able to attest to divine knowledge, even perhaps without the aid of an ecclesiastical official. Indeed, as he focuses on how the "lewed" might construct themselves as authoritative witnesses to divine truth, he turns to thinking about experience as a path to knowledge that might be as viable as that found in books. Surprisingly, he does so most forcefully through his personified Book.

Langland's Book and the Experience of Salvation

Like Lady Mede, Gluttony, and Anima, Langland's personified Book depicts a complicated but crucial intimacy between body and document as witnessing media that can testify on behalf of various communities, both "lewed" and clerical, and thereby offer divine knowledge. Book appears in passus 18 (C.20), just before the dreamer envisions the harrowing of hell. Awake after having listened to the Good Samaritan preach mercy and forgiveness to "alle manere men," the dreamer falls asleep once again. In his dream, he sees both the Samaritan and Piers Plowman riding into a town, which is preparing to watch a joust between Jesus and the devil to decide who should take possession of mankind. The dreamer then witnesses the crucifixion of Christ and the subsequent debate between the Four Daughters of God regarding the fate of mankind: whether all should remain condemned or be granted forgiveness and released from hell. The descriptions of Jesus' entry into Jerusalem, his trial and crucifixion, and his descent into hell to release the devil's prisoners make passus 18 arguably the most action-filled of B-text, and it has been read both as one of Langland's most dramatic and as one of his most saturated with legal imagery and language.[15] In particular, the Four Daughters' debate models various ways of culling evidence in support of an argument. While Truth and Righteousness use Scriptural citations to back up their argument that mankind should be left in hell to suffer for its sins, Mercy draws on "experience": "'Thorugh experience,' quod he[o], 'I hope thei shul be saved, / For venym fordooth venym—and that I preve by reson.'" (18.151–52). Agreeing with Mercy, Peace offers a royal document, a "patente" that proves God has forgiven mankind and has authorized Peace and Mercy to bail everyone out of hell.

Peace and Mercy construct a mutually supportive relationship between experience and official documents, imagining a "patente" as evidentiary corroboration of their argument to release mankind. Once Peace finishes her impassioned speech, Langland introduces Book, who collates the various kinds of probative materials marshaled in the debate—experience, legal documents, and Scriptural citation—as testifying witnesses to the divine Word. Although a witnessing Book is a striking personification even for a poem filled with odd personifications, neither Book nor his testimony is Langland's invention. For example, earthly elements appear in Matthew to testify to Christ's birth and passion, and they reappear in Augustine's exegetical treatise on John, in the pseudo-Augustinian sermon *De symbolo*, and Gregory's tenth homily on the Gospels.[16] A sermon included in the fourteenth-century Northern Homily Cycle is perhaps Langland's closest source for Book's speech, in that it explicitly translates "cognare" (the verb used by Gregory) as "witnessen," and it gestures toward a speaking book ("And sithen, for al that boc moht sai"). The sermon continues:

Hefen and erthe, and sun and se,
Bar witnes that cumen was he,

---

15. For discussions of the passus's legal imagery, see, for example, William J. Birnes, "Christ as Advocate: The Legal Metaphor of *Piers Plowman*," *Annuale Mediaevale* 16 (1975): 71–93. For a discussion of the passus's dramatic elements, see David C. Fowler, *Piers the Plowman: Literary Relations of the A and B Texts* (Seattle: University of Washington Press, 1961), 129–46. See also Stephen A. Barney, who notes of Jesus' sermon to the devils during the Harrowing of Hell that "for Jesus to speak at length extrabiblically has precedent in the French drama." *The Penn Commentary on "Piers Plowman,"* vol. 5 (Philadelphia: University of Pennsylvania Press, 2006), 73.

16. R. E. Kaske, "The Speech of 'Boke' in *Piers Plowman*," *Anglia* 77 (1959): 117–44. For an amplified list of possible sources for Langland's witnessing elements, see Barney, *Commentary*, 55–58.

> That suld mannes state amend,
> For heuin and sterne in witnes send,
> That he was cumen that broht us liht
> Into this warld, and makid briht
> The trowthe, that ar was mirk als niht,
> For thoru Crist, trow we now riht.[17]

In addition, in a formulation similar to the one in Book's speech, the fourteenth-century *Short Charter of Christ* lists a variety of witnesses to the Passion: "*his testibus:* / Witnesse the Earth that then did quake / And stonys great that in sunder brake / Witnesse my moder and St. Ihon, / And bystnders many a one."[18]

Book's speech (or the elements therein) is thus fairly commonplace in a range of doctrinal texts, Latin and vernacular. Langland tinkers with it most obviously by personifying Book as a testifying witness, which he emphasizes right from the beginning:

> Thanne was ther a wight with two brode eighen;
> Book highte that beaupeere, a bold man of speche.
> "By Goddes body!" quod this Book, "I wol bere witnesse
> That tho this barn was ybore, ther blased a sterre
> That alle the wise of this world in o wit acordeden—
> That swich a barn was ybore in Bethleem the citee
> That mannes soule sholde save and synne destroye." (18.229–35)

Langland specifically marks Book's body as a witnessing one, his two "brode eighen" denoting Book as an eyewitness to Christ's divine birth. Moreover, the designation of Book as a "beaupeere" establishes him as a ranking member of society, a figure of sufficient community status to provide credible testimony.[19] Perhaps drawing on the homiletic qualities of the speech, Lang-

---

17. *English Metrical Homilies from Manuscripts of the Fourteenth Century*, ed. John Small (Edinburgh: W. Patterson, 1862), page 98.

18. *The Middle English Charters of Christ*, ed. M. C. Spalding (Bryn Mawr: Bryn Mawr College, 1914), lines 21–28. Emily Steiner has discussed the formal and conceptual relationship between the *Charters of Christ* and *Piers Plowman* in *Documentary Culture and the Making of Medieval English Literature* (Cambridge: Cambridge University Press, 2003), 64–75.

19. "Beaupeere" is a somewhat vague Middle English term. Barney follows the *Middle English Dictionary*'s definition of "father-confessor," though as I discuss here, it can have more general connotations, including someone of good standing in a given community (which is one important requirement of being a witness in a court of law). Barney, *Commentary*, 55. As for Book's eyes, Kaske argues that they "can appropriately allegorize the relationship of the New Testament to both past and future." See "Speech," 126.

land emphasizes Book's voice by inserting "quod the Book" twice and adding some oral flourishes. For example, when describing the Passion, Book twice repeats "Lo!" as though calling out to a congregation:

> "And lo! how the sonne gan louke hire light in hirselve
> Whan she seigh hym suffer, that sonne and see made.
> The erthe for hevynesse that he wold suffre
> Quaked as quyk thyng and al biquasshe the roche.
> Lo! helle myghte nat holde, but opnede tho God tholede,
> And leet out Symondes sones to seen hym hange on roode." (18.245–50)

Langland's transformation of this text into the speech of a personified book sets up the specific stakes of Langland's inclusion of Book in his poem. Rather than merely offer a summary of Christ's life and death before the Harrowing of Hell, Langland uses Book to foreground his concern with the ability of personifications to express and teach Christian devotion, particularly the incarnational ideal of the divine Word. That he does so with a witnessing book suggests that he is particularly interested in how testimony might provide a way to think about the dreamer's access to the salvific knowledge contained within Book.

Beyond Book's immediate source-texts, we can locate Book's speech within a long history of books as mediators of the divine Word. The book surfaces as a penitential image in the Book of Revelation 5.1, in which the dreamer John sees that God holds a book written within and without (*librum scriptum intus et foris signatum*). Sealed with seven seals, the book cannot be opened until a wounded lamb takes it from God and opens it, revealing Christ's divinity. These episodes in Revelation set up two crucial features of the penitential book. First, the penitential book fundamentally controls access to God's Word. Only Christ can open the text, and those unable to open it never actually read or hear read the words within. Instead, John sees and hears the voices of many angels (*et vidi et audivi vocem angelorum multorum*), who mediate between the divine Word and John's understanding of it. Second, Revelation depicts God's book as an object to be witnessed, a symbol of God's Word rather than a legible text. This image of the penitential book thus carefully establishes both a gap and a link between the divine and the earthly: while John cannot read God's book nor even open it himself, he can witness the object that contains the Word and thus testify to its power. Indeed, the symbolic potential of the codex, what Jesse Gellrich calls the "myth of the book," imagines that divine *ordo* could be gathered into a kind of urtext, such that "the bond between image and referent, signifier and signified is highly motivated or natural."[20] In other words, because some books could fuse signifier and signified under the unity of the Word, they were crucial symbols of the link between divine wisdom and earthly signs. Accordingly, Langland's Clergie imagines books as the appropriate accoutrements of a utopian, heavenly society: "'For in cloistre cometh no man to [querele] ne to fighte,'" she says, "'But al is buxomnesse there and bokes, to rede and to lerne'" (10.301–2).[21]

Whereas John's testimony demonstrates that mythographic books can link the divine Word to earthly witnesses, personified, speaking books surface in the fourteenth century to complain about the laity who have found ways to access texts they have no business reading. In his *Philobiblon*, for example, Richard de Bury imagines books as the keepers of divine wisdom, which anyone can access: "There everyone who asks receives you, and everyone who seeks finds you, and to everyone that knocks boldly it is speedily opened."[22] But when Richard's books speak for themselves, they complain about all sorts of things, including misuse by "degenerate clerks" (*clerici degeneres*). In particular, because books have been expelled from the homes of the clergy and sold to laypeople, they protest, "We suffer from various diseases, enduring pains in our backs and sides; we lie with our limbs unstrung by palsy, and there is no man who lays it to heart, and no man who provides a mollifying plaster" (45). These personified books beg to be restored to clerks' cloistered studies, safe from rough laymen and the wives who are jealous of their husbands' love of books.

Richard's speaking books materialize one of his central points: that books harbor divine wisdom and thus can only be cared for properly by clerks trained to read sacred texts. His personified books, like Langland's Book, emphasize their own materiality, posing as diseased bodies decaying at the hands of ignorant laypeople. Moreover, as Richard's books worry about their material disintegration at the hands of ignorant or jealous abusers, they also

---

20. Jesse M. Gellrich, *The Idea of the Book in the Middle Ages: Language Theory, Mythology, and Fiction* (Ithaca, NY: Cornell University Press, 1985).

21. Shuffleton argues that throughout *Piers Plowman*, books are treated as the private property of clerks, who "know books kindly because of their institutional position." See "Missing Book," 59.

22. "Ibi te omis qui petit accipit, et qui quaerit invenit, et pulsantibus improbe citius aperitur." *The "Philobiblon" of Richard de Bury*, ed. Michael Maclagan and trans. E. C. Thomas (Oxford: Basil Blackwell, 1960), 16–17. For a discussion of Richard's "fetishistic" relationship between codicology and corporeality, see Michael Camille, "The Book as Flesh and Fetish in Richard de Bury's *Philobiblon*," in *The Book and the Body*, ed. Dolores Warwick Frese and Katherine O'Brien O'Keeffe (Notre Dame, IN: University of Notre Dame Press, 1997), 34–77. For a discussion of Richard's specific interest in the codex rather than other material texts, see Steiner, *Documentary Culture*, 18–19.

complain about a "pestilent multitude of creatures" among the laity, people who consider themselves able to preach and cite from sacred books without really understanding them (65). Richard's books moan, "As the silly parrot imitates the words that he has heard, so such men are mere reciters of all, but authors of nothing, imitating Balaam's ass, which, though senseless of itself, yet became eloquent of speech and the teacher of its master though a prophet" (67).

We can thus note two traditions that treat the relationship between books and witnesses available to Langland. On one hand, the Book of Revelation establishes mutually supportive links between God's Word, the symbolic codex, and earthly witnesses, and Scripture operates as the hinge between the divine Word and John's testimony of it. On the other hand, some fourteenth-century personified books argue that the Johannine experience of witnessing the Word should be confined to clerks to protect the Word from misuse. Langland's Book balances witnessing access and clerkly protection by bringing together the witnesses that might be understood to represent a "kynde" or experiential mode of knowing—natural, earthly eyewitnesses—and clerkly, textual ones, signaled by Peter's citation of Matthew. Indeed, Book focuses less on the miracle than on the testimony of those who can provide evidence of it:

> "And alle the elements," quod the Book, "herof beren witnesse
> That he was God and al wroghte the wolkne first shewed:
> Tho that weren in hevene token *stella comata*
> And tendeden hire as a torche to reverencen his burthe;
> The light folwede the Lord into the lowe erthe.
> The water witnesseth that he was God, for he wente on it;
> Peter the Apostel parceyved his gate,
> And as he wente on the water wel hym knew, and seide,
> *Iube me venire ad te super aquas.*" (18.236-44)

He goes on to claim that the sun, the earth, and the sea quaked with grief as they witnessed Christ's brutal hanging. Book's formulation lists witnesses horizontally, not ranking the claims of the witnessing water below Peter the Apostle's Latin quotation. Book thus brings together "experience" and clerkly learning.

Langland's personified Book is particularly invested in summarizing the miracle of the nativity and the Passion to prepare the dreamer for the Harrowing of Hell and Judgment Day. In offering a sermonlike speech, Book participates in the dramatic operations of the final passus, in which Christ enacts the gospels in front of a crowd, including the dreamer. For George Shuffleton, the end of *Piers Plowman* brings the immediate, communal experience offered by dramatic reenactments of Christ's life and death together with the textual citations scattered throughout the poem. As he puts it, in passus 18, "the poem still features textual learning, replete with documents and biblical quotations in an even greater density than in preceding passus, but now they are all on public display" (67). Indeed, Shuffleton extracts Book from the passus's supposed emphasis on "textual learning," arguing that Book ought not to be considered a kind of document or even a representation of *clergie*, but a kind of pure allegory that momentarily fuses the Book of Nature and God's Word, different from any documentary or textual materials that surface throughout *Piers Plowman*. Book's speech is to be encountered not as a citation, he claims, but as the divine Word emerging directly from the mouth of Scripture. But we ought not to dismiss so easily Book's textuality. Book is still a book, even if an especially transcendent one, and his materiality is crucial to his ability to express the eschatology passus 18 seeks to instruct. Book both participates in the dramatic enactment of the Harrowing of Hell and maintains the clerkly status of a commentary on it. As a witness to Christ's life and death whose testimony reveals the multiple kinds of witnesses working together in the service of verifying Christian eschatology, Book suggests that the Johannine understanding of the divine Word can be accessed and enacted in a number of ways and by a variety of readers, listeners, and observers, clerical and lay.

Yet Langland does not always offer such a mutually supportive relationship between eyewitness experience and bookish literacy, and he spends much of the poem struggling between the authoritative claims of experience and texts. He does so especially in the difficult third vision, where the dreamer turns to the question of grace: that is, whether humans are saved by grace alone or whether good works ("dowel") can offer the possibility of salvation. At the beginning of the vision, after asking many people where he might find "Dowel," the dreamer falls asleep. In this dream, he retreats to his interior consciousness, meeting Thought, who explains the working of Dowel, Dobet, and Dobest. But the dreamer shrugs off the lessons of Thought, telling him, "For more kynde knowynge I coveite to lerne" (8.110). He thus articulates the basic terms of the inner dream: what is the difference between what "bokes" and "kynde knowynge" can offer in the search for grace? The question leads the dreamer to personified figures that represent the human soul, including Thought and Wit, as well as those who represent "external" modes of accessing divine knowledge, including Dame Studie, Clergie, and Scripture. Not surprisingly, as these personifications try to define Dowel, Dobet, and Dobest for the dreamer, they emphasize tight links between moral development and formal models of education, including Scriptural exegesis. Clergy argues that Dowel means to know the articles of faith and "to bileve lelly, bothe lered and lewed"; he goes on to complain about incompetent priests and prophesizes that a king will soon come to reform the Church. The prophecy prompts the dreamer to ask if Dowel and Dobet are knights who will serve such a king, but before Clergy can answer, Scripture shows up.

When Scripture arrives, he answers the dreamer's question with a caveat about the reliability of material texts: "'I nel noght scorne,'" he says, "'but if scryveynes lye, / Kynghod ne knyghthod, by noght I kan awayte, / Helpeth noght to heveneward oone heeris ende, / Ne richesse right noght, ne reautee of lordes'" (10.331–34).[23] Scripture's admission that texts are susceptible to the fallibility of copyists reminds us that Scripture operates in material form, even as it expresses the immaterial Word. This reminder initiates Scripture's measured answer to the dreamer's questions about grace. At first, Scripture explains that only a few will be chosen to enter heaven, and the dreamer trembles with fear that he will not be among them. In response, the dreamer argues that only belief is required for redemption, and moreover, that even non-Christians might be redeemed: "For Crist cleped us alle, come if we wolde— / Sarsens and scismatikes, and so he dide the Jewes: / *O vos omnes sicientes, venite &c*" (11.119–20). Scripture, seemingly impressed with the dreamer's ability to cite from Isaiah, concedes that contrition and meekness could lead anyone to redemption: "'That is sooth,' seide Scripture; 'may no synne lette / Mercy, may al amende, and mekenesse hir folwe; / For thei beth, as oure bokes telleth, above Goddes werkes: / *Misericordia eius super omnia opera eius*'" (11.137–39). For Scripture, "oure bokes" provide the substance for this debate as well as the site of agreement between Scripture and the frustrated dreamer.[24]

The dreamer continues to argue until an irritated Scripture tells the dreamer that he simply does not understand himself well enough for such a complicated discussion. Insulted and exhausted, the dreamer falls asleep within his ongoing dream, and during this dream-within-a-dream he continues his conversation with Scripture, who cites from Matthew to preach that

---

23. For a discussion of this passage, see Simpson, *Introduction*, 96.

24. Shuffleton points out that Clergy offers to bring Conscience a bible to serve as a lesson about patience. As Shuffleton argues, "For Clergy, an intellectual yearning can best be satisfied by a material object. But again, the aim of this covetousness is kind knowing, the same type of intimate connection that exists between a clerk and his books, between owner and property." "Missing Book," 66.

God is both merciful and exacting in his justice. Outraged by the suggestion that clerical learning might be crucial for salvation, Trajan abruptly surfaces to interrupt the conversation. "'Ye, baw for bokes!'" he exclaims, going on to describe his own conversion as one that proves the futility of the kind of clerical authority Scripture advocates:

> "I, Troianus, a trewe knight, take witnesse at a pope
> How I was ded and dampned to dwellen in pyne
> For an uncristene creature; clerkes wite the sothe—
> That al the clergie under Crist ne myghte me cracche fro helle
> But oonliche love and leautee and my lawful domes." (11.141–45) [25]

Trajan was well known in the later Middle Ages as the pagan emperor who was saved by the sixth-century pope Gregory as a result of Trajan's sense of justice.[26] Langland's particular use of Trajan here illustrates his interest in the ways experiential testimony might operate as a fundamental discourse of justice and salvation, particularly as such testimony can dispute the authority of book learning. For Trajan, "taking witness" of his own conversion challenges the citational authority of Scripture and his "bokes." Indeed, as Frank Grady points out, one notable feature of Langland's version of Trajan is that "Trajan speaks—speaks of his own salvation, in his own voice, in the present moment" (24–25). In doing so, Trajan links his speech with the testimonial structures available in law rather than in theological discourse, acting as a witness of his own experiences rather than as a narrator of a dream or prophecy. Indeed, Trajan's self-referential manner of introducing himself as a testimonial subject ("'I, Troianus, a trewe knight, take witnesse'") posits witnessing as a critical intersection between legal and devotional models of grace, linking "love," "leautee," and "lawful domes."

The third vision goes on to offer a series of alternatives to "bokes" as pathways to salvation, including love, faith, and self-understanding. In fact,

---

25. This quotation is cited from Schmidt's first edition of *Piers Plowman*. In the second edition, the quotation from Trajan is in indirect discourse: "'Ye, baw for bokes!' quod oon was broken out of helle / Highte Troianus, a trewe knyght, took witnesse at a pape / How he was ded and dampned to dwellen in pyne / For an uncristen creature" (11.140–44).

26. For a description of the figure of Trajan from the lives of Gregory through twelfth-century theologians and Dante and Langland, see Gordon Whatley, "The Uses of Hagiography: The Legend of Pope Gregory and the Emperor Trajan in the Middle Ages," *Viator* 15 (1984): 25–63. For a concise summary of twentieth-century criticism on the legend of Trajan and *Piers Plowman*, see Frank Grady, *Representing Righteous Heathens in Late Medieval England* (New York: Palgrave, 2005), 20–22.

Trajan presents Paradise as a place where Scripture's "bokes" can be redefined to be more inclusive: "'Ther no clergie ne kouthe, ne konnyng of lawes!'" he states. "'Love and leautee is a leel science, / For that is the book blissed of blisse and of joye'" (11.165–67). Though he claims love and "leautee" ought themselves to be considered authoritative "books," his speech is littered with Scriptural axioms, illustrating, as Langland so often does, that the distinction between "lewed" and "clergie" is not easy to mark. More specifically, Langland shows that "taking witness" as Trajan means it and citing Scripture are not entirely distinct activities. But when Will awakens from his inner dream, he encounters Ymaginatif, who tries (unsuccessfully) to defend the authority of "clergie" over "lewed" models of devotion. Ymaginatif argues that while someone such as Trajan can be saved, his ignorance of clerical knowledge and eleventh-hour conversion will secure him a lower place in heaven than is reserved for those who are baptized. Significantly, to make this argument, Ymaginatif draws on multiple registers of witnessing:

> "Clergie and kynde wit cometh of sighte and techyng,
> As the Book bereth witnesse to burnes that kan rede:
> *Quod scimus loquimur, quod vidimus testamur.*
> Of *quod scimus* cometh clergie, a konnynge of hevene,
> And of *quod vidimus* cometh kynde wit, of sighte of diverse peple.
> Ac grace is a gifte of God, and of greet love spryngeth;
> Knew nevere clerk how it cometh forth, ne kynde wit the weyes:
> *Nescit aliquis unde venit aut quo vadit.*" (12.64–69)

In this passage, witnessing signifies "kynde wit," which is achieved through the "sighte of diverse peple." It also signifies Scriptural citation for a Latinate audience, as the "Book bereth witnesse to burnes that kan rede." Here, Ymaginatif takes up Trajan's opposition between Scriptural citation and witnessing by emphasizing an interactive relationship between "clergie" and "kynde wit," neither of which is wholly sufficient for redemption.

Trajan's testimony and Ymaginatif's sermon are both interested in the overlap between experiential and citational models of devotion and paths to redemption, and both figures broadly illustrate Langland's ambivalence about both clerical and extraclerical modes of demonstrating salvific knowledge. That the discussion about these paths to salvation coheres around Trajan and Ymaginatif is important, since Trajan is a quasi-historical figure, the only "real" figure to appear in *Piers Plowman*, as Grady points out. Ymaginatif, of course, is a personification, an embodiment of the psychological faculty that can construct and distinguish between images in the service of memory.[27] But Ymaginatif is depicted merely as a name, his body only once gestured to when he claims, "I sitte by myself in siknesse ne in helthe" (12.2). By imagining these characters conversing about the various definitions and salvific claims of "bokes," Langland posits "bokes" as the linchpin not only between personal experience and citational knowledge, but also between historical actor and personified abstraction.

In the third vision, then, "bokes" engineer theological discussions about the relationship between attested experience and Scriptural citation. At the end of the poem, Langland's Book collects the various threads of these discussions into a single personification that can exemplify both experience and book learning as witnessing evidence that supports the eschatological future he seeks to articulate. However, as we shall see, when Book takes an oath to burn himself to verify his promise of redemption, he troubles the unified ideal of experiential and bookish witnessing he presents in the first part of his speech. Indeed, Book's oath exposes that Langland's purpose in inserting a speaking Book into his poem is not merely to assert that the witness can blend the authoritative claims of "experience" and "auctoritee," but more specifically to think about how personification might mediate between earthly language and the divine Word. Book's oath recalls the problematic personifications of Gluttony and Anima, and we are asked to consider Book likewise as a personification in which the link between the body and what it represents is not so clear.

After listing the impressive variety of witnesses that either saw or reported on Christ's miraculous birth and violent death, Book confirms his testimony of the Passion with an oath to burn himself should Jesus fail to rise again:

"And I, Book, wole be brent, but Jesus rise to lyve
In alle myghtes of man, and his moder gladie,
And conforte al his kyn and out of care brynge,
And al the Jewene joye unjoynen and unlouken;
And but thei reverencen his roode and his resurexion,
And bileve on a newe lawe, be lost lif and soule!" (18.254–59)

Book's offer of his own body as a guarantee of Christ's certain resurrection enacts the martyrological structures of bodily effacement that testify to divine justice, typically over and above corrupt earthly judges.[28] In addition,

27. A. J. Minnis, "Langland's Ymaginatif and Late Medieval Theories of Imagination," *Comparative Criticism* 3 (1981): 71–103.

28. Critical work on Book's oath focuses on its half-line "but Jesus rise to lyve." Kaske understands "but" as indicating the future indicative, thus rendering the line "I, Book, will be burned,

if we recall Trajan's testimony when we read Book's introduction ("'I, Troianus, a trewe knight'"), we can also take into account the juridical underpinnings of Book's oath. An oath like this, where the burned body is offered as the conduit for divine justice, gestures to the oaths used in ordeal trial, particularly trial by fire. In such a trial, the accused would hold a hot iron in his hands and walk slowly through a marketplace and into a church, where he would drop the iron at the altar. Three days later, an ecclesiastical official would examine the accused's hand for blisters and wounds, thought to be unmistakable signs of guilt.[29] In this system, the oath and the ordeal were mutually exclusive. If one could prove his case with an oath or with oath-helpers (that is, people in good standing in the community who would attest to the accused's character or to his versions of events), he would not have to undergo an ordeal. Ordeal happened only when one needed what was called *lex aperta,* or "open," manifest proof. Ordeal trial thus assumes that the body is a more reliable source of divine evidence than words. Book's oath seems to rely on this standard: so sure is he of Christ's resurrection that he offers his own body as open proof.[30]

Book's testimony offers multiple forms of proof that Christ will return, and his oath crystallizes the various evidentiary media he brings together: his body will ensure Christ's return, his own vocal testimony and the testimony of others will corroborate that promise, and his written text will provide access to God's wisdom. Yet by putting an oath of self-destruction in the mouth of a speaking book, Langland emphasizes a paradox central to his testimonial speech. On one hand, Book is the sort of witness that can offer his body as a conduit for God's Word, but on the other hand, as a Bible or

---

but Jesus will rise" ("The Speech of Boke," 134–38). Richard L. Hoffman and E. Talbot Donaldson each convincingly refute Kaske's reading and translate "but" as "unless," and in doing so, render "lyve" as an infinite verb, not a future conditional. Joseph Wittig has settled the debate, reading the lines "And I, Book, will be burned, unless Jesus rises to live." Hoffman, "The Burning of 'Boke'" in *Piers Plowman,*" MLQ 25 (1964): 57–65; Donaldson, "The Grammar of Book's Speech in *Piers Plowman,*" in *Studies in Language and Literature in Honor of Margaret Schlauch,* ed. Mieczyslaw Brahmer, Stanislaw Helsztynski, and Julian Krzyzanowski (Warsaw: Polish Scientific, 196), 103–9; Wittig, "The Middle English 'Absolute Infinitive' and 'The Speech of Book,'" in *Magister Regis: Studies in Honor of Robert Earl Kaske,* ed. Arthur Groos et al. (New York: Fordham University Press, 1986), 217–40.

29. Robert Bartlett, *Trial by Fire and Water* (Oxford: Clarendon, 1988).

30. By the fourteenth century, ordeal trial had been denounced in English courts for over a century. Canon 18 of the Fourth Lateran Council prohibited priests from blessing the instruments used in the ordeal, effectively preventing the use of ordeal trial as a viable legal option. This is not to say, of course, that ordeal trial did not go on in fourteenth-century England, and ordeals are particularly central to the imaginative world of late medieval English romance, as in a text such as *Athelston.* For a discussion of oaths and ordeal trial in fourteenth-century English romance, see Nancy Mason Bradbury, "The Erosion of Oath-Based Relationships: A Cultural Context for *Athelston,*" *Medium Aevum* 73 (2004): 189–204.

other salvific text, his contents exceed his material form. Thus, Book's oath emphasizes the central question that emerges when we are confronted with a material, witnessing text: how are we to understand the competing modes of authority embedded in various testimonial media (bodily, vocal, and documentary)? Book's oath stages a complicated relationship between personification poetics, oral testimony, and documentary practice, a relationship Langland begins to explore in Lady Mede's trial and in his portraits of Gluttony and Anima.

Indeed, though they are perhaps a surprising group, Gluttony, Anima, and Book have much in common. All three take oaths that point out their existence at the seam between the immaterial and the material. As Elaine Scarry usefully explains, oaths function by "laying edge to edge of the extremes of the material and the immaterial," insofar as

> the body tends to be brought forward in its most extreme and absolute form only on behalf of a cultural artifact or symbolic fragment or made thing (a sentence) that is without any other basis in material reality: that is, it is only brought forward when there is a crisis of substantiation. As a result of this unanchored quality, the disembodied cultural fragment has a fluidity not shared by its physical counterpart.[31]

Gluttony and Anima both clearly suffer "a crisis of substantiation," as their bodies threaten to dissolve under the pressure to confess or give voice to the soul. It is more difficult to make the same claim about Book, who provides the dreamer the closest access to the transcendent Word and shows no sign of physical annihilation. But by reading Langland's oath-taking personifications together, we can see that Book, like Gluttony and Anima, exposes the friction between the transcendent Word and the material media that offer incomplete access to it. Thus, rather than understand Book only as personified Scripture or simply assign another signifier to him (such as the Book of Nature), we can read Book as simultaneously material and allegorical. As a personified, textual witness, he embodies both experience and "auctoritee."

Documentary Witnessing in Truth's Pardon

Recognizing the centrality of oath-taking and witnessing at the heart of Langland's explorations of personification, signification, and modes of sal-

---

31. Elaine Scarry, *The Body in Pain: The Making and Unmaking of the World* (Oxford: Oxford University Press, 1985), 127.

vific understanding permits a new reading of one of the most notoriously knotty passages in *Piers Plowman*. The tearing of the pardon scene (B.7) has generated more critical inquiry than any other episode in *Piers Plowman*, yet scholars have not entirely succeeded in clarifying the mysterious destruction of the ersatz pardon.[32] This is in part because critics have overlooked the fact that this pardon functions specifically "in witnesse of truthe," with the dreamer peeking over Piers's shoulder to read the text and subsequently watch its destruction. The passus begins just after Piers has finished plowing and before he embarks on a pilgrimage to find Truth. Worried about the possibility that Piers's fields will lie fallow while he goes on pilgrimage, Truth purchases a pardon for Piers and his heirs, telling Piers to return home to plow his fields. The pardon dictates who will receive salvation via Truth's pardon: kings and knights will be saved, as will patriarchs, prophets, bishops, and lawyers. Merchants, however, may not be:

Marchaunts in the margyne hadde manye yeres,
Ac noon *a pena et a culpa* the Pope nolde hem graunte,
For thei holde noght hir haliday as Holy Chirche techeth,
And for thei swere "by hir soule" and "so God moste hem helpe"
Ayein clene Conscience, hir catel to selle. (7.18–22)

Merchants have been excluded from salvation because they abuse oaths, using them to sell their goods rather than demonstrate their fidelity to divine truth.[33] Their careless oath-taking puts them dangerously close to the edge of condemnation. But Truth intervenes, telling the merchants that he has a papal bull which states that if they amend their ways and perform acts of charity, they will be saved. In gratitude, merchants everywhere praise Piers, who purchased the bull on their behalf.

When Piers receives Truth's pardon for himself and his heirs, a priest offers to read and explain it: "'For I shal construe ech clause and kenne it thee on Englissh'" (7.106). As Piers unfolds the pardon and reads it aloud (demonstrating at least some knowledge of Latin), he is surprised to find two lines of the Athanasian Creed:

---

32. For a small sampling of critical examinations of the pardon scene, see Nevill K. Coghill, "The Pardon of Piers Plowman," in *Style and Symbolism in "Piers Plowman,"* ed. Robert J. Blanch (Knoxville: University of Tennessee Press, 1969), 40–86; Rosemary Woolf, "Tearing the Pardon," in *"Piers Plowman": Critical Approaches*, ed. S. S. Hussey (London: Methuen, 1969), 50–75; David Lawton, "On Tearing—and Not Tearing—the Pardon," *Philological Quarterly* 60 (1981): 414–22; Denise Baker, "The Pardons of *Piers Plowman*," *Neuphilologische Mitteilungen* 85 (1984): 462–72; and Steiner, *Documentary Culture*, 121–42.

33. D. Vance Smith, *Arts of Possession: The Medieval Household Imaginary* (Minneapolis: University of Minnesota Press, 2003), 136–50.

> And Piers at his preiere the pardon unfoldeth—
> And I bihynde hem bothe biheld al the bulle.
> In two lynes it lay, and noght a le[ttre] moore,
> And was ywriten right thus in witnesse of Truthe:
> *Et qui bona egerunt ibunt in vitam eternam;*
> *Qui vero mala, in ignem eternum.* (7.107–10)

Enraged that he has been duped into buying a pardon that isn't a pardon at all, Piers angrily tears the document in two, vowing to leave his life of plowing to pursue prayer and penance. The pardon scene pits the material form of the document against the potentially redemptive citation of the Creed.

To navigate the relationship between a document that fails to fulfill its contractual promise and the Creed's simple model of penance, Langland inserts a third term, the witness. In doing so, he suggests that the pardon negotiates the probative claims of an individual text against the iterable force of documentary formulae and citation. Langland thus puts the pardon in the same paradox he puts Gluttony, Anima, and Book: material self-destruction may lead to salvation. Indeed, what Book merely promises, the pardon fulfills, when Piers rips it apart and chooses a life of prayer. This is not to argue that the pardon scene clearly promotes good works over clerical learning or ecclesiastical documents. Rather, recognizing the pardon as a witness expands what kinds of objects can be considered part of Langland's experiment in testimony and personification. Like Gluttony, Anima, or Book, the pardon uneasily occupies the space between the allegorical and the material.

If much of the pardon scene's tension is between the materiality of this individual pardon and the endurance of the truth of its contents outside any material form, the complicated relationship between the Latin Creed and the priest's English translation adds to these tensions. Simpson argues that throughout *Piers Plowman,* Langland attaches Latin and English to different, and contested, narrative modes: "If the vernacular lays claim to the experiential, the new, the contingent (the *seen*), it does so only in the shadow of a different kind of narrative, the sonorous, immutable, impersonal discourse of the Latin Creed—a text which is *read.*"[34] For Simpson, the hierarchical relationship between Latin and English relies on a gap between seeing and reading, between the kind of experiential Christian redemption in which someone such as Trajan can engage and the clerical authority asserted by those trained in Latin and Christian theology. Yet Langland's portrayal of the pardon as Truth's witness suggests that he resists understanding experiential

---

34. Simpson, "Desire and the Scriptural Text," 216.

witnessing and reading as different activities, even in the tension-filled pardon scene.³⁵

Significantly, a similar negotiation between eyewitnessing and reading also emerges in the C-text *apologia*, which famously replaces the pardon scene with Langland's most extensive, and most self-reflexive, discussion of authorship.³⁶ Staged as an interrogation between Will and Reason, the *apologia* defends the dreamer's ostensibly idle life against Reason's argument that he ought to perform manual labor in order to fulfill his material and spiritual duties. Asserting himself as a clerk, the dreamer explains that his "tools" consist of liturgical texts and his primer, then claims that his contemplative work sets him apart from the kind of labor executed by less educated men:

> And also moreover me thynketh, syre Resoun,
> Me sholde constrayne no clerc to no knaves werkes,
> For by the lawe of *Levyticy* that oure lord ordeynede,
> Clerkes ycrouned, or kynde understondynge,
> Shold nother swynke ne swete ne swerien at enquestes
> Ne fyhte in no faumewarde ne his foe greve. (C.5.53–58)

The dreamer contrasts all sorts of manual activities with the contemplative, clerkly work of a poet, but his insertion of oath-taking is striking. Why might Langland want to disengage oath-taking from writing here? The citation of the "law of Leviticus" offers some insight. Beyond dictating how clerks were to dress and conduct themselves, Leviticus 5:4–5 states, "The person that swears and utters with his lips that he would do either evil or good and binds it with an oath and his word, and having forgotten it afterward, understands his offence, let him do penance for his sin."³⁷ Leviticus puts quite a bit of pressure on the oath, making it stand in for the intentions of its speaker even when what was promised has been forgotten or the intentions have changed. For a writer like Langland, whose work was likely appropriated by the rebel leader John Ball in 1381, this kind of contract is particularly dangerous.³⁸ By

---

35. By the end of the poem, according to Simpson, Langland has produced a picture of active reading, in which "experience" and "auctoritee" are not necessarily at odds.

36. See Kathryn Kerby-Fulton, "Langland and the Bibliographic Ego," in *Written Work: Langland, Labor, and Authorship*, ed. Steven Justice and Kathryn Kerby-Fulton (Philadelphia: University of Pennsylvania Press, 1997), 67–143; and David C. Fowler, "*Piers Plowman*: Will's 'Apologia pro vita sua,'" *YLS* 13 (1999): 35–47.

37. "Anima quae iuraverit et protulerit labiis suis ut vel male quid faceret vel bene et id ipsum iuramento et sermone firmaverit oblitaque postea intellexerit delictum suum agat paenitentiam pro peccato."

38. Steven Justice, *Writing and Rebellion: England in 1381* (Berkeley and Los Angeles: University of California Press, 1994).

disentangling oath-taking from the kind of work a clerk or a poet might perform, the narrator renounces the possibility that his writing might be used as a kind of "evidence" in support of an ideological or political position he might never have intended.

Thus, we can understand the dreamer's dismissal of swearing as anxiety about the potentially close relationship between an author and a witness who, under the authority of an oath, attests to the incontrovertible truths of his works. Perhaps, under the politically pressured conditions of the 1380s, Langland wanted to disengage witness from author, perhaps even retreating to the individuated authenticity of the dream-vision as a way of mitigating the possibility that *Piers Plowman* could be read as a testifying document by those using it in the service of dissident ideological claims.[39] Yet, as we shall see in the next section, fifteenth-century Langlandian poetry brings the witnessing document and the vernacular author back together. Texts in the *Piers Plowman* tradition construct their political critiques by effacing the individual dreamer and vernacular author and replacing them with documentary anonymity.

Langlandian Witnessing in the *Piers Plowman* Tradition

Thus far, this chapter has argued that Langland uses episodes of witnessing to negotiate the overlaps and frictions between "experience" and "auctoritee" as modes of spiritual expertise. Langland's fullest expression of testimony as a multifaceted model of spiritual knowledge emerges in Book's speech, when he collapses the differences between eyewitness experience and textual authority by imagining a testifying, salvific book with a body and a voice. But throughout *Piers Plowman*, Langland draws on witnessing speech-acts, particularly the oath, to experiment with whether and how personification might offer access to spiritual, moral, and ethical truths. This section turns to fifteenth-century Langlandian texts to see how Langland's thinking about the relationship between the experiential eyewitness and the clerical text was deployed with increasingly ideological urgency and specificity.

The fifteenth-century texts that deliberately imitate and expand upon *Piers Plowman* depict witnessing as a mode of political engagement. At the turn of the fifteenth century, as Grady argues, English poetry began to shift

---

39. There are numerous discussions of the role of *Piers Plowman* in the Rising of 1381. For extended accounts, see Anne Middleton, "Acts of Vagrancy: The C-Version 'Autobiography' (C.5.1–108) and the Statute of 1388," in *Written Work: Langland, Labor and Authorship*, 208–317; and Justice, *Writing and Rebellion*.

away from the visionary authority of the individual dreamer toward the authorizing conceits of bureaucratic reportage and legal discourse. In particular, these authorizing conceits were used to discuss and satirize topical politics regarding Richard's deposition. "The two motifs are certainly related," Grady writes. "It is logical to assume that a crisis of political authority—the deposition and its aftermath—would present a problem for political poetry trying to speak authoritatively about that crisis. Trading dreams for documents turns out to offer some potential solutions."[40] The turn to documents perhaps protected the poet from the confessional pitfalls of dream-visions and permitted him to speak with a social voice. Still, dream-vision remains an important genre in the fifteenth century, and much of the *Piers Plowman* tradition is, in fact, dream-vision.[41] The witness brings together the visionary authority of the dreamer and the legal or bureaucratic authority of testimony, so the witness provides a powerful voice with which to critique the king. Specifically, poems included in the *Piers Plowman* tradition deploy the witness as an outside observer of royal systems of power that can respond to political upheaval. In "Richard the Redeless," for example, the narrator laments that he is troubled over the bitter criticism of Richard's reign: "for it passid my parceit and my preifis also, / How so wondirffull werkis wolde haue an ende."[42] Locating his narratorial fallibility in his inability to "perceive and prove" the end to Richard's story, this speaker translates the uncertainty of Langland's dreamer into an imperfect witness.

Mum and the Sothsegger offers an extended meditation on Langlandian witnessing. Written between 1402 and 1409, *Mum* centers on the reign of Henry IV, and it worries about the false flatterers who surround the king and argues for the need for royal "truth-tellers." Structurally, it calls upon *Piers Plowman* by featuring a dream-vision as well as the narrator's pilgrimage in search of a "sothe-segger." The dreamer's quest to find a truth-teller provides the narrative conceit for a satirical look at what constitutes "truth" in contemporary politics and law. More specifically, it considers how keeping mum undercuts the need for royal justice that works according to ethics and truth rather than a political system that supports those who merely agree with the king in order to curry favor.

40. Frank Grady, "The Generation of 1399," in Steiner and Barrington, *The Letter of the Law*, 206.
41. The term "*Piers Plowman* tradition" is Helen Barr's, and it denotes a series of four texts produced between 1399 and 1415: *Pierce the Plowman's Crede, Richard the Redeless, The Crowned King,* and *Mum and the Sothsegger.*
42. "Richard the Redeless," in *The Piers Plowman Tradition*, ed. Helen Barr (London: J. M. Dent, 1993), 17–18. Quotations from *Mum* will also be cited parenthetically from this edition, by line number.

In Langlandian fashion, *Mum* turns to testimony to conceptualize the vexed status of a royal counselor, particularly in delicate bureaucratic matters. *Mum* begins with a striking definition of what it means to witness well: first, it says, attend to the gospel, where you will see for yourself the sins of your king. Armed with this knowledge, you must then interrogate him to draw out a confession. Such interrogation should be pursued until the king sees the wisdom of drawing out the truth. When you "haue wittenes the with that thou wel knowes," you will be able to convince your king of the wisdom of keeping a truth-teller in his retinue:

> For whenne thy tente and thy tale been temprid in oone,
> And menys no malice to man that thou spekys,
> But forto mende hym mukely of his misse-deedes,
> Sory for his synne and his shrewed taicches,
> And the burne be y-blessid and balys cunne eschewe
> And thrifty and towarde, thou shal thanke gete. (90–95)

Pushing the king into testimonial dialogue—that is, interrogating him and getting him to confess—not only keeps the king honest, it also unites the truth-teller's intention ("tente") with his words ("tale"). The truth-teller thus operates as a double agent: he draws the king into confessional honesty that will protect the crown from the duplicitous desires of flatterers and power-hungry lords, and he offers his own testimony of the king's foibles, bearing witness to the king's misdeeds as a kind of thermometer for the health of the realm.

Later, when Mum emerges to extol the virtues of staying silent rather than draw confessions out of the king, he introduces himself to the narrator as "Mum thy maister." Mum goes on to explain that he remains close to sovereigns by refusing to contradict them and by flattering them. Frustrated, the narrator accuses Mum of serving only himself, at the expense of the realm: "'Thou wol not putte the in prees but profit be the more, / To thy propre persone, thou passes not the bondes / Forto gete any grucche for glaunsyng of boltes'" (267–69). Nonetheless, the narrator finds himself intrigued with Mum's counseling strategies, and he goes on a quest to search for a truth-teller and to investigate what he repeatedly calls "my matiere of Mum" (326, 396). Mum is thus established, in Langlandian fashion, both as a personified interlocutor for the narrator and his object of study. The "matiere of Mum" can be defined as the exploration of how silence can function in a system of counsel that, as the beginning of the poem asserts, requires a counselor to testify to his knowledge of the crown's crimes and sins.

Mum argues throughout the poem that such truthful testimony would negate the material benefits garnered by being a flattering yes-man. But when he specifically addresses the problem of remaining mum as a courtroom witness, he oddly belies his own arguments. Citing a legal axiom, "*qui tacet consentire videtur*," he warns that those who remain silent in the face of "silde-couthe thingz" will be considered legally liable for those deeds (745–50). Mum continues,

> And eeke in lond-is lawe I lernyd by anothir:
> Yf a freke for felonye is frayned atte barre
> For traison or for trespas and he a tunge haue
> And wil not answere to the deede he is of indited,
> But stont stille as a stoone and no worde stire,
> But he be deef or dum to deeth shal he wende,
> As atteynt for the trespas, and is a trewe lawe. (751–57)

Here, Mum states that silence in the courtroom is akin to self-destruction, since refusing to testify to the truth in cases of treason or trespass will lead to the same death reserved for those who commit these crimes. It is a strange speech for Mum, particularly given his impassioned defense of flattery, praise, and silence in the face of a sovereign's misdeeds. But it becomes less strange in the wider context of Langlandian testimonial discourse. Mum suggests that he can exist as the personified representation of flattering silence only in certain contexts: here, within the intimacy of royal counsel and maintenance. When called upon to testify in a court of law, his very existence—as the embodiment of flattery and silence, of keeping mum—is put in jeopardy. Like Langland's Gluttony, Mum's status as personification finds its limits in testimony: if called upon to testify in a court of law, he cannot continue to perform the silence and flattery that is his essence as Mum.

The narrator, pleased with Mum's admission that silence can sometimes be self-destructive, compares courtroom truth-telling to exposing the wounds on a sick plant. The link between wounds and social sins is ubiquitous throughout the Middle Ages, particularly in confessional manuals and penitential treatises, and surely this is where the narrator takes the imagery of telling the truth as lancing a physical wound. But the imagery assumes new meaning when read as a reprisal of Langland's investigation of the interface between personification, testimony, and text. "'For thou has rubbid on the rote of the rede galle,'" the narrator tells Mum, "'And eeke y-serchid the sore and sought alle the woundz'" (770–71). The narrator reads Mum's confession as saying that legal testimony would destroy him as a path to healing, but such "healing" would erase Mum: like Gluttony, if Mum suddenly "healed" the social wounds created by flatterers such as himself by speaking truth to crown, he would be redeemed out of existence. After Mum warns those who refuse to provide truthful legal testimony, the narrator goes on a dream-vision quest to learn where he can find a bona fide truth-teller. In his dream, he encounters a wise beekeeper, who explains a hive as an ideal model of governance, imagining himself as the sovereign. He is, the narrator discovers, the truth-teller he has been searching for, and the beekeeper implores the narrator to write down his words to give to the king: "'And furst feoffe thou therewith the freyst of the royaulme, / For yf thy lord liege alone hit begynne, / Care thou not though knyghtz copie hit echone, / And do write eche word and wirche there-after'" (1284–87).

When the narrator wakes up, he discovers a bag full of "pryue poyse," which details the vices and virtues of bishops and lords of the realm. This bag of books powerfully extends Langland's experiments in the relationship between witnessing and personification. It includes "real" documents, such as a quire that lists bequeathed goods and a collection of visitation papers for bishops and priests, and fictional documents, such as a "rolle of religion" that details monks' misuse of their endowments. Emily Steiner argues that the bag represents a satirical investigation of how public poetry and bureaucratic documents allow "society to disclose itself to public view, and, in doing so, to translate disclosure into incrimination and reparation" (182). Accordingly, she claims, the kind of counsel poetry that is authorized by the truth-teller can operate like a public document, one that reveals social ills and thus helps them to be disclosed, punished, and healed. Likewise, Helen Barr reads the bag of books as a strategic image that divests the poet of the political liability of criticizing the realm.[43] She argues that by featuring a sack full of bureaucratic documents, the *Mum*-author suggests that political criticism is embedded in legal and documentary formulae, rather than in the personal gripes of an individual author or the words of a single poem. Both Steiner and Barr recognize that the power of the bag of books is its disengagement from any particular author, so that truth-telling becomes a collective rather than an individual pursuit.

When we focus on the description of one specific document embedded in the long list of legal and bureaucratic texts, the "raggeman rolle," we can also understand the bag of books as an extension of the poem's arguments about witnessing. When the narrator mentions a "raggeman rolle that Ragenelle hymself / Hath made of mayntennance and motyng of the peuple"

---

43. Barr, *Piers Plowman Tradition*, xiii–xiv.

(1565–66), he cites the legal text that documents the accusations made in both criminal and civil courts. Those who transported these rolls from the complainants to the courtrooms were known as "ragmen," and so the term comes to signify both the document and the bureaucratic official in charge of that document.[44] In *Mum*, "Ragenelle" also signifies the devil, who has produced a text that proclaims the abuses imposed on the public by the practices of maintenance that Mum espouses. By naming "Ragenelle" as the author and as the carrier of the "raggeman rolle," the *Mum*-poet momentarily reminds us of the complicated link between material document and personification. The name functions like Book, in that it refers both to an embodied personification and to the material form that conveys testimony. Like Langland, then, the *Mum*-poet suggests that personification can navigate between the communal claims of anonymous bureaucratic and legal documents and the individual testimony lobbied by a dreamer or vernacular poet.

Mum and the Sothsegger offers a rich example of how Langland's experiments in witnessing and personification offer the fifteenth-century *Piers Plowman* tradition an opportunity to conceptualize testimony as a political and ethical imperative. In *Mum*, witnessing documents are a source of disembodied authority, in which testimony can be detached from any individual source and thus derive its power from the collective voice it assumes. Thus legal documents take on the power to attest to political critiques on behalf of the community as a whole. But in the sixteenth century, as we shall see, the individual voice of the witness—named Piers the Plowman—reemerges as an important source of political critique. Significantly, it does so via the implicit authoritative claims of print technology, thus expanding upon Langland's experiments in the relative efficacies of body, voice, and document.

Langlandian Witnesses in Print

The author of *Mum and the Sothsegger* takes Langlandian explorations of testimony and personification into the political sphere of the court, investigating the complicated relationship between individuals offering spoken testimony and the material texts that can serve in their stead. The bag of books offers not simply a catalogue of the kinds of bureaucratic documents circulating at the turn of the fifteenth century, but an exploration of the way

---

44. See John Alford, *Piers Plowman: A Glossary of Legal Diction* (Cambridge: D. S. Brewer, 1988), 125. In her discussion of the "raggeman rolle," Steiner argues that it, like the rest of these documents, inserts vernacular alliterative poetry into the bureaucratic and legal poetics of public discourse. *Documentary Culture*, 183.

personification might inform even the most official or formulaic bureaucratic document. In the sixteenth century, the relationship between testimony and personification is taken up in the service of Reformation politics, as "Piers Plowman" and his brethren, the "simple plowmen," surface as stock figures in the service of arguments against the rhetorical bombast and financial bloat of the Church.[45] More specifically, the texts that feature a witnessing Piers center on print technology as an ideological medium. What this suggests is that the Reformation Piers, a witness in the case for political and doctrinal reform, may help articulate some of the political stakes of early modern print culture.

Jesse M. Lander has shown that Protestant reformers often imagined an alliance between anti-Catholic polemic and the printing press, in which print technology could be formulated as a system dedicated to spreading doctrinal truth.[46] At the same time, plowmen (and "Piers Plowman") emerge as representatives of reformist ideology, even revising Langland's medieval Catholicism to suit the needs of Protestant polemic. These two developments are not unrelated. Sixteenth-century "Plowman texts" focus on granting power to laborers and others outside institutional systems of authority by closing the gap between the simple (that is, illiterate) laborer and the sophisticated (that is, literate) clerk.[47] Notably, to close the gap, they turn to reportage as a form of authority that unites manuscript and print and brings together the "voice" of the testifying plowman and the print technologies that disseminate that voice among a wide audience. "Reportage" thus puts in play multiple kinds of testimonial media, drawing on both the voice and the document alike to authorize the ideological principles to which "Piers the Plowman" can attest.

Robert Crowley was the first to print *Piers Plowman*, producing three editions of the poem in 1550. These versions include a preface from "the printer to the reader" as well as a program of marginal notes that tends to be anti-Catholic, even if mildly so. The preface is most overt in its insertion of Langland into a radical agenda, locating the poem's philosophical and theological imperatives alongside those of Wyclif:

> In whose tyme it pleased God to open the eyes of many to se hys truth, giving them boldenes of herte, to open their mouthes and crye oute agynst

---

45. See, for example, John N. King, *English Reformation Literature: The Tudor Origins of the Protestant Tradition* (Princeton, NJ: Princeton University Press, 1982).

46. Jesse M. Lander, *Inventing Polemic: Religion, Print, and Literary Culture in Early Modern England* (Cambridge: Cambridge University Press, 2006).

47. The phrase "Plowman texts" is from Sarah A. Kelen, *Langland's Early Modern Identities* (New York: Palgrave, 2007).

the workes of darckenes, as dyd John Wicklyfe, who also in the those dayes translated the holye Byble into the Englishe tonge, and this writer who in reportynge certayne visions and dreames, that he fayned hym selfe to have dreamed, doth most christianlie enstructe the weake, and sharplye rebuke the obstynate blynde.[48]

One of Crowley's main purposes in his preface is to detach Langland from prophecy, which he says misconstrues Langland's intent: "And that which foloweth and geveth it the face of a prophecy," he writes, "is lyke to be added by some other man than the first autour" (f. iir).[49] Crowley rejects reading Langland prophetically by constructing a complicated series of authorial and editorial claims to authenticity, and these claims turn on the kind of witnessing reportage that surfaces in fifteenth-century Langlandian texts. "This writer," as Crowley puts it, "who in reportynge certayne visions and dreames, that he fayned hym selfe to have dreamed, doth most christianlie enstructe the weake." In turn, the reader is to "loke not upon this boke therefore to talke of wonders past or to com but to emend thyne owne misse, which thou shalt fynd here most charitably rebuked" (f. iir). For Crowley, "reportynge" is the operative verb. Like the poems in the *Piers Plowman Tradition*, Crowley's *Piers* substitutes the individual authority of the dreamer with the iterability of the witnessing text. Here, eyewitness reports triumph over other, particularly medieval, ways of accessing redemptive knowledge, including dream-vision and prophecy. Reporting also shores up his own printing project more broadly. Crowley begins his preface by locating the poem's authorship (attributed to "Roberte Langlande, a Shropshire man") and its year of first publication, which he strains to authorize via his own eyewitness and scholarly expertise:

For the tyme when it was written, it chaunced me to se an auncient copye, in the later ende whereof was noted, that the same copye was written in the yere of oure Lorde. M.iii.C and nyne, which was before thys present

---

48. *The Vision of Pierce Plowman, Now Fyrste Imprynted.* STC 11906, ed. A. W. Pollard et al. (London, 1926), folio iir.
49. In offering this caveat, he may be positioning his editions against other sixteenth-century constructions of *Piers Plowman* as a prophetic voice in the service of royal politics. British Library MS Sloane 2578, for example, includes in its varied collection of political prophecies a fragment of the B-text. See Sharon L. Jansen, "Politics, Protest, and a New *Piers Plowman* Fragment: The Voice of the Past in Tudor England," *Review of English Studies* n.s. 40.157 (1989): 93–99. For a description of MS Sloane 2578's contents, see Jansen, "British Library MS Sloane 2578 and Popular Unrest in England," *Manuscripta* 29 (1985): 30–41.

> yere, an hundred & xli yeres. And in the seconde side of the lxviii leafe of thys printed copye, I finde mention of a dere yere, that was in the yere of oure Lord. Miii.hundred and .L. John Chichester than being mayre of London. So that this I may be bold to report, that it was fyrste made and written after yeare of our lord. M.iii.C.L. and before the yere M.iiii.C. and .ix, which meane space was lix yeres.[50] (f. iir)

Crowley's "bold report" that *Piers Plowman* was first made between 1350 and 1409 is based both on his chance encounter with an "auncient copye" and on his careful codicological investigation into "thys printed copye."[51] Locating his editorial authority in both manuscript and print editions, Crowley pays close attention to the hermeneutic pitfalls of having multiple printed copies of *Piers Plowman* in circulation. For example, he admits that while some editions of the poem might support prophetic readings, his does not: whereas "diuerse copies" might depart from the (nonprophetic) intentions of the author, the copy he has followed closely follows the original—presumably the "auncient copye" he was able to witness. By insisting that he has been able to see for himself an "auncient copye" of *Piers Plowman*, Crowley draws on the commonplace use of the term "ancient" to describe medieval texts, a method that transformed the Catholic Middle Ages into a distant past that could be appropriated and assimilated by early modern writers. Moreover, Crowley imagines a mutually supportive relationship between the "ancient" manuscript and this printed copy in his pursuit of a "true" version of Langland's poem.

Reportage is also the primary method of authorization in a text that imagines Piers the Plowman to testify directly to parliament on behalf of the "poore comens." In the mid-sixteenth-century *Pyers Plowmans Exhortation*, Piers begins his catalogue of complaints (which include problematic property distribution in the wake of the widespread closure of religious houses) by suggesting that parliament focus on the plight of the poor so that "in all regions wher as it shalbe reported how that we of thys realm haue expelled all vayne tradicions of men / and receyued the true religion

---

50. Kelen points out that Chichester was mayor of London from 1369 to 1370, not in 1350. Crowley likely calculated 1350 from Activa Vita's speech discussing the effects of a famine; in some manuscripts, Activa Vita says Chichester was mayor in 1350. See *Langland's Early Modern Identities*, 28.

51. The tag of "auncient" applied to medieval texts was a common rhetorical practice in early modern texts that sought to absorb medieval writers within a new Protestant culture. Spenser's *Shepheardes Calendar* is one example.

of Christ."⁵² Piers uses the term "reported" to extend the reach of his formal complaint beyond parliament, claiming its power to produce reports throughout the realm not merely of parliament's good will toward the poor, but of England's reception of true (that is, anti-Catholic) doctrine. Notably, Piers's mode of reform is to ask members of parliament to trust their own witnessing experience in contradistinction to the clerical and educated claims of "fatte priestes" and "fatte marchau*n*tes": "But he that wyll be conuersaunt with the come*n* sorte of the poore comens, shal (if he not stop his eares, nor hyde not his eyes) both heare se & *per*ceyue the case to be farre otherwise" (f. 1v).

Sixteenth-century reformers may have seen in Langland the possibility of appropriating clerical models of authority on behalf of a new ideology that positioned an "unlearned" laity as the proper representatives of theological and doctrinal ideals for a religious community. For Langland, however, witnessing offered a conceptual model for linking together experiential and textual modes of doctrinal knowledge. Examining closely how Langland depicts oath-taking reveals his investment in the way legal language can help express spiritual exploration. Witnessing provides Langland the opportunity to play with the relative probative and contractual authorities of the body and the document, and his Book depicts his most powerful and urgent investigation of testimonial media with respect to the divine Word. Moreover, the Langlandian witness endures into the fifteenth and sixteenth centuries, when it is taken up for a range of purposes: to critique royal systems of maintenance and flattery and to contend with the incorporation of a Catholic medieval past into a reformist present. For sixteenth-century reformers, the voice of "Piers Plowman" could be disseminated through the medium of print, and "reporting" became a crucial vocabulary term in the rhetorical service of transforming the medieval voice of the individual Piers into the ideological claims of a reformist collective.

Indeed, the idea that a witness might provide a position from which reform can be argued and preached is crucial to the Wycliffite criticism of the Church bubbling up toward the end of the fourteenth century. The next chapter examines how one early fifteenth-century Lollard tract deploys the negotiation between testimonial *vox* and witnessing text to address the very real possibility of self-destruction under the 1401 *De heretico comburendo* statute, which authorized capital punishment for relapsed heretics. As that

---

52. *Pyers plowmans exhortation unto the lordes, knightes and burgoysses of the parlyamenthouse*, STC 19905 (London: Imprinted by Anthony Scoloker dwelling in the Sauoy tentes without Templebarre, 1550).

chapter shows, witnessing remains a central but vexed mode of political and doctrinal engagement throughout the fifteenth century, deployed by conservative ecclesiastical officials and radical Lollard resistors alike to negotiate their respective claims to the "true" Church and to articulate the bonds of their respective theological communities.

five

Witnessing, Presence, and Lollard Communities

THE TRIAL RECORDS of accused Lollards produced in the fifteenth century, coupled with the printed compilations of Lollard "martyrs" in the sixteenth century, are critical to thinking about the procedural and conceptual legacy of witnessing in the later Middle Ages. As Andrew Cole has shown, the persecution of heresy in late medieval England, which began with the Blackfriars Council in 1382 and gathered steam with the institution of the *De heretico comburendo* statute in 1401 and Archbishop Arundel's "Cruel Constitutions" in 1409, depends on the mutual support of ecclesiastical and secular justice.[1] Accused Lollards trapped by this massive campaign were subject to both canon and common law, a procedural fact that significantly changed how defendants could be interrogated. More broadly, witness accounts of Lollard interrogations help us think about the relationship between historicity—that is, biographical or historical truth, verified by documentary evidence—and the individual testimony that animates that historicity. As Christina von Nolcken has argued, Wycliffite and Lollard texts are an "obvious test case" regarding our ability to capture and interpret the past because they exhibit little individual inventiveness or authorial flair, instead illustrat-

---

1. Andrew Cole, *Literature and Heresy in the Age of Chaucer* (Cambridge: Cambridge University Press, 2008), 3–22.

ing a kind of dogmatic repetition of the same phrases and structures in the service of producing a dangerous heterodox culture.[2]

Nowhere is such dogmatic repetition more obvious than in the legal records of Lollard interrogations. Despite the leeway given scribes and notaries to transform the sometimes tedious narrative of witness testimony into a concise text,[3] accused Lollards were asked to respond to a stock set of questions designed to draw out a consistent picture of their heretical beliefs and practices.[4] The basic tenets of what was considered heresy at the turn of the fifteenth century were drawn from Wyclif's writings; interrogators typically focused on his arguments against the miracle of Eucharistic transubstantiation and those in favor of disendowment of the clergy, as well as on his complicated arguments about Scriptural truth and the literal sense, first articulated in his *Trialogus* and spectacularly enacted in his English translation of the Bible.[5]

The resulting legal documents work to suppress the individual voice or specific beliefs of the defendant. Thus, rather than offering access to the life and beliefs of any particular individual, these documents illustrate how inquisitional process and witness testimony were used to produce a uniform picture of heterodox thinking and to authorize draconian tactics of persecution. By providing a consistent illustration of the heresies that were attacking the moral sanctity of Church doctrine, ecclesiastical and royal officials could assemble the testimonies of individual defendants into a collective and dangerous counterculture. Yet, as this chapter shows, witnessing rhetoric was also used by Lollard thinkers to counteract ecclesiastical control over the depiction of heterodox communities. For example, the writer of the Wycliffite tract *Apology for Lollard Doctrine* deploys witnessing to insist that his challenges to Church doctrine do not attack faith itself. In doing so, he establishes his testimony as a verification of his adherence to the "true" Church:

> First, I witnes bifor God Almiȝty, and alle trewe cristunmen and women, and ȝowe, þat I haue not ben, nor is, nor neuer schal, of myn entent ne

2. Christina Von Nolcken, "A 'Certain Sameness' and Our Response to It in English Wycliffite Texts," in *Literature and Religion in the Later Middle Ages*, ed. Richard G. Newhauser and John A. Alford (Binghamton, NY: Medieval and Renaissance Texts and Studies, 1995), 191–208.

3. For a discussion of the editorial latitude given notaries, see chapters 2 and 4.

4. See Anne Hudson, "The Examination of Lollards," *Bulletin of the Institute of Historical Research* 46 (1973): 145–59.

5. For a discussion of the production of the Wycliffite Bible out of Wyclif's arguments on translation and Scriptural truth, see Mary Dove, *The First English Bible: The Text and Context of the Wycliffite Versions* (Cambridge: Cambridge University Press, 2007).

purpos, to sei any þing a3en the general feiþ; neiþer entent to bigile, or deseyue, ani man or woman, in ani vnprofitable to perpetual 3el of soule; ne agein seying to þe wordis, ne sentence, of ani seint, seying feithfulli.[6]

The flexibility of witness testimony to define and persecute Wycliffite heresy on one hand and to defend against such persecution on the other drives the *Examination of William Thorpe* (also known as the *Testimony of William Thorpe*), a peculiar document that shrewdly transforms Thorpe's official deposition into his own autobiographical, testimonial text. The *Testimony* presents itself as a first-person account of Archbishop Arundel's interrogation into Thorpe's unauthorized preaching. Purportedly written in 1407, a year after Thorpe's arrest in Shrewsbury, it details his production of a text on behalf of "dyuerse freendis" who have requested that he document his "aposynge and answeringe."[7] Though there is some historical evidence to corroborate that this interrogation actually occurred, including a notebook of the diocesan official John Lydford that contains articles drawn up against a "William Thorpe,"[8] the historicity of Thorpe's testimony remains shadowy. We do not know, for example, whether this particular interrogation ever took place, nor do we know what happened to William Thorpe afterward. As Rita Copeland has put it, "As a life, Thorpe barely exists beyond the page."[9]

Thorpe's existence at the edge of historical verification provides a critical view of how late medieval witness testimony, particularly the testimony produced under the ecclesiastical persecution of heretics, negotiates the relationship between historical and testimonial truths. With this in mind, this final chapter examines what it means to construct a Lollard testimony at the beginning of the fifteenth century, when efforts to eradicate heretics and their writings were ramped up with an unprecedented urgency. In 1401 the parliamentary statute *De heretico comburendo* officially sanctioned burning relapsed heretics to death, and ecclesiastical and secular officials proved

---

6. *An Apology for Lollard Doctrines,* ed. James Henthorn Todd, Camden Society vol. 20 (London: John Bower Nichols and Son, 1842), 1.

7. Lines 20, 26. All citations for the *Examination* are by line number as given in *Two Wycliffite Texts,* ed. Hudson. Hereafter cited parenthetically. For a discussion of the arrest of William Thorpe in 1406, see Maureen Jurkowski, "The Arrest of William Thorpe in Shrewsbury and the Anti-Lollard Statute of 1406," *Historical Research* 75 (2002): 273–95.

8. See Hudson's introduction to *Two Wycliffite Texts,* xlvii–l.

9. Rita Copeland, "William Thorpe and his Lollard Community," in *Bodies and Disciplines: Intersections of Literature and History in Fifteenth-Century England,* ed. David Wallace and Barbara A. Hanawalt (Minneapolis: University of Minnesota Press, 1996), 201. For a response to Copeland's claims about Thorpe's shadowy existence in extant documents, see Fiona Somerset's review of *Pedagogy, Intellectuals and Dissent in the Later Middle Ages* in *Medium Aevum* 72 (2003): 140–41.

their willingness to follow through on this threat when they burned William Sautre that same year. In 1410 John Badby became the first layperson to be killed under the statute. Thorpe's *Testimony* depicts his keen awareness of the material consequences of his responses to Arundel, as well as his sense that the document that will emerge from the interrogation might be used to support efforts to imagine Lollardy as a united assault on the sanctity of Church practices and systems.

Specifically, this chapter examines Thorpe's strategies of producing a testimony of resistance, one that redefines the role of a witness in a heresy inquisition. Rather than acquiesce to Arundel's attempts to get him to abjure, Thorpe documents his Lollard beliefs and practices for a receptive audience, whom he calls witnesses, outside the interrogation room. The debate between Arundel and Thorpe largely centers on how testimony and documents can sharpen the distinctions between orthodox and heretical communities, with Arundel insisting that his official list of complaints against Thorpe testifies to Thorpe's heresy. Rather than merely deny the complaints, however, Thorpe reframes Arundel's documents to accommodate a different ideal of testimony, one that calls upon presence as its central term and key strategy. In doing so, Thorpe stretches the definition of witnessing to imagine a document that both deploys and exceeds the conditions of its production. As both a speaking witness and a self-aware "notary" of his own interrogation, Thorpe offers a sophisticated staging of his own testimony, writing it as a dramatic debate with serious consequences for himself and for his audience of witnesses.[10] Thorpe thus transforms what should be a negotiation for his own self-preservation into an example of how Lollard witnesses could use the very tactics of their inquisitors to authorize the beliefs and practices of heterodox textual communities.[11]

Documents, Witnesses, and the Struggle for Authority

In 1382 Archbishop William Courtenay and the Blackfriars' Council described and condemned a series of constitutions drawn from Wyclif's works because they were worried that the academic arguments of a university man had somehow escaped the ivory tower and "infected" the laity.

---

10. For an argument that Thorpe's *Testimony* draws on the rhetorical principles of drama, see Ritchie D. Kendall, *The Drama of Dissent* (Chapel Hill: University of North Carolina Press, 1986).

11. The phrase "textual community" is Brian Stock's. He uses it to describe communities that cohere around a set of core texts. See *Listening for the Text* (Baltimore: Johns Hopkins University Press, 1990).

Accusing a group of Oxford theologians of being runaway preachers, the Council blamed these teachers for contaminating lay communities outside the university. Much of the fear-inducing rhetoric formulates Wycliffite doctrine as a "pestilence" that might infiltrate even the healthiest of communities. For example, Roger Dymmock begins his 1395 condemnatory response to the Lollard *Twelve Conclusions* by accusing Lollards of hiding poison (*uenenum pestiferum heretice pravitatis*) behind fancy language and the pretense of sanctified truth (*uariis coloribus ueritatis et diuersis ymaginibus sanctitatis*).[12] Similarly, according to the chronicler Henry Knighton, England required an "antidote" for the poison Lollards spread through the realm. He attests that the pestilence of Lollardy must be treated so the body politic might be healed:

> And unless God soon shorten the days of their asperity, and provide some antidote to their evil, I testify that this realm of England will be unable to sustain their deceits and their malice. Hence the verses:
>
> > If all the world were parchment, and the trees one reed,
> > The seas a pool of ink, and all mankind a mighty scribe,
> > They would not serve to tell the wicked tale.[13]

Knighton amplifies the ubiquitous metaphor of pestilence by turning from the infected body of the realm to the world-as-text; for Knighton, the diseased body politic will wither before it is able to record the Lollards' rampage. Indeed, his "testimony" of the realm's demise suggests that writing itself suffers under the pervasive disease of heresy.

In response to the toxicity of Lollard preaching, ecclesiastical officials took up the Lollard body as its object of inquiry and punitive canvas, claiming that the "pestilence" of Lollardy could be eradicated only with the destruction of the bodies from which it issued forth. In 1401 Thomas Arundel, Archbishop of Canterbury and Thorpe's adversary, convened a clerical council to sentence the accused Lollard William Sautre to death by fire. Parliament was in session during his burning at Smithfield, and they sent representatives to Arundel's council to offer lay support of its aims to address what was seen as "widespread" errors and heresies throughout the realm.[14] That support

---

12. *Rogeri Dymmok Liber Contra XII Errores et Hereses Lollardorum*, ed. H. S. Cronin (London: Kegan Paul, Trench, Trubner & Co., 1922), 14.
13. *Knighton's Chronicle*, ed. and trans. G. H. Martin (Oxford: Clarendon, 1995), 305–6.
14. For a discussion of the events leading up to the *De heretico comburendo* statute, see Paul Strohm, *England's Empty Throne* (New Haven, CT: Yale University Press, 1998), esp. 32–62.

came in drastic form: parliament approved the *De heretico comburendo* statute to burn any heretics who refused to abjure their beliefs publicly, specifically so that such punishment might "inspire fear in the minds of others."¹⁵ Notably, the language of the statute shifts the martyrological terms taken up by Langland's Book. If Book's contents exceed his material form—such that his narrative of salvation history can survive the possibility of his fiery self-destruction—this statute supports the fantasy that the fiery destruction of Lollard bodies could effectively erase Lollard doctrine. Indeed, Henry's addendum to the statute asserts the need for violent measures "so that this wicked sect, preachings, doctrine, and opinions should cease from now on, and should completely be destroyed."¹⁶

Six years after parliament authorized the *De heretico comburendo* statute, Arundel drafted what are known as the "Cruel Constitutions," a series of articles that prescribed methods for dealing with unauthorized preachers such as Thorpe. The most extreme articles closely regulate how theology was to be taught and accessed, forbidding the study of Wyclif's works and warning of the dangers of translating Scripture from one language to another. Other articles detail how officials were to find and punish suspected heretics.¹⁷ The Constitutions' explanation of due process for searching out and interrogating heretics shows the attempt to discipline Lollards through the proliferation of official documents, building upon and transforming the standard inquisitional procedure that was formalized by Innocent III in the Fourth Lateran Council. As described in the introduction to this book, *inquisitio* differs from *accusatio* or *denunciatio*—the trial procedures used in English criminal courts—primarily in its use of a judge to present charges against a defendant, rather than an individual accuser. In *inquisitio,* the judge acts on behalf of the public, who makes the defendant's *infamia* (public fame of criminal activity) known. As in all trial procedures in England, the defendant has a right to know the witnesses testifying against him and to hear their testimony (or hear it read).¹⁸

---

15. "easdem coram populo in eminenti loco comburi faciant, ut huiusmodi Punitio metum incutiat mentibus aliorum." *Rotuli Parliamentorum,* vol. 3 (London, 1767–77), 467.

16. *Statutes of the Realm,* vol. 2 (London: Dawsons, 1816), 126. Cited and discussed by Strohm, *England's Empty Throne,* 67–69.

17. *Concilia Magnae Britanniae,* ed. David Wilkins (London: Gosling, Gyles, Woodward, and Davis, 1737). Nicholas Watson has shown the wide-ranging effects of these Constitutions on the production and circulation of theological writing in English: see "Censorship and Cultural Change in Late-Medieval England: Vernacular Theology, the Oxford Translation Debate, and Arundel's Constitutions of 1409," *Speculum* 70.4 (1995): 822–64.

18. For a summary of *inquisitio* procedures (as well as the argument that inquisition was not a system specifically designed to prosecute heresy), see Kelly, "Inquisition and the Prosecution of

In the second half of the thirteenth century, the jurisprudential subfield of *inquisitio heretice pravitatis* ("inquisition of heretical depravity") developed specifically to address the peculiar challenges of prosecuting heresy, which was considered a crime of belief as much as one of "action."[19] *Inquisitio heretice pravitatis* loosened the evidentiary requirements of *inquisitio* in several ways, mostly having to do with what testimony could be admitted and how it should be publicized. For example, the names of witnesses could be suppressed if the judge felt that providing them would put the witnesses in danger, and criminals and other "infamous" witnesses were permitted to testify.[20] Moreover, witness testimony could be self-incriminatory, because a judge could demand that a witness testify "about themselves and about others" (*de se et de aliis*). Thus, in regular inquisitional procedure, witness testimony was sought to determine whether a defendant was sufficiently infamous to merit a trial. In contrast, in the inquisitional procedure used for heresy, the testimony given during a trial could *produce* the infamy necessary to begin trial proceedings against the witness who had given testimony against the defendant.

In addition, given the (perceived or actual) slipperiness of accused heretics, procedures of *inquisitio heretice pravitatis* permitted heretics to be prosecuted and punished *in absentia*. To do so, a judge, working on the knowledge of the accused's infamy, would issue a citation at the accused's parish church. After a reasonable wait for the accused to respond to the summons and appear in court, the trial could proceed. The thirteenth article of Arundel's Constitutions builds upon this procedure by proliferating the number of citations that could be produced and the places they could be posted. Not content with merely posting a single citation in the parish church, Arundel authorizes multiple documents to be posted where a heretic was born and where he was thought to have preached. This article exhibits how ecclesiastical officials produced infamy under the auspices of merely

---

Heresy," in *Inquisitions* I.439–51. For a discussion of *accusatio, denunciatio,* and *inquisitio* in the Fourth Lateran Council, see the introduction to this book.

19. Innocent III determined that heretics were those who believed, received, or defended heretical ideas, and Gregory IX confirmed this definition in 1231. See Kelly, "Inquisitorial Due Process and the Status of Secret Crimes," in *Inquisitions* II.414.

20. H. C. Lea claims there was another shift: in standard *inquisitio* process, if a witness changed his or her testimony, the second version would not be admitted into evidence, but in heresy cases, witnesses were allowed to change their testimony so long as the changed testimony incriminated the accused. Notably, however, he does not offer specific evidence of this claim. *History of the Inquisition of the Middle Ages* (New York: Russell & Russell, 1955), 434. Kelly points out that "infamous" witnesses could be used in cases of treason and simony as well, and so this shift was not specific to heresy trials. *Inquisitions* I.446.

seeking it, since these documents, posted in multiple parishes, would publicize the accusations against an individual to activate the *infamia* necessary to begin trial proceedings. In addition, the article dismisses the need for witness testimony should the accused fail to present himself at court:

> We do ordain, will, and declare, for the easier punishment of the offenders in the premises, and for the better reformation of the church divided and hurt, that all such as are defamed, openly known, or vehemently suspected, in any of the cases aforesaid, or, in article of the catholic faith, sounding contrary to good manners, by the authority of the ordinary of the place or other superior, be cited personally to appear, either by letters, public messenger being sworn, or by edict openly set at that place where the said offender commonly remains, or in his parish church, if he have any certain dwelling house; otherwise, in the cathedral church of the place where he was born, and in the parish church of the same place where he so preached and taught: and afterwards, certificate being given that the citation was formerly executed against the party cited being absent and neglecting his appearance, it shall be proceeded against him fully and plainly, without sound or show of judgment, and without admitting proof by witnesses and other canonical probations. And also, after lawful information had, the said ordinary (all delays set apart) shall signify, declare, and punish the said offender, according to the quality of his offence, and inform aforesaid; and further, shall do according to justice, the absence of the offender notwithstanding.[21]

The mere verification that the citation was properly executed could mitigate the need for witness testimony during the trial. Thus the absence of the heretic was a procedural inconvenience, but it did not affect the ability to

---

21. "Volumus, ordinamus, et declaramus, ob faciliorem punitionem delinquentium in praemissis, et reformationem scissurae ecclesiae ex hoc laesae, quod diffamati, detecti, sive denunciati, sive vehementer suspecti in aliquo casuum praedictorum, sive alio articulo quocunque in fide catholica aut bonis moribus male sonante, auctoritate loci ordinarii, alteriusve superioris citentur personaliter, si apprehendi poterunt, per literas sive per nuncium publicum juratum; sin autem per edictum, ad locum habitationis ipsius delinquentis, ubi morari communiter consuevit, et in ecclesia sua parochiali, si certum habuerit domicilium, publice propositum; alioquin in ecclesia cathedrali loci originis suae, et in ecclesia parochiali ipsius loci, in quo sic praedicavit, et docuit; ac recepto certificatorio legitimo de citatione huiusmodi executa, contra sic citatum etiam absentem et comparere negligentem, in poenam contumaciae suae huiusmodi summarie et de plano, absque strepitu et figura judicii, ac lite non contestata, ad testium receptionem, et alias probationes canonicas procedatur; habita quoque informatione legitima, idem ordinarius, omni dilatione semota, sententiet et declaret, puniatque secundum qualitatem delicti, modo et forma superius expressatis, ulteriusque faciat quod est justum, ipsius contumacis absentia non obstante." *Concilia Magnae Britanniae* 3:319.

excommunicate him. Indeed, Wyclif himself was condemned as a heretic in 1413, nearly 30 years after his death.²²

The *De heretico comburendo* statute and Arundel's Constitutions demonstrate two related issues at the heart of fifteenth-century prosecution of heretics in England. First, they depict the Lollard body as a site of heretical belief, insofar as they imagine Lollardy as an infection that has made its way from Oxford into the body politic. To root out this infection, they seek the actual bodies of Lollards to be "healed" through confession and abjuration or to be burned and eradicated. Second, they construct a tight link between the Lollard body and the documents used to search out and transform it. The Constitutions in particular replace the absent Lollard with a series of official citations and documents, mitigating the need for testimony (either by the defendant or by corroborating witnesses). These two pieces of legislation triangulate the body of the Lollard, accusatory documents, and witness testimony in an effort to ensure that Lollardy could be constructed as a frightening attack on the health of the church and realm, one that could be controlled only by verifying the narrative of heretical infection with an impressive paper trail.

In the service of controlling and destroying the bodies from which Lollard pestilence emanates, the depositions of Lollard trials end with the fusion of the Lollard body and the official documents designed to record the heretic's abjuration. The defendant was required to sign the documents explicitly "with myn owen hand a cross," and one copy of the deposition was to be enrolled in the official register while the other was to remain with the accused "unto my lyves ende."²³ It is not entirely clear how this was supposed to happen, as Rebecca Krug points out. Perhaps the document was supposed to be displayed, or kept in a drawer, or even kept on one's person until death.²⁴ But it is clear that legal officials sought to rein in the body of the heretic with its hefty documentary apparatus.²⁵

However, whereas fifteenth-century legislation tried to make the Lollard body the central linchpin in its campaign against heresy, the testimonies of

---

22. Joseph H. Dahmus, *The Prosecution of John Wyclyf* (New Haven, CT: Yale University Press, 1952).

23. See the documents collected in *The Heresy Trials in the Diocese of Norwich, 1428-31*, ed. Norman P. Tanner, Camden 4th Series, vol. 20 (London: Royal Historical Society, 1977).

24. Rebecca Krug, *Reading Families: Women's Literate Practice in Late Medieval England* (Ithaca, NY: Cornell University Press, 2002), 143-44.

25. Significantly, Thorpe's 1406 arrest document ends by insisting on the delivery of his body to prison: "Quorum corpora vobis mittimus in cancellaria vostrum virtute brevis predicti." See "Appendix: Public Record Office C 250/4, no. 23," in Jurkowski, "The Arrest of William Thorpe," 294-95.

accused Lollards envision the Lollard body as a site of resistance and theological privilege. For example, in a letter detailing his 1403 interrogations for unauthorized preaching, the convicted Lollard Richard Wyche explains that on the way to the first interrogation, he fell off a horse and hurt his leg. He then goes on to describe in detail the gastrointestinal distress he suffered in prison:

> And our good Lord, out of his grace, has afflicted me through a great constriction of the stomach, on account of which I now have and have been having great pain at times purging my stomach, so that for nine days I have not had so much as one purgation, and hemorrhoids have twice gripped me and have bled rather profusely, such that it is shameful to mention it. However, I must do so or not survive, and my purgation is as difficult as the purging of it. These are my secrets.[26]

By emphasizing the material conditions of his time in prison, Wyche retrieves his own body from the symbolic economy constructed by his accusers, turning that economy upside down. His inability—or, perhaps, his refusal—to "purge" his stomach draws on commonplace language in late medieval confessional manuals, which imagine confession as a kind of "vomit" that cleanses the body and the soul of its sins. Here, his constipation enacts his resistance against his accusers' desire for a full confession and abjuration, "enclosing" Lollard secrets in his body.

Likewise, Margery Baxter, accused of sometimes housing the known Lollard William White and storing his books, makes her own body a central feature of her arguments against the orthodox claims against her. According to her household servant, Joanna Clyfland, Margery once told her that crosses were merely objects produced by "lewed wrights," and that if Joanna wanted to see a cross she could just look at Margery holding her arms outstretched.[27] Margery then goes on to state that she harbors a "charter of sal-

---

26. "In quo continuo, etc. habens cibum et potum competenter, gracias agens Deo. Et bonus Deus noster ex sua gracia visitavit me per magnam strictitudinem in ventre, per quam habeo et habui magnam penam aliquando pergare ventrem meum, quia aliquando per novem dies non habui quantitatem unius purgacionis et emeraudes tenuerunt me bis et sanguinarunt quodammodo fortiter, et sic quod pudor est dicere. Tamen oportet me ita facere vel non vivere et purgacio mea est dura sicut purgacio eius. Ista sunt secreta mea." F. D. Matthew, "The Trial of Richard Wyche," *The English Historical Review* 5.19 (1890): 541. For a discussion of Wyche's letter, see Copeland, *Pedagogy*, 161–63.

27. "Et ista iurata asseruit se libenter videre velle veram crucem Christi. Et prefata Margeria dixit, 'vide,' et tunc extendebat brachia sua in longum, dicens isti iurate, 'hec est vera crux Christi, et istam crucem tu debes et potes(t) videre et adorare omni die hic in domo tua propria, et adeo

vation" in her womb.[28] Calling upon Marian imagery to suggest an organic (and distinctly female) connection to God's Word, Baxter imagines her body to contain legal documents ecclesiastical authorities cannot access.[29] In doing so, she constructs her own body as a sacred enclosure that holds secret, salvific knowledge that can survive bodily and textual persecution. Though Baxter's claim is a startling one, reading it alongside Wyche's letter suggests a wider picture of resistant Lollard rhetoric that imagined the body as a kind of reliquary that held "secrets" or documents beyond the access of ecclesiastical officials.[30]

Like Wyche and Baxter, Thorpe writes his *Testimony* in the shadow of the *De heretico comburendo* statute, knowing that his refusal to abjure for unauthorized preaching will lead him, as Arundel tells him more than once, to follow Sautre to Smithfield. But unlike Wyche or Baxter, Thorpe never features his own body in his depiction of his interrogation. Admittedly, he does repeatedly claim that Arundel and his assistants "manassed him," and at the end of the interrogation, he reiterates that he was "rebuked and scorned and manassid on ech side" by Arundel's assistants (2224). But beyond those vague gestures, Thorpe provides no physical details of his incarceration, nor does he use his body as a site of resistance. Instead, Thorpe emphasizes his own presence as a witness on behalf of an absent audience. In doing so, he constitutes his interrogation as an opportunity to outline and explain his beliefs to those beyond the closet in which Arundel has confined him. As he explains to Arundel and his assistants early in the interrogation,

"I make þis protestacioun before ȝou alle foure þat ben now here present, coueitynge þat alle men and wymmen, which now ben here absent,

---

tu in vanum laboras quando vadis ad ecclesias ad adorandas sive orandas aliquas ymagines vel cruces mortuas.'" *Heresy Trials* 44.

28. "Margeria, ut asseruit isti iurate, habuit et habet unam cartam salvacionis in utero suo." *Heresy Trials* 49. For a discussion of Baxter's "charter," with reference to the *Charters of Christ* specifically and to Trinitarian metaphors of conception and pregnancy generally, see Andrew Galloway, "Intellectual Pregnancy, Metaphysical Femininity, and the Social Doctrine of the Trinity in *Piers Plowman*," *YLS* 12 (1998): 117–52.

29. For a discussion of Baxter's use of Marian imagery, see Rita Copeland, "Why Women Can't Read: Medieval Hermeneutics, Statutory Law, and the Lollard Heresy Trials," in *Representing Women: Law, Literature, and Feminism*, ed. Susan Sage Heinzelman and Zipporah Batshaw Wiseman (Durham, NC: Duke University Press, 1994), 253–86. For a discussion of Margery's idea of a "text" inaccessible to ecclesiastical authorities, see Steiner, *Documentary Culture*, 231–22, and Krug, *Reading Families*, 132–34.

30. Other Lollard depictions of trials comment on their accusers' physical roughness: the author of the *Opus arduum*, for example, takes care to mention being shackled in steel manacles. Cited in Curtis V. Bostick, *The Antichrist and the Lollards* (Leiden: Brill, 1998), 50.

knowen þe same: þat, whateuer þing before þis tyme I haue thou3t or don or seid, eiþir what þat I schal now here do or seie eiþir ony tyme heraftir, I belieue þat al þe olde lawe and þe newe, 3ouen and ordeyned bi þe counseile o þre persoones of þe holi Trinite, weren 3ouen and written to þe saluacioun of mankynde." (306–13)

Thorpe here imagines his testimony to exceed the temporal and spatial constraints of its occurrence, reaching beyond the four present interrogators to the absent men and women awaiting the text of this interrogation.

Thorpe's production of an absent audience directly opposes Arundel's staging of the interrogation. As Thorpe tells it, he was brought before Arundel after sitting for several months in a prison at Saltwood Castle. At first, he says, Arundel "stood in a greet chaumbre" surrounded by many people, but when he saw Thorpe, he retreated into a "priuy closet" with only a physician named Malvern, a parson, and two lawyers (171–79). The retreat into a small interrogation room ostensibly gives Arundel the upper hand, isolating Thorpe from his supporters and forcing him to engage directly with the authorities. It also follows standard *inquisitio* proceedings, which were supposed to be conducted in secret.[31] But by invoking an audience of absent men and women, Thorpe rhetorically reaches beyond the closet and reframes the role of the Lollard body in heresy interrogations. Instead, he constructs an opportunity to theorize his own presence as a testifying witness, both during the interrogation and as a document that will endure beyond his future at Smithfield. In doing so, Thorpe produces what looks like a Lollard sermon for an imagined audience, rather than a set of responses to a standard inquisition or even a text that bears witness to his experiences in Arundel's interrogation room.

In turning away from his own body to focus on "presence," Thorpe formulates his testimony as a text without a body, a document that can be detached from the particularities of his inquisition. The clearest statement of this transformation of his heretical body into documentary presence comes when he defines his interrogation as truth that will be continually witnessed by fellow believers. Responding to the specific charge of unauthorized preaching, Thorpe explains,

3he, þe peple to whom we prechen, be þei feiþful eiþer vnfeiþful, schulen be oure lettris þat is oure witnesse-berers; for truþe whanne it is sowen may not ben vnwitnessid. For alle þei, þat ben conuertid or saued bi herynge of

---

31. Lea, *History of the Inquisition*, 406.

Goddis word and worchen þeraftir, ben witnesse-berers þat þe truþe þat
þei herden and diden after is cause of her saluacioun. (774–79)

Thorpe establishes that his *Testimony* will function as an extralegal document that constructs an audience of readers as witnesses who can testify to the truth of his beliefs. In conceptualizing his absent audience as witnesses, Thorpe draws upon an Augustinian model of readers as witnesses. In Book 10 of his *Confessions,* Augustine begins his theory of memory by explaining his text as a revelation of truth to which his readers must attest. "Therefore I speak out, and in this hope I rejoice when I rejoice in a wholesome way," he writes. "This I wish to do in my heart before you in confession, and in my writing before many witnesses" (*multis testibus*).[32] Augustine's invention of a witnessing audience extracts his *Confessions* from the isolation from which it was produced, translating the confession of his inner contrition into an exemplary text that can testify to the spiritual efficacy of his life's narrative. Augustine is one of Thorpe's favorite patristic authorities, and like Augustine, Thorpe offers an autobiographical narrative that can move beyond the immediate circumstances of its composition. For Thorpe as for Augustine, witnessing transforms autobiographical narrative into iterable document, transforming individual biography into exemplary testimony.

Moreover, by specifically representing his absent audience as witnesses and letter-bearers, Thorpe reconstitutes the inquisitional procedure Arundel attempts to follow. With interrogations conducted in secret, often with the mere presumption of infamy, inquisitors could proceed to convict and punish an accused heretic without calling upon witnesses to testify either on behalf of or even against the defendant. As Arundel makes clear in his Constitutions, a series of citations and official documents could substitute for the witnesses required in English canonical and even civil courts. So when Thorpe conceptualizes his audience both as his witnesses and as his letter-bearers, he co-opts the ecclesiastical power to replace witness testimony with official documents. His testimony not only serves as his defense against Arundel's accusations, it more broadly rejects the legal system that has dissolved the safeguards designed to ensure a fair trial based on clear proofs and public infamy. Indeed, when Thorpe reconstitutes his interrogation into a production of a text that will reach a community of absent witnesses, he does so specifically against the official documents Arundel has at his disposal. And the battle between documents—on one hand, Arundel's official articles of complaint and, on the other, Thorpe's *Testimony*—turns

---

32. Augustine, *Confessions,* trans. R. S. Pine-Coffin (New York: Penguin Classics, 1972), 10.1.

on the witnessing authority they each can claim. Arundel begins by explaining to Thorpe how this interrogation will go. After Thorpe forsakes his own opinions one by one, he says, Thorpe will then give up his friends.

To Arundel's frustration, Thorpe responds with a lengthy articulation of his beliefs one by one rather than admitting to his crimes and abjuring. Arundel then instructs one of his clerks to fetch the "certificate" from Shrewsbury that details the "errours and þe eresies" against Thorpe. Arundel is very careful to enumerate the authenticating instruments that announce his administrative authority: "'Take hidir anoon þe certificat þat cam to me from Schrouesbirie vndir þe bailyes seelis,'" he tells his assistant, "'witnessynge þe errours and þe eresies whiche þis losel haþ venymously sowen þere'" (618–20). He reads it aloud and then smugly puts it back in the cupboard. Later, when Thorpe again stalwartly refuses to abjure, Arundel again retrieves the document from the cupboard and performs his discovery of an official corroboration of Thorpe's open preaching. "'Lo, here it is certified and witnessed aȝens þee bi worþi men and feiþful of Schrouesbirie þat þou prechedist þere opinli in seint Chaddis chirche þat þe sacrament of þe auter was material breed after þe consecracioun. What seist þou?'" (929–32). The cycle repeats: with every article of interrogation, Arundel retrieves the document with great pomp, unrolls it, and reminds Thorpe that this list of heresies has been "certified" by trusted witnesses and ecclesiastical seals.[33] He even wants Thorpe to help produce documents that will lead to other interrogations of heretics:

> "and hem þat wol not leue þees dampnable opinyouns þou schalt putten vp, publischinge her names, and make hem knowen to þe bischop of þe diocise þat þese ben inne, eiþir to þe bischopis mynystris. And ouer þis I wole þat þou preche no more, to þe tyme þat I knowe bi good witnesse and trewe þat þi conuersacioun be suche þat þin herte and þi mouþ acorden trewli in oon, contrariing alle þe lore pat þou hast tauȝt herbifore." (358–64)

Arundel first insists that Thorpe "publish" the names of other heretics, leaning on the *de se et aliis* process used by ecclesiastical authorities to use witness testimony to produce *infamia*. He then suggests he will know that Thorpe has truly abjured when Thorpe's statements accord with what he feels in his heart, taking up language from confessional manuals that imagine confessional discourse to reveal what is hidden in one's heart and soul.[34]

---

33. See, for example, lines 1629–31.

34. For the similarities between the work of a confessor and that of an inquisitor, see Bernard Gui's thirteenth-century inquisitional manual, which equates the inquisitor with a "medicus

The gap between what happens in one's heart and what one says by mouth was specifically at stake in late medieval heresy investigations, particularly in terms of the oaths inquisitors required of accused heretics.[35] *Inquisitio heretice pravitatis* sought to draw out the poisonous beliefs festering in the hearts of heretics to skirt around the ecclesiastical axiom that the Church does not judge secret crimes. Accordingly, it was designed to bring the beliefs of the accused out of his heart and into his mouth, thereby making his beliefs "public" and punishable. To accomplish this, the procedure required an oath *ex officio*, which forced the defendant to swear to tell the truth and before charges were even named as well as to pledge fidelity to Church law. Any silence in response to questions or claims of innocence could be turned into a potential charge of false witness, since the defendant had already vowed to adhere to official doctrine. (In contrast, English common law did not consider it perjury to plead "not guilty," even if the defendant were convicted of the charges against him.[36]) The oath rendered any perceived gap between what the defendant felt in his heart and what he said under oath a confirmation of heretical belief and a breach of the vow with which the proceedings began.

Accused heretics took advantage of this procedural reliance on the oath. For example, Richard Wyche dramatizes the paradoxical design of the inquisitional oath when he bargains with his interrogators about how he will pledge to tell the truth. Wyche claims that, on advice of his interrogators, he will take an oath to obey Church doctrine with reservations in his heart (*in corde tuo limitatum*). The promise emerges out of complex negotiations in which Wyche agreed to obey the law of the Catholic Church because, as he asserts, the law of the Church is the law of God. In other words, he will easily pledge fidelity to the "true Church," reserving in his heart his belief that the ecclesiastical hierarchy of the current Church perverts the truth of its doctrine. Yet he also knows that according to inquisitional procedure, he must pledge an oath "according to the intention of the judge," rather than according to his own conscience. The interrogator reassures him that his lord merely wants to procure an oath *pro forma*; Wyche is thus willing to accept one that expresses his reservations and pledges his faith to Church doctrine "as it pertains to me."[37]

---

animarum." *Manuel de L'Inquisiteur*, ed. and trans. G. Mollat (Paris: Belles Lettres, 2006), 8.

35. For a succinct discussion of the history of oath-taking in ecclesiastical courts and the argument that Wyche's "mental reservations" dramatize his dissent against the construction of the public record, see Copeland, *Pedagogy*, 166–70.

36. See Leonard W. Levy, *Origins of the Fifth Amendment* (Oxford: Oxford University Press, 1968): 43–82; and H. A. Kelly, "The Right to Remain Silent: Before and After Joan of Arc," in *Inquisitions* III.992–1026.

37. "Dixi, volo libenter si dominus meus voluerit facere sicut vos dicitis et recipere a me

Similarly, when Arundel insists that Thorpe take an oath to forsake his heretical opinions, Thorpe responds to Arundel with silence, instead complaining to his absent audience that Arundel's request is "an vnleeful askynge" (366). Undeterred, Arundel reiterates that he knows "bi good witnesse and trewe" that Thorpe has preached without Church authorization, and he goes on to enumerate that these witnesses come with official documentary authentication: "'I wole ȝeue credence to þese worschipful men, which haue writun to me and witnessen vndir her seelis þat þou prechidest þus openly þese forseid errours and heresies þere among hem'" (639–42). Arundel conceptualizes "true" witnesses as the sealed documents he keeps in a cupboard inside the "privy closet." Like the oath-taking negotiations depicted in Wyche's letter, this scene depicts the fissures between Thorpe's beliefs, held in his heart and expressed in the extralegal document he produces for an absent audience, and the official documents Arundel uses as evidence against Thorpe.

The battle over the use of testifying documents and oaths emerges particularly in Arundel's repeated attempts to get Thorpe to swear upon a book and renounce his heretical beliefs. Generally speaking, Wycliffite doctrine rejected such oath-taking practices, which Thorpe carefully explains to Arundel: "'Sir, I vndirstonde a book is no þing ellis, no but a þing compilid togidere of diuerse creaturis, and so to swere bi a book is to swere bi dyuerse craturis; and to swere bi ony creaturis boþe Goddis lawe and mannes lawe is þeraȝen'" (336–38). Thorpe continues to say that he has no problem swearing by "'Goddis ordynaunce or word comaundid of God'" (343). Thorpe's resistance specifically turns on the transcendence of the material oath-text, in his rejection of it as a "creature": that is, as a mere earthly object.[38] When Arundel again insists, more strenuously this time, that Thorpe place his hand upon the book and swear that he will refrain from preaching without official authorization, Thorpe elaborates upon his rejection of oath-taking. He begins by explaining that he and other Lollards know very well that no bishop would give them authorization papers unless they obey "þe bondis or terms" prescribed by the Church authorities. "And herfore," he says,

---

istud iuramentum limitatum in corde meo, hoc est, quod teneor obedire legi Dei, in quantum ad me pertinet. Eciam dixit: Ne dubites. Tunc dixit cancellarius: Per Deum, tu iuras sicut nos volumus antequam recesseris. Non respondi ei verbum. Et miles surrexit. Et cum stetisset in hostio domus, dixit: Richarde, in fide, vis tu tenere pactum de istis que dixisti? Eciam, si dominus meus voluerit tenere pactum de quibus vos dixistis. Eciam, scias illud pro certo recessit." Matthew, "Trial of Richard Wyche," 534–35.

38. See Margaret Aston, *Lollards and Their Books* (London: Hambledon, 1984).

"þou3 we haue not 3oure letter neiþer lettris of oþir bischopis writun wiþ enke vpon parchymyne, we dur not herfore leeue þe office of prechynge, to whiche prechinge alle presits aftire her kunnynge and her power ben bounden bi dyuerse witnessingis of Goddis lawe and of greet doctours, wiþouten ony mencioun makynge of bischopis lettris." (761-66)

Initially, Thorpe engages with the orthodox requirement that preachers carry official papers with them, simply taking issue with the terms and limitations these authorizing letters would impose: they are, he says, "sumtyme to straite and sumtyme to large" (758). But he soon dismisses the very idea that he needs any kind of documentary authentication by returning to the empty materiality of these letters. Parchment and ink are no match for the "dyuerse witnessingis" of Scripture and patristic commentary. Thorpe's dismissal of material letters here draws upon the Wycliffite reconceptualization of the Johannine union between God and Word. For Wyclif, the literal sense of Scripture exceeds both the specificities of language and the material text, such that Scripture can be "indestructibly true" (*infringibiliter veram*).[39] Wyclif's take on John's ideal of Christ-as-book argues that Scripture surpasses the "sensible signs" (*signa sensibilia*) that make the divine Word intelligible to mankind.[40]

For Thorpe, the Wycliffite argument that scriptural truth cannot and should not be contained in material texts undergirds his refusal to take an *ex officio* oath. Thorpe elaborates his argument for disengaging the divine Word from material texts when Arundel asks him specifically to describe his beliefs about oath-taking. In response, Thorpe narrates a story in which he witnessed a conversation between a theologian and a lawyer about the problem of oaths, and he extrapolates out of this story a theory of book-oaths that returns to his definition of true witnesses as letter-bearers. Thorpe explains that the lawyer argued that if a sovereign asks someone to lay his hand upon a book and kiss it to certify obedience, he or she must do it. The theologian countered that such an oath does not permit any kind of resistance if the sovereign asks something immoral or illegal. Thorpe then explains the "moral" of the story:

---

39. *On the Truth of Holy Scripture*, trans. I. C. Levy (Kalamazoo, MI: Medieval Institute, 2001), 202; see *De Veritate Sacrae Scripturae*, ed. R. Buddensieg (London: Wyclif Society, 1905), I:114.19.

40. *On the Truth of Holy Scripture* 99; *De Veritate Sacrae Scripturae* I.110.20. For a discussion of these passages in Wyclif and of Wycliffite thought on the material book and its influence on late medieval vernacular devotional works, see Nicole R. Rice, *Lay Piety and Religious Discipline in Middle English Literature* (Cambridge: Cambridge University Press, 2008), 62-77.

> "for euery book is noþing ellis, no but dyuerse creaturis of whiche it is made. þerfore to swere vpon a book or bi a book is to swere bi creaturis, and þis sweringe is euer vnleeful. þis sentence witnessiþ Ierom and Crisostom pleynli, blamynge him greetli þat bryngeþ forþ a book for to swere vpon, amonestynge clerkis þat in no wyse þei compellen ony lyf to swere wheþer þei gessen a man to swere trewe or fals." (1684–90)

At first, Thorpe merely reiterates a point he has made a few times: since a material text is nothing but a series of "diuerse creaturis," it does not offer any specific access to God's judgment, which exists conceptually in Scripture rather than in the particularities of an individual language or text. He then supplements his exemplary narrative by saying that Jerome and Chrysostom both plainly bear witness to this "sentence," noting that both admonish those clerks who use books to corner men into swearing oaths. By first refusing to adhere to Arundel's official witnessing practice of requiring book-oaths and then calling upon "plain witnesses" to support his argument, Thorpe effectively transforms Arundel's interrogation about oaths into an attestation of divine truth's detachment from books. In doing so, he redirects the authority of witnessing away from the deceptive work of inquisitional oaths and material texts and toward "plain" Scriptural citation.

By this point, Arundel has realized that this interrogation has become a battle over hermeneutic authority rather than a proper inquisition. His first move is to take all of Thorpe's books away, as he explains to his assistants:

> "Lo, sere, þis is þe bisinesse and þe maner of þis losel and siche oþer: to pike out scharpe sentencis of holy writ and of doctours for to maynteyne her sect and her loore aȝens þe ordenaunce of holi chirche. And herfore, losel, it is þat þou coueitist to haue aȝen þe Sauter þat I made to be taken fro þee at Cauntirbirie, forþi þat þou woldist gadere out þereof and recorde scharpe verses aȝens vs. But þou schalt neuere haue þat Sauter neiþir ony oþer book, til þat I wite þat þin hert and þi mouþ acorden fulli to be gouerned bi holi chirche." (888–95)

His next move is to probe Thorpe's knowledge of Scripture and patristic commentary in the absence of his research materials. He focuses particularly on why Lollards use Scriptural citations to upbraid priests, rather than secular authorities: "'Whi, losel,'" he asks, "'wolt þou not and oþer þat ben confedrid wiþ þee sechen out of holy writt and of þe sentence of doctours as scharpe auctoritees aȝens lordis and knyȝtis and squyeris and aȝens oþer seculer men, as ȝe done aȝens preestis?'" (1573–76). Thorpe's answer not only demonstrates his facility with patristic authorities, it also illustrates how he imagines his *Testimony* to deflect the threat of death that Arundel repeatedly holds over his head. Calmly, Thorpe explains,

> "But, sere, siþ Crissostem seiþ þat presits ben as þe stomke of þe peple, it is ful nedeful in prechinge and also in comownynge to be moost bisie aboute þis presthode, siþ bi þe viciousenesse of prestis boþe lordis and comuns be moost synfull effect and led into þe werst ende." (1580–84)

Thorpe's first purpose here is to display his knowledge of Scriptural hermeneutics, meeting the Archbishop's pointed questions with the same arsenal of patristic citations.[41] But he deftly turns away from a discussion of Chrysostom to a condemnation of proud priests, which Arundel pursues. Arundel ultimately fails in his attempt to get Thorpe to renounce his reproach of orthodox priests. In fact, as Arundel doggedly reframes his questions in the hope of getting Thorpe to answer differently, his assistant pulls him aside and whispers, "'Sere, þe lengir þat ȝe appose him, þe worse he is; and þe more þat ȝe bisie ȝou to amende him, þe more weyward he is'" (1621–23).

Naturally, Thorpe's refusal to submit to Arundel's "manassing" perplexes and enrages Arundel, ultimately wearing him down. Toward the end of the interrogation, Arundel insists, one last time, that Thorpe surrender to the authority of the Church as authenticated in Arundel's official documents: "'Submitte þee þan now here wilfulli and mekeli to þe ordenaunce of holi chirche whiche I schal schewe to þee'" (2063–65). Of course, Thorpe coyly avoids the specific terms of the demand, saying that he is perfectly ready to obey Christ as the head of "holi chirche," as well as to "þe lore and þe heestis and to þe counseilis of euery plesyng membre of him" (2067–79). For Arundel, it is too much to bear, and he punches the cupboard that holds the official rolls and documents, promising that he will make Thorpe "'as sikir as ony þeef þat is in Kent!'" (2074). In a narrative haunted by the mere specter of bodily punishment, this is the only moment of physical aggression, and it is an especially impotent one.

Thorpe's purpose in describing the moment Arundel punches the cupboard is to deflate Arundel's ecclesiastical and legal power to enact violence, depicting that violence as both self-inflicted and weak. When Arundel punches the cupboard, he attacks the very vessel that contains his official witnesses, the documents that authorize his menacing interrogation of Thorpe.

---

41. For a discussion of Thorpe's facility with university discourse, see Fiona Somerset, "Vernacular Argumentation in *The Testimony of William Thorpe*," in *Clerical Discourse and Lay Audience in Late Medieval England* (Cambridge: Cambridge University Press, 1998), 179–215.

Rather than violently destroy the Lollard body that could harbor alternative, secret legal documents, Arundel can only commit violence against an inert cupboard that houses his official arrest document and the depositions of witnesses who have testified against Thorpe. Thorpe thus uses this moment to perform a model of resistance that differs from other resistant strategies. Wyche and Baxter both envision their own bodies as the containers of "secrets" or authorizing texts, turning the kind of documentary inaccessibility Arundel brandishes around on itself. But this tactic is dangerous: the *De heretico comburendo* statute gives ecclesiastical authorities ultimate power over the Lollard body, whether it harbors a secret document of salvation or not. Thorpe's translation of his bodily presence at his defense into a documentary presence that transcends the time and space of the interrogation succeeds in devastating the overlap between Lollard body and Lollard opinion upon which Arundel's authority depends. The cupboard scene illustrates the success of Thorpe's disembodied testimony: rather than carry out violence upon this testifying Lollard, Arundel has no choice but to carry out violence against his own documentary witnesses.

Thorpe's Presence, Real Presence, and Eucharistic Doctrine

Thorpe's strategy for resisting the threat of a fiery death without abjuring his beliefs depends on his complex management of material presence and textual absence. He conceptualizes his interrogation as the impetus for a witnessing document that can reach beyond the confines of Arundel's "privy closet," constructing an absent audience of witnesses that transcends the interrogators' presence. His repeated use of the term "presence" to describe the work of his *Testimony* captures an ongoing issue at the center of Lollard heresy persecutions: the presence of Christ's body in the transubstantiated host. As Miri Rubin has explained, orthodox sacramental doctrine promises Eucharistic presence, insofar as a consecrated host loses its accidental properties of bread and wine in favor of the substance of Christ's body.[42] Heterodox thinking challenged this ideal of presence by arguing that a consecrated host retained its accidental properties, even as it contained the substance of Christ's body. Thorpe's specific intervention in debates about Eucharistic presence is to explore the way the laity was expected to access a consecrated host. Rather than consume the host, as the parable of the Last Supper pre-

---

42. Miri Rubin, *Corpus Christi: The Eucharist in Late Medieval Culture* (Cambridge: Cambridge University Press, 1991).

scribes, medieval congregants typically witnessed it, watching as the priest murmured "*Hoc est corpus meum*" and then turned to face the congregation and elevate the host for all to see. For Thorpe, as for other Lollard writers, this witnessing moment is a source of frustration about the unavailability of Christ's presence to a layperson's senses and, more broadly, about the relationship between external sight and inward faith.

The doctrine of Eucharistic presence is central to all kinds of devotional writing in the fourteenth and fifteenth centuries, both Lollard and otherwise. Wyclif had invigorated debates around presence several decades before Thorpe's *Testimony* when he began to question the doctrine of transubstantiation. In a 1378 sermon, for example, Wyclif suggested that it was enough to venerate a consecrated host in the same way as a crucifix: that is, as a sign.[43] Likewise, in *De apostasia*, he argues that a consecrated host that contains Christ's body exists in multiple registers:

> The reason for this multiplication of Christ's soul is that it is more principally the Person of the Word than the body. The immaterial qualities, however, which find their subject in the soul of Christ, are multiplied along with it throughout the host. These include knowledge, justice, and the other virtues of Christ's soul which do not require Christ's corporeal pre-existence wherever they might be present.[44]

He goes on to say that there are several ways the body can be present in the consecrated host: corporeally, dimensionally (by which he means visibly or palpably), spiritually, and figuratively. In his *De Eucharistia*, Wyclif turns to the logic of materiality by discussing the moment the priest breaks apart the consecrated host. The priest breaks the host, not the body of Christ, he states, adding that the consecrated host is a sign of the body of Christ, not the body itself.[45]

In the second half of the fourteenth century through the first half of the fifteenth, Wyclif's skeptical stance on Eucharistic sacramentality was used

---

43. I. C. Levy, *John Wyclif: Scriptural Logic, Real Presence, and the Parameters of Orthodoxy* (Milwaukee, WI: Marquette University Press, 2003), 230.

44. "Et causa huius multiplicacionis anime Christi est, quod ipsa est principalius ipso corpore persona verbi. Qualitates autem immateriales, que subiectantur in anima Christi, commultiplicantur cum ipsa per hostiam, ut sciencia, iusticia et alie virtutes anime Christi, que non requirunt, ubicunque fuerint, Christi preexistenciam corporalem." *Tractatus de apostasia*, ed. Michael Henry Dziewicki (London: Trubner & Co., 1889), 224. Cited and translated by Levy, *John Wyclif*, 290.

45. "Satis ergo est ad honorem et potenciam sacerdotis quod ipse benedicit, consecrat et conficit sacramentum; quod est hostia consecrata et non corpus Chriti sed eius signum vel tegumentum." *De Eucharistia Tractaus Maior*, ed. J. Loserth (London: Trubner & Co, 1892), 16.

to test accused heretics about their beliefs. Two years after censuring Wyclif in 1380, the Blackfriars Council examined Nicholas Hereford, John Aston, and Philip Repingdon, all of whom abjured their beliefs about Eucharistic accident by confessing mechanically that the consecrated host is truly the body of Christ.[46] Unsatisfied with their rote responses, the Council articulated its desire for stronger confessions that would admit, following Church teachings, that the body of Christ is identically, truly, and really present in the sacrament of the altar (*corpus Christi est in sacramento altaris, identice, vere, et realiter, in propria praesentia corporali*). Indeed, the Church's stance insisted on Christ's "plentitudinous presence" in the sacrament of the altar, and Church officials argued in increasingly strident terms that the consecrated host is Christ's body.[47] In one particularly blunt version from the 1420s, for example, Thomas Netter, the Provincial Prior of London, argues that a consecrated host is definitively a "pure body without bread" (Rubin 330).

Nicholas Love, a Carthusian monk and prior of Mount Grace in Yorkshire, directly takes on Lollard arguments against transubstantiation with a bit more nuance. He admits that this sacrament requires special faith. Nonetheless, he argues that Christ is corporeally present in the consecrated host:

> For alle oþer þinges pasede þat we haue mynde of we conceyuen in spirite & in herte so þat þereby we haue not þe bodily presence of hem. Bot in þis gostly mete & sacramentale commemoracion of oure lorde Jesu he is verreyly & bodily present wiþ vs vnder an oþere forme bot soþely in his owne proper substance verrey god & man.[48]

For Love, the miracle of the Eucharist is that it performs the devotional work of images that help the faithful turn their minds and hearts to God. Unlike those images, however, the Eucharist is actually the body and blood of Christ, not simply a symbol of or prod toward it. Yet if orthodox views on the sacrament of the altar maintained the corporeality of the consecrated host, those who rejected transubstantiation used philosophies of Eucharistic corporeality to their advantage. For example, Walter Brut, charged with

---

46. "panis quem tenet sacerdos in maibus suis, fit vel efficitur, virtute verborum sacramentalium, vere et realite, diem corpus Christis numero." *Fasciculi zizaniorum*, ed. Rev. Walter Waddington Shirley (London: Longman, Brown, Green, Longmans, and Roberts, 1858), 330.

47. For an outline of the late medieval Church's stance on the sacrament of the altar, see David Aers, "The Sacrament of the Altar in the Making of Orthodox Christianity or 'Traditional Religion,'" in *Sanctifying Signs* (Notre Dame, IN: University of Notre Dame Press, 2004), 1–28.

48. Nicholas Love, *The Mirror of the Blessed Life of Jesus Christ*, ed. Michael G. Sargent (Exeter: University of Exeter Press, 2005), 224.

heresy in 1393, insists that the sacrament ought to be consumed, then cites Matthew to explain that the consumed host must be excreted. He uses this citation as proof against transubstantiation, since, he says, even Jesus notes that the disciples at the Last Supper chewed, swallowed, and excreted the bread.[49] Likewise, Margery Baxter focuses on the materiality of the Eucharist as consumed food when she argues that if a consecrated host really were the true body of Christ, each day millions of Christs would be consumed and then excreted into vile-smelling pits.[50]

The graphic arguments lobbied by Brut and Baxter rely on the idea that the Eucharist must be ingested to enact its sacramental power, and by pursuing the corporeal ideal of transubstantiation to its logical limit, each mocks the idea that a consecrated host does not retain its accidental properties. But, as mentioned above, most medieval congregants seldom ingested the host, instead witnessing it as the priest held the consecrated host aloft during Mass.[51] Thus, the *Lay Folk's Mass Book* instructs the laity to revere the sight of the host by kneeling and lifting up their hands, since "that same es he thou lokes opone."[52] And late medieval Eucharistic poetry often emphasized the power of seeing the sacrament, as one poem from the Vernon manuscript does:

I þe honoure wiþ al my miht
In fourme of Bred as I þe se,
Lord, þat in þat ladi briht,
In Marie Mon bi-come for me.
þi fflesch, þi blod is swete of siht,
þi Sacrament honoured to be,
Of Bred and Wyn wiþ word i-diht;
Almihti lord, I leeue in þe.[53]

---

49. *Registrum Johannis Trefnant*, ed. William W. Capes (London: Canterbury and York Society, 1816), 339.

50. "mille tales deos et postea tales deos comedunt et commestos emittunt per posteriora in sepibus turpiter fetentibus, ubi potestis tales deos sufficientes invenire si oueritis perscrutari." *Heresy Trials*, 45.

51. See Eamon Duffy, *Stripping of the Altars*, 2nd ed. (New Haven, CT: Yale University Press, 2005), 91–130. Between 1215 and 1222, a London synod carefully outlined when the congregation was allowed to see the host, warning priests to elevate it only once the words *Hoc est corpus meum* had been uttered to prevent idolatry of an unconsecrated host. For a discussion about how theologians marked the exact moment of consecration, see V. L. Kennedy, "The Moment of Consecration and the Elevation of the Host," *Mediaeval Studies* 6 (1944): 121–50.

52. *The Lay Folks' Mass Book*, ed. T. F. Simmons, EETS 71 (London: Trubner, 1968), 38.

53. *The Minor Poems of the Vernon MS* 25. See also 178 for a similar formulation of seeing the consecrated host.

The turn away from consuming toward seeing the Eucharist seems to emerge from two concerns. First, as the anonymous lyric *On the Feast of Corpus Christi* explains, many people failed to take it seriously when they consumed the sacrament regularly: "ffor folk war howsild so comunly, / þai toke þe les reward þarby, / Ne þam-self þai wald noght ȝeme / Als to þe sacrament suld seme" (183). Second, it was too much work for the individual priest to distribute pieces of the host to every congregant. Accordingly, the fifteenth-century chaplain John Audelay instructs the laity to worship the sacrament upon sight, arguing that witnessing the host enacts the relationship between external sight and inward belief: "Hayle! þi glorious Godhed hit may not be sene, / Hayle! with no freelte of flesly ȝene; / Hayle! I beleue truly in þis bred þat ȝe bene, / Verey God and mon."[54]

For Audelay and other orthodox officials, witnessing the host offers a chance to reiterate the sacrament's miracle: while the consecrated host still looks like bread, faith allows true believers to recognize it as Christ's body. Yet for some fifteenth-century writers, the fact that some congregants could only witness the host from afar only exacerbates the gap between clerical and lay audiences.[55] For example, in one fifteenth-century antagonistic debate about lay access to the Eucharist, expecting the laity to witness the host is understood as a deliberately deceptive tactic on the part of the Church. *Jack Upland's Rejoinder* (ca. 1420) is the third text in a back-and-forth between Jack Upland, a layman critical of fraternal corruption, and Friar Daw, an orthodox representative who defends friars' rights to itinerant preaching. In the *Rejoinder*, Upland reproaches priests who deliberately obscure the sacrament of the altar:

> we sey alle þe sacrid oste þat is sene with eye
> is verey cristes body; but thy sette seyþ not soo
> but ȝe sey þer is cristes body, but ȝe tel not where;
> but crist seyþ þis is my body & not þer is my body
> whi ȝe templers messe sellers, grante ȝe not cristes wordes
> syþ ȝe chafyr þus þerwith, by gylyng þe pupil
> lete ȝoure sette write ȝoure byleue of þis sacrid osste,

---

54. *The Poems of John Audelay*, ed. Ella Keats Whiting, EETS 184 (Oxford: Oxford University Press, 1931), 8.15–18.

55. See Aers, who states, "the laity were encouraged to make prayers and readings which might often bear little relation to what was being enacted at the east end of their church. The Mass thus embodied and fostered the clearest division between clergy and laity." *Sanctifying Signs*, 72.

& preche it as ȝe write it, & sette þerto ȝoure sele
& j am sikir of my feyþ ȝe schul be stoned to deþe[56]

In this rather confusing claim, Upland seems to focus on priests' garbling of the consecrating words by saying "*There* is Christ's body" rather than correctly understanding Christ's phrase, "*This* is my body." Indeed, Upland says, even if priests were aware of their misstatement, they fail to show where Christ's body appears. Upland seems to argue obliquely that the host retains its accidental properties, scoffing that the priest has failed to produce the promised body of Christ because he has misstated the consecrating words. Worse, he has beguiled his congregation into believing that the unchanged host has become Christ's body, despite evidence to the contrary.

To prevent the dissemination of the false doctrine of transubstantiation, Upland recommends that priests write down their beliefs and "preche it as ye write it," then authorize the written text with the kind of seal Arundel's documents boast. Based on such clear documentary evidence of their iniquity, Upland says, priests would be stoned to death. The quick turn from arguing against transubstantiation to daring the clergy to document their false beliefs turns the ecclesiastical claims against unauthorized preaching against ecclesiastical authorities themselves. Crucial to Upland's argument is the easy jump from the materiality of Christ's body to the material documents Upland challenges Friar Daw to produce. For Upland, official documents (sealed with the material accoutrements of authorization) would reveal the emptiness of the consecrated host, not the heresy of those who challenge the doctrine of transubstantiation.

Unlike Upland, Thorpe never engages in direct debate with Arundel regarding Eucharistic presence. Instead, he subtly and powerfully challenges the idea of transubstantiation by turning away from the problem of the consecrated host to his own presence as a preacher. Repeatedly pressing Thorpe to explain his views on the sacrament of the altar, Arundel often points to an accusation written in his roll that states that Thorpe preached "'opinli in seint Chaddis chirche þat þe sacrament of þe auter was material breed after þe consecracioun'" (931–92). Rather than answer this charge directly, Thorpe instead challenges the orthodox link between outward sight of the Eucharist and inward belief by narrating a story that describes a congregation's thoughtless, automatic responses to liturgical ritual:

56. "Upland's Rejoinder 2," in *Jack Upland, Friar Daw's Reply, and Upland's Rejoinder*, 5–13.

> As I stood þere in þe pulpitte, bisiinge me to teche þe heestis of God, oon knyllide a sacringe belle, and herfor myche peple turned awei fersli and wiþ greet noyse runnen frowardis me. And I, seying þis, seide to hem þus "Goode men, ȝou were better to stoonden here stille and to here Goddis word! For, certis, þe vertu and þe mede of þe moost holi sacrament of þe auter stondiþ myche moore in þe bileue þereof þat ȝe owen to haue in ȝoure soulis þan it doiþ in þe outward siȝt þerof. And þerfore ȝou were better to stond stille quyetefulli and to heeren Goddis worde, siþ þoroȝ heeringe þerof men comen to veri bileue." And oþer wise, ser, I am certeyne I spak not þere of þe worschipful sacrament of þe auter. (936–46)

Thorpe insists that this congregation would be better off staying where they are and listening to God's words rather running to see another priest elevate a transubstantiated Host. He uses this moment to espouse his Wycliffite rejection of idols and images, arguing that "outward sight" cannot offer access to the inward soul, where the real sacrament resides. He thus disputes the kinds of arguments offered in fifteenth-century orthodox poetry that contend that witnessing the host should be enough for any congregant who truly believes in the consecrated host and who trusts that what his or her outward eye cannot see, the soul can.

But Thorpe moves beyond any traditional Lollard argument about the flimsiness of images when he strikingly envisions his own sermon as a substitute for the consecrated wafer at the Church across the square. Rather than turn toward a wafer that remains material bread, he tells the crowd, this audience should stay to hear him speak. Elizabeth Schirmer points out that Thorpe's refusal to address the question of his beliefs about Eucharistic presence strips his discussion of the Eucharist of the miracle, and he instead focuses on his real-life experiences and those of his audience.[57] Significantly, he emphasizes hearing rather than sight as the mode of sacramental access. He notes the "greet noyse" of the crowd when the sacring bell rings and asks them to "stond stille quyetefulli" to hear God's word, "siþ þoruȝ heeringe þerof men comen to veri bileue" (943–45). Thorpe turns away from the relationship between outward sight and inward belief Arundel wants to draw out of him. Instead, Thorpe shifts from describing a listening audience to addressing a listening Arundel in order to emphasize the link between his imagined absent audience and the present one. By doing so, he can imagine his answers to Arundel's questions as a kind of "sermon" preached to those witnesses who will read the transcript of his interrogation as an exemplary

---

57. Elizabeth Schirmer, "William Thorpe's Narrative Theology," *SAC* 31 (2009): 272–73.

text. He thus transfers the discussion about Eucharistic presence into one about his own presence as a preacher, first for a public at St. Chad's Church, then for Arundel and his assistants, and finally for the absent witnesses whom his *Testimony* addresses.

Rather than worry about whether Thorpe will confess to openly preaching against transubstantiation in public, Arundel now seems to care more about how Thorpe might explain the difficult relationship of subject and accident: "'I trowe þee not, whateuere þou seist, siþe so worschipful men haue witnessid aʒens þee. But siþ þou denyest þat þou seidest not þus þere, what seist þou now? Dwelliþ þer after þe consecracioun of þe oost material breed or nai?'" (947–50). For Arundel, Thorpe's words are no match for the documentary witnesses he contains in his cupboard, yet he insists that Thorpe provide him with a direct answer in the interrogation so that he can gather clear evidence of Thorpe's heretical beliefs. And Thorpe readily answers Arundel's question. He patiently explains the events of the Last Supper and then tells Arundel, "'þe worschipful sacrament of þe auter is verri Cristis fleisch and his blood in forme of breed and wyne'" (968–69). Remarkably, Arundel concedes that the sacrament is Christ's body in the form of bread, though he remains confused that the rest of Thorpe's "sect" teaches that the host is bread in substance. Thorpe refuses to get into the academic debates about *accidentem sine subiecto* (though shows off his facility with these debates), instead turning, once again, to witnessing as the most certain form of theological knowledge: "'Ser, bi open euydence and bi greet witnesse a þousand ʒeer after þe incarnacioun of Crist, þe determynacioun which I haue confessid here bifore to ʒou was accept of al holi chirche as sufficient of saluacioun of alle hem þat wollen bileue it feiþfulli and worchen þeraftir charitabli'" (1042–66). In eschewing university discourse for "great witnesses," Thorpe returns to his earlier claim that his own witnesses will bear his teachings *extra muros*. For Thorpe, witnessing offers the best, most "open" kind of evidence of the righteousness of his beliefs, and, moreover, it allows him to imagine the enduring presence of his teachings in an audience of absent witnesses. By "greet witnesse" he can claim that his complicated arguments about Eucharistic presence reach back to early, uncorrupted Church doctrine, and, by extension, he can suggest that his own status as a witness in this interrogation inserts him into this sacred genealogy.

Arundel soon realizes he will get nowhere with Thorpe about Eucharistic sacramentality or anything else, and the interrogation ends much as it began. Thorpe reiterates his willingness to submit to the teachings of Christ and the "true" Church, and Arundel slumps in defeat. He bids the constable to return Thorpe to prison, and Thorpe sighs in relief to be away from his interrogators:

> And I was þanne gretli confortid in alle my wittis, not oonly forþi þat I was þan delyuered for a tyme fro þe siȝt, fro þe heeringe, fro þe presence, fro the scornynge and fro þe manassinge of myn enemyes, but myche more I gladid in þe Lord forþi þoruȝ his grace he kepte me so boþe amonge þe flateryngis specialli, also amonge þe manassingis of myn aduersaries [þat] wiþouten heuynesse and agrigginge of my conscience I passid awei fro hem. (2238–45)

Thorpe here restates his investment in presence, mirroring his initial claim that he writes his *Testimony* for an absent audience of men and women. Bodily presence, for Thorpe, manifests in the witnessing bodies of his interrogators ("þe siȝt . . . þe heeringe . . . þe presence"), but they are not true witnesses. The only true witness is his own testimonial text, a treatise for those will disseminate his beliefs.

Testimony, Martyrology, and Thorpe's Mysterious End

We do not know what happened to Thorpe after he returned to prison at Saltwood Castle. There is no record of his formal trial for heresy, nor is there a record of his abjuration or punishment. Hudson fantasizes that "it is tempting to think that Thorpe escaped from the archbishop's hands at some time between the conversation recorded in the present text and that formal investigation" (xlvi), and she even suggests that Thorpe might have run away to Prague like Peter Payne, another English Lollard, did in 1413. The biographical sketchiness of Thorpe's life after his *Testimony* certainly lends itself to such imaginings. As Copeland sympathizes, "There is a certain attractiveness in looking for another career that can be recovered in nearly all of its significant profile, to find a way of imagining the life of Thorpe which leaves almost no imprint on the historical record" (*Pedagogy* 192). But Thorpe's own *Testimony* resists such a biographical reading. Indeed, his strategy of ignoring his own bodily existence in favor of a documentary presence that could be "witnessed" by an absent audience allows him to slip away both from Arundel's legal authority and from our scholarly desire to recover a "real" William Thorpe.

Codicologically speaking, we know a bit more. The text of Thorpe's *Testimony* survives in three manuscript versions (one English, two Latin) and one early printed version. The ownership and provenance of these texts are difficult to trace, but both Latin manuscripts are written in Bohemian hands, and it seems that Thorpe was known in Bohemia, perhaps through his acquaintance with Jan Hus.[58] Sometime around 1531, Richard Bayfield, a monk of Bury St. Edmonds, imported several books from abroad, including a text called *A boke of thorpe or of John Oldecastelle*.[59] This short text was subsequently taken up by the Protestant reformist John Bale, who reprinted parts of Thorpe's Latin *Testimony* in 1543 (later collected in the *Fasciculi zizaniorum*). In 1563 John Foxe gathered together the narratives of fourteenth- and fifteenth-century heretics such as Badby, Oldcastle, and Thorpe and placed them alongside Reformation figures such as Anne Askew and Thomas Cranmer in his multivolume *Acts and Monuments*. Indeed, Foxe is Thorpe's most important champion in England, inserting his *Testimony* into English ecclesiastical history as a reformist martyrology.

The sixteenth-century impulse to construct Thorpe as a martyr seems almost anticipated in his own text. Hudson suggests that the *Testimony* can be understood as a "substitute saint's life," insofar as Thorpe offers his own life as evidence of the truth of his beliefs in the face of the Church's relentless persecution of Lollards.[60] His quasi-hagiographical narrative indeed turns often to his own experiences, rather than Scriptural citation or academic discussion, to argue on behalf of Lollard doctrine, and he even begins his *Testimony* with an autobiographical account of his upbringing and education. There, he suggests his life might be understood as inspirational, perhaps even saintly:

> And so þanne I, ymagynynge þe greet desire of þese sondir and diuerse frendis of sondri placis and cuntrees, acoordinge alle in oon, I occupiede me herwiþ diuerse tymes so bisili in my wittis þat þoruȝ Goddis grace I perseyued, bi her good mouynge and of her cheritable desir, sum profit þat myȝt come of þis writing. For truþe haþ þis condicioun: whereeuere it is enpugned, þer comeþ þerof odour of good smel, and þe more violently þat enemyes enforsen hem to oppressen and to wiþstoonde þe truþe of Goddis word, þe ferþir þe swete smel þerof strecchiþ. And no doute, whanne þis heuenli smel is moued, it wol not as smoke passe awei wiþ þe wynde; but it wol descende and reste in summe clene soule þirstinge þeraftir. (41–51)

---

58. See Hudson, xxvi–xxxvii, and Copeland, *Pedagogy*, 191–93.
59. Aston, *Lollards and Their Books*, 220.
60. Likewise, Little compares Thorpe to St. Cecelia: *Confession and Resistance* 64.

By constructing a diverse, international audience, Thorpe imagines his text's broad dissemination, and he claims that God's grace has given him the foresight to imagine its wide-ranging benefits. His turn to the "good smell" of truth draws upon a common hagiographical metaphor, and he amplifies it by imagining that violence against truth would merely strengthen its odor. Of course, as discussed above, that violence never materializes in the *Testimony*. That he imagines it here, however, suggests that Thorpe tries to shape his narrative to fit the generic requirements of martyrology. Yet the *Testimony* does not narrate a martyr's trial. Thorpe does not suffer physically as Christ had, and he provides little material evidence of his own bodily or even emotional distress in the face of Arundel's "manassing." He does not even offer a conditional martyrology like Langland's Book—a statement that would say something like "If I were to be violently struck or killed, then I will have suffered for my beliefs."

This chapter opened by considering the relationship between biographical certitude and testimony, suggesting that the pervasive threat of bodily violence and death puts particular pressure on the ways testimonial narrative can be read biographically. We might now ask a similar question of martyrology: that is, how does the martyrological threat (or promise) of violent death structure its testimony? Death is, of course, a critical feature of any martyrological narrative, the moment when the martyr transcends his or her body and the earthly world in favor of divine exemplarity. Yet Thorpe's death remains a mystery. By turning to the construction of Thorpe as a Protestant martyr in Foxe's enormous mythographic project, we can extend our thinking about Thorpe's testimonial presence. Whereas Thorpe's sketchy biography foregrounds the gaps between personal testimony and documented biography, the unconventionality of his narrative within Foxe's martyrology foregrounds the gaps between testimony and exemplarity.

Tracking the martyrological fate of William Thorpe in Foxe's *Acts and Monuments*, however, potentially offers a skewed perspective of the sixteenth-century sanctification of convicted Lollards. Though Foxe lists a number of Lollards in his treatise, most Lollards were not particularly venerated for their deaths, and Lollard doctrine itself generally sneered at the kind of iconographic worship martyrology encourages. One notable exception is Richard Wyche. After his 1403 interrogation for heretical preaching, Wyche went on to live the life of a clerk without incident until 1440, when he was burned publicly for inciting rebellion.[61] Chronicle accounts describe

---

61. For an account of Wyche's 1440 trial and the events that led up to it, see Christina Von Nolcken, "Richard Wyche, a Certain Knight, and the Beginning of the End," in *Lollardy and the*

an unprecedented and unrepeated response to his death, including pilgrimages to the site of Wyche's execution.[62] Even John Oldcastle, who emerges as a central figure in fifteenth- and sixteenth-century chronicle accounts and literary discussions of Lollardy and dissent, does not provoke such devotion.

Thorpe oddly achieves his status as a martyr in the sixteenth century, since his violent death was never witnessed, his end never accounted for.[63] Indeed, the very open-endedness of Thorpe's life transforms him into an elastic figure for reformist polemic that can attest to the immediate history of anti-Catholic martyrology and offer an example of steadfast resistance for Protestant reformers. The ideal of Thorpe as a martyrological witness is robustly expressed in John Foxe's ecclesiastical history of England, *Acts and Monuments*. As a grand compilation of myriad manuscript and printed sources, this work establishes the credibility of Foxes's history—and by extension, of his reformist doctrine—by calling upon eyewitness reports and handwritten documents. As John N. King puts it, "Even when he does not consult manuscripts directly, he accords quasi-talismanic significance to *monuments* concerning the history of the 'true' church throughout the ages."[64]

Foxe conceives the materiality of his own project to link the apostolic tradition of early Christian martyrs to sixteenth-century reformers, a link made possible by Wyclif and his followers. He does so by imagining his text as a critical witness to a new history. He begins by lamenting the fact that he is contributing yet another book to a world already saturated with the printed word:

> Seeing the worlde is so replenished with suche an infinite multitude of bookes, dayly put foorth euery where: I shall seme (perhaps) to take a matter inhand superfluous and needeles, at thys present time to sette out so great a volume as this is, especiallye touchinge writing of historyes, considering now adaies the worlde is pestred not onelye with a superfluous

---

Gentry in the Later Middle Ages, ed. Margaret Aston and Colin Richmond (New York: St. Martin's, 1997), 127–54; and Richard Rex, "Which Is Wyche? Lollardy and Sanctity in Lancastrian London," in *Martyrs and Martyrdom in England, c. 1400–1700,* ed. Thomas S. Freeman and Thomas F. Mayer (Suffolk: Boydell, 2007), 88–106.

62. See Rex, "Which Is Wyche?" 93–96.

63. Noting the absence of martyrological cults around executed Lollards, Thomas S. Freeman claims, "Only Thorpe's account of his own examinations qualifies as a popular Lollard martyrological work." "Over Their Dead Bodies: Concepts of Martyrdom in Late Medieval and Early Modern England," in *Martyrs and Martyrdom,* 8.

64. John N. King, *Foxe's "Book of Martyrs" and Early Modern Print Culture* (Cambridge: Cambridge University Press, 2006), 47.

plenty therof, but of all other treatises, so that bookes maye rather seme to lacke Readers, then Readers to lacke bookes. Howe be it I doubt not but manye good men doo both perceiue, and inwardlye bewayle this insatiable grediness of wryting and printing, which to say the truth, for my part I do as much lament as many man else may do beside.[65]

Nonetheless, he claims, his compilation rescues reformists from the "pit of oblivion," extracting these martyrs out of obscurity:

For first of all, they geue a lyuely testimonye that there is one aboue which ruleth all, contrary to the opinion of the godless, and the whole nest of Epicures: Like as one said of Harpalus in times past, that his doings did liuely testifie that there was no God, because in suffering of him a great space together, God semed to neglect all care of reasonable creatures: So contrarywise, in these men we haue an assured and plaine witness of God, in whose lyfe appeared a certaine force of divine nature, and in their death a farre greater signification, whiles in such shaprenes of tormentes wee behelde in them a strength so constant aboue mans reache, a redynes to answer, patience in prison, godlynes in foreuing, cherefulnes in suffering, besides the manifold sense and feling of the holy ghost, which they learned in many of their comfortes, and we by them. (143)

Foxe's justification for putting together such an enormous book relies on his production of layers of witnesses: first, the martyrs themselves who offer "lively testimony" of righteous doctrine, and second, those who "behold" these martyrs, either as eyewitnesses or as readers of *Acts and Monuments*. Indeed, the series of woodcuts that Foxe uses to illustrate the violent trials and executions of his martyrs offers readers a way to act as "eyewitnesses" to these martyrologies.[66]

Thorpe's testimony poses a particular challenge for Foxe's agenda: there is no record of Thorpe's existence after his return to Saltwood prison, either in the *Testimony* or in other documents. Since Foxe asserts in the preface to *Acts and Monuments* that a martyr's death offers "far greater signification" of divine presence than even the events of his life, Thorpe's mysterious end is a

65. Princeton University, William H. Schiede Library MS 11.1.2, page 143. All citations of *Acts and Monuments* are from this 1563 edition unless otherwise noted.

66. For a discussion of how Foxe's woodcuts offered a visual counterpoint to the martyrological narratives, see the series of essays in the "Visual Culture" section of *John Foxe and His World*, ed. Christopher Highley and John N. King (Suffolk: Ashgate, 2002), esp. Andrew Pettegree, "Illustrating the Book: A Protestant Dilemma," 133–44; and Thomas Betteridge, "Truth and History in Foxe's *Acts and Monuments*," 145–59.

difficult conundrum, and Foxe works strenuously to ensure that Thorpe fits in with his compilation of martyrological witnesses. In the apparatus around Thorpe's narrative, Foxe overtly meditates on the witnessing claims of voice, manuscript, and document to certify the truth of Thorpe's *Testimony*. He begins with a preface that praises Thorpe as "a warrior valiant under the triumphant banner of Christ," going on to insist repeatedly that Thorpe's story is his own: "written by the said Thorpe, and storied by his own pen, at the request of his friends, as by his own words, in the process hereof, may appear" (249). Foxe's reiterations of Thorpe's authorial "ownership" explicitly posit the narrative as an extralegal document, a text not written by the officials trying to censor Thorpe and other Lollards, as well as a direct link back to Thorpe's own body and voice. Indeed, Foxe instructs the reader to learn the doctrinal truth professed by Thorpe and to marvel at his status as God's witness, "for thou shalt behold here in this man, the marvelous force and strength of the Lord's might, spirit, and grace, working and fighting in his soldiers, and also speaking in their mouths, according to the word of his promise, Luke xxi" (143).

Foxe then turns from Thorpe's authorial presence to his own editorial status, and he certifies the authenticity of Thorpe's document by tracing its manuscript heritage and by claiming its proximity to living eyewitness sources. Attributing the first printing of Thorpe to William Tyndale, Foxe insists that he has stayed faithful to Tyndale's version and praises him for managing both to retain Thorpe's voice and to clarify the language for a modern audience: "The English though the saide Maister Tindall did somewhat amend, and frame it after our manner: yet not fully in all wordes, but that some thing dooth remaine, sauering the olde speache of that time" (143). With this admission in mind, Foxe shores up his claims to editorial authenticity while lamenting the loss of Thorpe's voice:

> To the text of the story we have neither added nor diminished, but, as we have received it copied out and corrected by Master William Tindal, (who had his own handwriting), so we have here sent it, and set it out abroad. Although for the more credit of the matter, I rather wished it in his own naturall speache, wherin it was first written. Notwithstandyng, to put away all doubt and scruple herein, this I thought before to pre-monish and testifie to the reader touching the certeintie hereof: that they bee yet a lyve, which haue seen the selfe same copy in his own old Englishe, resembling the true antiquitie both of the speache and of the tyme, the name of whom, as for the record of the same to avouch, is Master Whitehead. (143)

He further mentions that a "maister Whithead" saw the "true auncient copy in the hands of George Constantine," who then verified the text both to Foxe and to the printer.

The term of verification here—an eyewitness to an "auncient copy"—is familiar from Crowley's preface of his 1550 print versions of Langland's poem, in which he makes sure to corroborate the authenticity of his text by referring to the "ancient copies" to which he had access.[67] In *Acts and Monuments*, Foxe amplifies the kind of editorial authority Crowley asserts by adding his fantasy of Thorpe's "speache," which could presumably seep through the original text, since it was penned by Thorpe himself. Indeed, as if trying to harness Thorpe's authentic voice, Foxe appends a *Testament*, an apocryphal text purportedly written by Thorpe at the time of his death, dated to around 1460; it first appears in the 1530 Antwerp edition of Thorpe's narrative. The *Testament* continues Thorpe's criticisms of the Church, focusing on greed and lechery among priests. The *Testament* offers some closure to the trenchant problem of Thorpe's life after his return to Saltwood prison.[68] Perhaps it offered a similar sense of closure for Foxe. But the *Testament* does not answer questions about the end of Thorpe's life any more than the *Testimony* provides significant biographical corroboration of Thorpe's existence. Indeed, what purpose the *Testament* holds, either in Foxe's text specifically or in the fifteenth- and sixteenth-century legacy of the Thorpe narrative more generally, is not entirely clear. It certainly offers more blatant reformist rhetoric, exhibiting none of the narrative qualities of Thorpe's *Testimony* and instead tracking the kinds of abuses against which Foxe defines Protestant doctrine. It also, significantly, shores up the martyrological potential of Thorpe's life:

> And I that am a most unworthy and wretched caitiff, shall now, through the special grace of God, make to him pleasant sacrifice with my most sinful and unworthy body: beseeching heartily all fold that read or hear this end of my purposed testament, that, through the grace of God, they dispose verily and virtuously all their wits, and able in like manner all their members, to understand truly, and to keep faithfully, charitably, and continually, all the commandments of God. (284–85)

---

67. For a discussion of Crowley's use of the phrase "auncient copy" to authorize his printing project, see chapter 4.

68. "It has always seemed unlikely that such a prominent heretic was neither induced to recant nor brought to the stake, and indeed was never heard of again." Richard Rex, "Thorpe's *Testament*: A Conjectural Emendation," *Medium Aevum* 74.1 (2005): 110.

Foxe emphasizes this martyrological potential in his 1563 edition of *Acts and Monuments* by moving directly from the *Testament* to a half-page woodcut depicting a bearded man in a barrel, hands held aloft, with a scroll issuing forth from his mouth that says "Lorde Iesus Christ helpe me." Men on horseback and on foot surround him, stoking the fire beneath the barrel as flames encircle his body. Beneath the woodcut is a short narrative titled simply "An Artificer, a Lay Man" (172).

The narrative describes an anonymous layperson condemned for arguing against transubstantiation, and it is suspiciously close to the story about John Badby's 1410 burning that Thomas Hoccleve includes in his *Regiment of Princes*. Foxe's (lengthy) version goes like this:

> And when as the sentence of his condemnatio(n) was geuen against him, and that this valia(n)t Martyr of Christ should be caried into a market place without the citie to be included in a pype or tunne, for so muche as Cherillus Bul was not then in use amongst the byshops, as it happened the prince the eldest sonne of kyng Henry was there present: this man as a good Samaritane, indeuored him selfe to saue the life of him, whome the unshamefast Leuites & Phariseis sought to put to death: he admonished and counseled him that hauing respect unto him selfe, he should spedely withdrawe him self out of these daungerous Laberynthes of opinions, adding oftentimes threateninges, the which might haue daunted any mans stomack. But this valiaunt champion of Christe neglecting the princes fayre wordes and vanquishing all mens deuises, fully determined, rather to suffer any kinde of tormente were it neuer so greuous, then so great Idolatry and wickednes. Whereupon being inclosed in the pype or tonne, he was torme(n)ted by the raging flame. The innocent soule moste miserably roring and criynge out in the middest of the fier. With whiche horrible crie the Prince beynge moued, he cometh agayne unto the man to reclaime hym unto life. (that pytie and mercye whyche commen sence of nature wrought in him, the same by this cruel new deuyse or new crueltie of so strau(n)ge death, was double in him augme(n)ted) he com(m)undede pe fyer to be drawen backe and take(n) away, he comforted him which was torme(n)ted, promysing him yet hope of his lyfe, if he would consent unto his counsels: adding moreover that he should haue certayne yearly stipend geue(n) him out of the kynges treasury, asmuch as sold suffice for his suste(n)atio(n). But againe he refused the offer of wordly promyses, without al doubt being more veheme(n)tly inflamed with the spirite of God then with any earthly desire. Wherefore when as yet he continued unmouable in his former mynde, the prince commaunded him straight to be put againe into

the Pype or Tunne, and that he should not afterward loke for any grace or fauour. But as he could be allured by no rewardes, euen so was he nothing at al abashed at their tormentes, but as avaliaunt champio(n) of Christe, he perseuered inuincible vnto the ende. Notwithout a great and mooste cruell battaile, but with muche more greatere triumphe of victory, the spirite of Christ hauing all wayes the upperhande in this members, maugre the fury rage & power of þe whole world. (172–73)

Compare Thomas Hoccleve's description of Badby's execution:

> My lord the Prince—God him save and blesse—
> Was at his deedly castigacioun
> And of his soule hadde greet tendrenesse,
> Thristynge sore his sauvacioun.
> Greet was his pitous lamentacioun
> Whan that this renegat nat wolde blynne
> Of the stynkynge errour that he was ynne.
> This good lord highte him to be swich a mene
> To his fadir, our lige lord sovereyn,
> If he renounce wold his error clene
> And come unto our good byleeve ageyn,
> He shold of his lyfe seur been and certain;
> And souffissant lyflode eek sholde he have
> Unto the day he clad were in his grave.[69]

Hoccleve goes on to describe the prince's valiant but ineffective attempts to convert Badby, details Foxe also includes. What are we to make of Foxe's inclusion of Badby's trial and execution under the rubric of an anonymous layperson?

It is possible that Foxe wanted to include Badby within the list of convicted Lollards he depicts in his 1563 edition of *Acts and Monuments,* a list that includes John Ball, John Purvey, Richard Wyche, William Sautre, and William Swinderby. But by following Thorpe's *Testament* with Badby's narrative, without identifying it as Badby's, Foxe effectively provides Thorpe's story with a conclusion not offered in either his *Testimony* or his *Testament.* Indeed, the last few lines of Thorpe's *Testament* occur at the top of the page, followed by the woodcut and description of the execution of the anonymous "layman" (figure 1). The page layout thus gives the sense of continua-

---

69. Hoccleve, *Regiment,* lines 295–308.

truely, and to kepe faithfully, charitably, and continually all the commaundementes of God, and so than to pray deuoutly to al the blessed trinitie, that I may haue grace with wisdom & prudence from aboue, to end my life here in this forsaid truthe and for this cause, in true faith and stedfast hope, and perfit charitie. Amen.

¶ An Artificer a Lay man.

1410.

After this priest folowed an hand= ecraftes mā, in the yeare of our Lorde M. iiii. C. x. he held this opinion, that it was not the bo= dy of Christ really, the whiche was sacramentally vsed in the churche: when as he could by no meanes be perswaded from the constancie of this opinion, but that he had wholy determined with him self to die therin, he was deliuered ouer to the seculer power. And when as the sentence of his condemnatiō was geuen against him, and that this valiant Martyr of Christ should be caried into a mar= ket place without the citie to be inclused in a pype or tunne, for so muche as Cherillus Bul was not then in bre amongst the byshops, as it happened the prince the eldest sonne of kyng Henry was there present: this man as a good Samaritane, indeuored him selfe to saue the life of him, whome the vnshamefast Leuites & Phariseis sought to put to death: he admoni= shed and counseled him that hauing respect vn to him selfe, he should spedely withdrawe him selfe out of these daungerous Laberynthes of opinions, adding oftentimes threateninges, the which might haue daunted any mans sto= mach. But this valiaunt champion of Christe neglecting the princes fayre wordes and van= quishing all mens deuises, fully determined, rather to suffer any kinde of tormente were it neuer so greuous, then so great Idolatry and wickednes. whereupon being inclosed in the pype or tonne, he was tormēted by the raging flame. The innocent soule moste miserably ro= ring and cryeng out in the middest of the fier. With whiche horrible crie the Prince beyng moued, he cometh agayne vnto the man to re= claime hym vnto life:(that pytie and mercye whyche commen sence of nature wrought in him, the same by this cruel new deuyse or new crueltie of so straūge death, was double in him augmēted) he cōmaunded ye fyer to be drawen backe and take away, he comforted him which was tormēted, prompsing him yet hope of his lyfe, if he would consent vnto his counsels: ad= ding moreouer that he should haue certayne yearly stipend gene him out of the kynges trea sury, asmuch as shold suffise for his sustētatiō. But againe he refused the offer of worldly pro= myses, without al doubt being more vehemēt= ly inflamed with the spirite of God then with any

A miraculous example of constancy

tion, rather than a turn to a new martyr narrative. We are perhaps implicitly instructed to visualize the burning of this anonymous layman and read the description of his execution as Thorpe's own end. It certainly offers a definitive end to Thorpe's life, one that supports the martyrological aims of Foxe's compilation.

Seven years later, possibly chagrined by the disapproval lodged by critics such as Nicholas Harpsfield and Thomas Harding, Foxe omitted both the woodcut and the anonymous narrative after Thorpe's *Testament*, instead moving directly on to a description of John Purvey's trials and execution. In the 1570 edition, Foxe cagily avoids offering any real closure to Thorpe's life and instead adds this conclusion:

> What was the end of this good man, and blessed servant of God, William Thorpe, I find as yet in no story specified. By all conjectures it is to be thought that the archbishop Thomas Arundel, being so hard an adversary against those men, would not let him go; much less it is to be supposed, that he would ever retract his sentence and opinion, which he so valiantly maintained before the bishop; neither doth it seem that he had any such recanting spirit. Again, neither is it found that he was burned; wherefore it remaineth most likely to be true, that he, being committed to some straight prison, according as the archbishop, in his examination before, did threaten him there (as Thorpe confesseth himself), was so straightly kept, that either he was secretly made away with, or else he died there by sickness.[70]

Foxe's conjecture has been reiterated a number of times by modern scholars (Copeland and Rex, for example), exposing our discomfort with the openness of Thorpe's narrative. Attending to Thorpe as a witness, with all the complexities that term signifies, does not offer the kind of closure that Foxe seeks. But it does suggest a more accurate account of what the *Testimony of William Thorpe* can and cannot provide to scholars who want to try to "recover" a voice from the past. Indeed, like many Lollard depositions, Thorpe's *Testimony* challenges those looking for the "real" Thorpe, a historically verifiable human being who stood up for his beliefs when doing so could lead to public death. The value of the *Testimony* is not so much in providing a link to the distant past as it is in exposing the desire for that link and the mechanisms by which we imagine it. To what can we, as scholars of the medieval past, attest? What can we witness in the documents and texts left us?

70. John Foxe, *Acts and Monuments*, ed. George Townsend, vol. 3 (London: Seeley, Burnside, and Seeley, 1843), 285.

coda

Witnessing the Middle Ages

THE QUESTIONS posed at the end of the previous chapter deserve a sustained answer, beginning with a brief summary of what this book has tried to accomplish. As this book has shown, medieval witnessing might be understood both heuristically—that is, as a method to retrieve evidence that can uncover truth, whether legal, ethical, or doctrinal—and hermeneutically—that is, as a method of interpretation that can produce an explanation, start a discussion, or point to gaps in what is considered evidentiary. Because witnessing can be both heuristic and hermeneutic, it worked in the Middle Ages to produce cultural ideologies and obligations as well as to critique them. Those critiques, this book claims, emerge most dynamically and powerfully in vernacular literary texts, which cite, restage, and experiment with the legal and devotional witnessing practices charged with authenticating and disciplining communal obligations.

Witnessing is heuristically and hermeneutically crucial in our own discussions of how scholarship can retrieve and interpret evidence of a medieval past. Notably, as I discuss in this coda, the term "witness" is used in philological criticism to describe the documents that can attest to the events, people, or customs of the Middle Ages. I argue here that the use of the term in this context confers a sense of authenticity onto these documents by attaching a kind of presence to them. In other words, when philological convention refers to medieval documents and texts as "witnesses," it implies that these texts can offer authentic and immediate access to the words or thoughts of someone who was "really there," recording an event we can now only understand through those documents. Here, in assessing how the term "witness" functions to authorize certain modes of medievalist scholarship, I offer some suggestions regarding what the critical stakes of medieval testimony might be.

Oath-Taking and the Production of Evidence

This book has described witnessing as crucial to formations of and challenges to doctrinal, legal, and ethical communities. In doing so, it has depicted witnessing broadly as a diverse set of practices and forms, including the hue and cry, formal depositions, and even prayer. When considered under the rubric of "witnessing," all of these practices try not only to authenticate a truth-claim or an event but also to attest to a community's beliefs and ethics. Moreover, this book has shown that a wide range of texts feature witnessing to explore how communities articulate and police their boundaries. Vernacular poetry, sermon exempla, outlaw ballads, and fictional legal documents alike describe witnessing to imagine communities outside of official ecclesiastical and legal prescriptions. In doing so, these texts all use witnessing to examine the relationship between the divine Word and human words, between divine knowledge and human judgment. They juxtapose multiple models of witnessing to depict dynamic transactions between bodily, oral, and documentary testimony, transactions that reveal the complex ways witnessing practices could claim the authority to articulate community customs and project communal ideals.

As this book has illustrated how witnessing encompasses a wide range of practices that can define, articulate, and police community ties, it has throughout turned its attention to the oath, an important and ubiquitous practice that sought to yoke together divine justice and human systems of law. The oath relied on formulaic language to do so, proclaiming God as a witness alongside the oath-taker. The efficacy of oaths relied on a series of community networks, as when, for example, compurgatory oath-helpers were called upon to attest to a public reputation or when family and neighbors were called upon to authenticate a last will and testament. Oaths were also where vernacular writers could explore how human language and law interacted with divine justice and, in turn, how such a link between the divine Word and earthly language helped sanctify doctrinal or ethical community ties. In the *Man of Law's Tale*, for example, divine justice exposes the iniquity of the false knight's oath in front of a crowd of onlookers, which can then be transformed into a Christian community under the guidance of a converted Alla. Likewise, in the *Pistel of Swete Susan,* the Elders manipulate the dual function of the oath as a call to divine justice and an assertion of community standing to mask their sexual aggression and protect their reputations. In *Piers Plowman,* Langland takes oaths as an opportunity to examine the relationship between personification allegory and documentary materiality, while William Thorpe dismantles the fantasy that book-sworn oaths can harness the divine Word to extract his testimony from the legal purpose it was supposed to serve.

Oath-taking is a site of contention in these texts because it straddles any demarcating lines between heuristic and hermeneutic. Designed as a mode of discovery, as a formula that can make divine judgment visible to a watchful community, in the hands of writers such as Langland or Thorpe it becomes an opportunity for interpretation and literary invention. Indeed, vernacular writers from the period repeatedly saw in the oath the possibility of exploring how human language can mold—rather than simply reveal— divine judgment and "truth." Their depictions of oaths foreground the ways different truths might be constructed from the same evidence, and they demonstrate that the determination of what constitutes evidence can sometimes be a strategic, even tautological, shaping of events into a narrative that is then authenticated by an oath. Similarly, as I discuss below, examining the ways witnessing shapes our scholarship with respect to the past can reveal our own strategic modes of evidence gathering and narrative production.

Philological and Historical "Witnesses"

Whereas witnessing was a central mode of thinking about the relationship between language, community, and divine justice in the Middle Ages, it also offers us a way to think critically about our own relationships to language, texts, and the past. In his account of the long history of scholarly research and editorial practices, D. C. Greetham has noted that "one of the indeterminacies of textual research is its relation to the disciplines that rely on the discovery and interpretation of evidence."[1] Indeed, he insists that textual and editorial research—that is, the search for "evidence"—should seek not to uncover an origin or an unassailable truth about the object of study, but to recognize and articulate textual variance. Greetham particularly examines

---

1. D. C. Greetham, "Textual Forensics," *PMLA* 111.1 (1996): 33.

the reliance on "textual witnesses," a phrase that refers specifically to manuscripts that can uniquely establish a text's authoritative version or origin. Fifteenth-century humanists such as Lorenzo Valla, Greetham states, developed a heuristic model of textual "testimony," distinguishing between "internal" and "external" evidence as a way to root out forgeries from "authentic" versions of texts.[2] As scholars, we continue to comb these material artifacts, these "witnesses," to see how and to what they can testify about the past. Following Valla, we often divide the documents that constitute our research into "primary" and "secondary" witnesses, suggesting perhaps that "primary" witnesses are closer to a textual origin or the author's hand.[3] Such archival work is, of course, necessary for assessing and analyzing the extant materials of the distant period we study, offering critical and exciting insights into the medieval world. Here, however, I want to think briefly about what it means to use the term "witness" to describe archival work and to suggest that our own critical and historicist practices are mired in the same kinds of complications about the rhetoric of authority and "truth" that are at the heart of late medieval experiments in witnessing.

The critical practices of the "New Philology," a phrase coined by Stephen G. Nichols in a 1988 issue of the *Romanic Review*, raise "questions about the status of history, historicism, and contextual referentiality" by dismantling a post-Auerbach philological tradition, which sought to produce an edited text that could ossify the textual variance endemic to manuscript culture.[4] As Nichols put it two years later in his introduction to the 1990 *Speculum* volume dedicated to the New Philology, "The high calling of philology inherited by Auerbach's generation installed a preoccupation with scholarly exactitude based on edited and printed texts."[5] In contrast, the New Philology sets out to return to the indeterminacy of an open-ended manuscript culture, in which the production, translation, and rewriting of texts emerged out of the cultural conditions of a polyglot world that was an admixture of

---

2. See Anthony Grafton, *Forgers and Critics: Creativity and Duplicity in Western Scholarship* (Princeton, NJ: Princeton University Press, 1990).

3. We might take Lee Patterson's assertion into account with respect to internal and external textual witnesses: "At heart, external evidence is nothing other than the fact that a particular reading occurs in one or more manuscripts, that is, attestation; internal evidence is nothing other than the fact that there are on many occasions more than one reading, that is, variation. Both internal and external evidence are evidence of originality; both are, in themselves, equally factual, equally objective, equally historical." See "The Logic of Textual Criticism and the Way of Genius: The Kane-Donaldson *Piers Plowman* in Historical Perspective," in *Negotiating the Past: The Historical Understanding of Medieval Literature* (Madison: University of Wisconsin Press, 1987), 77.

4. Stephen G. Nichols, "Editor's Preface," *Romanic Review* 79.1 (1988): 1.

5. Stephen G. Nichols, "Philology in a Manuscript Culture," *Speculum* 65.1 (1990): 3.

oral and literate practices and conventions. Those who advocated the aims of the New Philological practices suggested that it could perhaps release medieval studies from the exegetical stranglehold of Roberstonianism and from the resolutely formalist work of the New Critics.[6] Moreover, as Steven Justice has said, the materialist practice of returning to the manuscript or printed text to explore its polyvocality rather than to construct and solidify a single master text allows us to "reconstitute not only the array of texts we might come to know, but also the texts we know already" (7). With this in mind, he suggests, the New Philology might offer important methodological tools that help produce a productive "skeptical historicism."

This "skeptical historicism" might also help posit an alternative to the New Historicist practices that reinvigorated Early Modern studies several decades ago, practices that were resoundingly asserted in the 1980 publication of Stephen Greenblatt's *Renaissance Self-Fashioning*. Indeed, the New Philology seems haunted by the promises and practices of the New Historicism, as the contributors to the 1990 *Speculum* volume repeatedly demonstrate. For example, Gabrielle M. Spiegel imagines the New Philology as a critique of the practices of Foucauldian cultural history. For Spiegel, the failure of such historicist practice is that it dismantles the differences between text and context; she claims that "the problem becomes even more severe when we remember that so-called 'documentary' representations of reality (charters, laws, fief lists, economic data, accounts of trade or wars, not to mention cat massacres and cockfights) are equally included within the compass of the social construction of reality."[7] Literary texts and historical context are not the same, Spiegel warns, and the analytic methods used for one should not be imported to use for the other. In addition, she reminds us that historical documents do not provide unproblematic access to a clear "truth" and should not be used to construct master narratives that can then be used to decode the playful ambiguities of literary discourse.[8] For her, the New Philology offers the possibility of historical inquiry engineered by the belief that texts represent geographically and temporally situated instances,

---

6. Though Patterson does not discuss the "New Philology" specifically, see his discussion of the work of Robertsonian exegetics and the New Criticism on the production of medieval studies as a discipline: "Historical Criticism and the Development of Chaucer Studies," in *Negotiating the Past: The Historical Understanding of Medieval Literature* (Madison: University of Wisconsin Press, 1987), 3–39. For a thorough assessment of the New Philology since 1990, see Sarah Kay, "Analytical Survey 3: The New Philology," *New Medieval Literatures* 3 (1999): 295–326.

7. Gabrielle M. Spiegel, "History, Historicism, and the Social Logic of the Text in the Middle Ages," *Speculum* 65.1 (1990): 69.

8. See also Richard Firth Green, "John Ball's Letters: Literary History and Historical Literature," in *Chaucer's England: Literature in Historical Context*, ed. Barbara A. Hanawalt (Minneapolis: University of Minnesota Press, 1992), 176–200.

thus allowing scholars to focus on the locality and material specificities of the text or artifact at hand. The effect of such work, she suggests, is to give analytic weight to both the literary and the historical without absorbing one into the other. Thus, the promise of the New Philology is that the material specificity of the text will open up a way to return to the historical without transforming historical documents into literary artifacts or vice versa.

Recently, a challenge has been issued in medieval literary studies to be "post-historical." For Elizabeth Scala and Sylvia Federico, the editors of *The Post-Historical Middle Ages*, this means taking up Paul Strohm's "strategic disregard of the literary/non-literary divide," particularly in examining the usefulness of the term "text."[9] Paying attention to the wide register of witnessing in the later Middle Ages performs this metacritical work, and it does so specifically by calling attention to the ways various media—the body, the voice, the document—all lay claim to, even compete for, the authoritative designation of "text." As this book has shown, *Piers Plowman* is particularly dedicated to dramatizing the multiple ways the idea of "text" can be invoked, manipulated, and used as a tool of power. In addition, the poem's numerous editions, emendations, and marginal glosses have been a wellspring of historical evidence for editors and readers of the poem's variants. Yet as Lee Patterson has noted, such scholarly work often grounds itself in the authority of assessment, insofar as "external evidence" might be understood as material, historical, and unassailable, while "internal evidence" can be considered the product of individual interpretation and thus can be seen as unreliable, even whimsical or idiosyncratic.[10] Chapter 4 demonstrated that Langland examines the conceptual boundaries between idiosyncratic experience and communal knowledge derived from books and documents. We might use Langland's sustained investigation of the witness as a hinge between individual experience and communal knowledge to redraw the boundaries between "external" and "internal" evidence, reconsidering our own reassurances of what constitutes incontrovertible data and what suspiciously emerges from the singular mind of the reader, editor, or scholar.

The calls to question the status of historicism as a dominant mode of analyzing medieval texts and culture emerge from an enduring discussion in medieval studies that both uses the New Historicism and critiques it as a discipline that celebrates the Renaissance as a radical shift in the history of the

9. Sylvia Federico and Elizabeth Scala, "Getting Post-Historical," in *The Post-Historical Middle Ages*, 7. Paul Strohm's text to which they refer here is *Theory and the Premodern Text* (Minneapolis: University of Minnesota Press, 2000).

10. "The Logic of Textual Criticism and the Way of Genius: The Kane-Donaldson *Piers Plowman* in Historical Perspective," in *Negotiating the Past*, 77–78.

subject, at the expense of the Middle Ages. To offer one especially pointed example, Stephen Greenblatt announced in *Renaissance Self-Fashioning* that "in the sixteenth century there appears to be an increased self-consciousness about the fashioning of human identity as a manipulable, artful process."[11] This statement has, not surprisingly, raised hackles among some medievalists.[12] David Aers famously responded by countering that *Renaissance Self-Fashioning* is innocent of the analysis of medieval culture it would need to satisfyingly support its argument, and Patterson similarly argued that Greenblatt's assertion shows how "the Middle Ages has functioned as an all-purpose alternative to whatever quality the present has wished to ascribe to itself."[13] For Patterson, medieval selfhood can be characterized by "the dialectic between an inward subjectivity and an external world that alienates it from both itself and its divine source."[14] Significantly, this dialectic is forcefully visible in witness depositions such as Margery Baxter's as well as in vernacular texts that take witness testimony as the impetus for thinking about the relationship between an inward self and its articulation to an external world, both earthly and divine. The *Testimony of William Thorpe* also offers a prime example of the way internal subjectivity might be structured by the external discourses, such as testimony, that claim to express it.

Strikingly, Greenblatt's New Historicist aims require the authenticating testimony of a medieval witness to authorize the temporal and conceptual boundaries he seeks to produce. His argument about the status of the printed book in Thomas More's self-fashioning turns to Foxe's *Book of Martyrs* and begins, curiously, with William Thorpe. Noting Thorpe's technique of falling silent in response to Arundel's histrionic questioning, Greenblatt argues that Thorpe seeks to act like Christ at his inquisition:

> A long tradition of suffering for the faith lies behind this eloquent silence, a tradition reaching back to Christ's own initial silence before Caiaphas: "And the chief priest arose and said to him: answerest thou nothing? How is it that these bear witness against thee? But Jesus held his peace" (Matt.

---

11. Stephen Greenblatt, *Renaissance Self-Fashioning* (Chicago: University of Chicago Press, 1980), 2.

12. For an assessment of the status of New Historicism in Chaucer studies specifically, see David Matthews, "Recent Chaucer Criticism: New Historicism, New Discontents?" *Modern Philology* 106.1 (2008): 117–27.

13. David Aers, "A Whisper in the Ear of Early Modernists; or, Reflections on Literary Critics Writing the 'History of the Subject,'" in *Culture and History, 1350–1600*, ed. David Aers (Detroit, MI: Wayne State University Press, 1992), 177–202.

14. Lee Patterson, *Chaucer and the Subject of History* (Madison: University of Wisconsin Press, 1991), 8.

26: 29–39). Caught in a terrifying situation and facing the rage of the great and powerful, the heretic William Thorpe, like the imprisoned Thomas More, found refuge in an identification with Christ. (77)

Greenblatt further claims that Thorpe's identification with Christ marks "a simultaneous affirmation and effacement of personal identity" (77). Greenblatt's turn to Thorpe as More's self-fashioning predecessor is particularly notable given his citation of Matthew, which specifically depicts Christ as a witness. Though he presumably wants to show the centrality of the printed book in dramatic depictions of abjuration and relapse, Greenblatt here takes Thorpe as a flesh-and-blood figure, a biographical person from the past whose real-life experiences serve as a backdrop for those of Thomas More. He misses the layered ways in which Thorpe functions as a Christ-like witness, testifying not only to the structures of power that animate his text and perhaps merit its inclusion in Foxe's compilation, but also to how a text, and, perhaps, a life, from the turn of the fifteenth century can all too easily be assimilated into a process of self-fashioning that has been declared a product of the sixteenth century. Greenblatt does not distinguish between Thorpe as historical actor and Thorpe as textual agent. At the very least, he treats Thorpe like More, although More's biography can be assessed through multiple extant documents and texts in a way that Thorpe's cannot.

This suppression of the boundary between a historical or biographical figure and literary persona specifically occurs in his discussion of Thorpe as a witness, and it seems the implicit use of "witnessing" in his New Historicist work authorizes the archival translation of literary or historical presence into full biography. A few years ago, Greenblatt wrote a biography of Shakespeare, titled *Will in the World: How Shakespeare Became Shakespeare*, in which he begins with and ends with the same caveat about the insufficiency of historical data in reconstructing a life. For example, when he discusses the order of Shakespeare's works, he writes, "After many decades of ingenious research, scholars have reached a relatively stable consensus, but even this time line, so crucial for any biography, is inevitably somewhat speculative."[15] Later, in his "Biographical Notes," he reminds us, "All biographical studies of Shakespeare necessarily build on the assiduous, sometimes obsessive archival research and speculation of many generations of scholars and writers" (391). Undeterred by Greenblatt's careful caveats, the playwright Charles Mee responded with enthusiasm for the book's "authentic" reporting of

---

15. Stephen Greenblatt, *Will in the World: How Shakespeare Became Shakespeare* (New York: Norton, 2004), 18.

Shakespeare's life. "At last," he says, "the book Shakespeare has deserved: a brilliant book written by a virtual eyewitness who understands how a playwright takes the stuff of his life and makes it into theater."

Mee's designation of Greenblatt as a "virtual eyewitness" to Shakespeare's life—and to the apparently intimate relationship between Shakespeare's life and his works—demonstrates how witnessing sometimes operates as a shorthand for a kind of historical realism or authenticity, muddying the line between history and fiction in a way that would surely make Spiegel uncomfortable. It also demonstrates that the term can be extended to conceptualize as "eyewitnesses" those who were certainly not present at the event, turning the New Historicist scholar and biographer into a legalistic figure with personal and immediate access to historical truths. The term thus can transform a series of archival documents, or, as Greenblatt would put it, "speculations," into a realized life that both emerges from those documents and precedes them. Notably, the same year he published *Will in the World*, Greenblatt praised David Riggs's biography of Marlowe as a "fine, full-blooded biography," similarly using language that suggests the possibility that an assiduous researcher who makes full use of archives can animate a series of texts and in doing so, re-embody a historical figure and give life to the past.[16] In these biographical accounts of early modern playwrights and poets, the philological vocabulary of manuscript "witnesses" comes to describe the idiosyncratic work of the individual scholar.

Witness Testimony and Premodern Biography

In pointing out these cases in which the term "witness" signals the historical accuracy and power of biography, I certainly do not want to scold the reviewers for their praise of these works. Rather, I want to suggest that we might consider witnessing as a way to refine and rehabilitate the scholarly opportunities of premodern biography. Indeed, another scholarly avenue that may emerge through the consideration of witness testimony in late medieval legal and literary culture is the possibility of biographical work in medieval studies. As Daniel Birkholz has claimed, for medieval scholars, "biographical desire is never absent from the system of literary interpretation. Literary-historical personae, from patrons to authors to scribes to readers, are constructed in response to unsatisfactory prevailing wisdoms."[17]

16. David Riggs, *The World of Christopher Marlowe* (New York: Henry Holt, 2004).
17. Daniel Birkholz, "Biography After Historicism: The Harley Lyrics, the Hereford Map, and the Life of Roger de Breynton," in *The Post-Historical Middle Ages*, 168.

Birkholz does not advocate a recuperative kind of biography, in which the "real" or "hidden" life of a person is uncovered and detailed. Such work would not only be impossible, given the extant materials we have from the Middle Ages, it would work against the more complex aims of biography: that is, to imagine how a life can understood as and rendered into a historical artifact or set of artifacts.[18] Witness testimony could put a decidedly legalistic spin on such a project: how do legal documents account for, even judge, a life? How can historical and literary personae be constructed out of interrogations, or last wills and testaments, or writs of complaint? What are the historical and the literary drives that shape testimonial discourse?

Witness testimony foregrounds that such questions are always diachronic, insofar as they probe the ways the Middle Ages might have imagined and constructed personae. Witnessing also foregrounds our own desires to animate those personae, to know them, and even to judge them ourselves. By paying attention to the forms and practices of witnessing, as well as to the implicit claims of authenticity and truth witnessing assumes, we can read across the past and the present to conceptualize what it means to produce and to analyze the "evidence" of a life. Indeed, we can ask ourselves by what means we produce and analyze the Middle Ages itself. If we, as scholars of the Middle Ages, are witnesses to it, then we must take care to recognize our own roles as *narratores* of the past. Like the Man of Law, we too sometimes uneasily navigate evidence and narration, truth and fiction. Like Piers Plowman, we must always question the media by which truth is mediated and manufactured. And like William Thorpe, in attesting to the medieval past and to our own scholarly desires, we seek to produce texts that will exceed their own moments of production.

---

18. For an interesting discussion of this issue vis-à-vis the editorial work of gathering external textual evidence, see John M. Bowers, "*Piers Plowman*'s William Langland: Editing the Text, Writing the Author's Life," *YLS* 9 (1995): 65–94.

works cited

Primary Sources

An Apology for Lollard Doctrines. Ed. James Henthorn Todd. Camden Society. Vol. 20. London: John Bower Nichols and Son, 1842.
Aspin, Isabel. *Anglo-Norman Political Songs.* Oxford: Anglo-Norman Text Society, 1953.
Audelay, John. *The Poems of John Audelay.* Ed. Ella Keats Whiting. Oxford: Oxford University Press, 1931.
Augustine, *Confessions.* Trans. R. S. Pine-Coffin. New York: Penguin Classics, 1972.
———. *The Works of St. Augustine: Sermons.* Ed. John E. Rotelle. New York: New City, 1995.
Barr, Helen, ed. *The Piers Plowman Tradition.* London: J. M. Dent, 1993.
Bede. *The Ecclesiastical History of the English Nation.* Ed. J. A. Giles. London: Henry G. Bohn, 1849.
Bernard Gui. *Manuel de L'Inquisiteur.* Ed. and trans. G. Mollat. Paris: Belles Lettres, 2006.
Bevington, David, ed. *Medieval Drama.* Boston: Houghton Mifflin, 1975.
Biblia Latina cum Glossa ordinaria. Vol. 3. Turnhout: Brepols, 1992.
The Book of Vices and Virtues. Ed. W. Nelson Francis. Oxford: Oxford University Press, 1942.
Bracton, Henry. *De legibus et consuetudinibus Angliae.* Trans. Samuel E. Thorne. Cambridge, MA: Harvard University Press, 1968.
Caesarius of Heisterbach, *Dialogue on Miracles.* Trans. H. von E. Scott and C. C. Swinton Bland. New York: Harcourt, Brace, and Co., 1929.
Calendar of Patent Rolls, Edward III. Vol. 12: 1361–64. London: Public Record Office, 1912.
Calendar of Patent Rolls, Edward III. Vol. 14: 1367–70. London: Public Record Office, 1913.
Chaucer, Geoffrey. *The Riverside Chaucer.* 3rd ed. Ed. Larry D. Benson et al. Boston: Houghton Mifflin, 1987.
Christine de Pizan. *The Book of the City of Ladies.* New York: Norton, 1988.
Commentaire sur Daniel. Trans. Maurice Lefèvre. Sources Chretiennes 14. Paris, 1947.
Commentarii on Danielem. Ed. F. Glorie. Turnhout: Brepols, 1968.
Commentary on Daniel. Trans. Gleason L. Archer. Grand Rapids, MI: Baker, 1958.
Concilia Magnae Britanniae. Ed. David Wilkins. London: Gosling, Gyles, Woodward, and Davis, 1737.

Dan Michel's Ayenbite of Inwit. Ed. Richard Morris. London: Trubner and Co., 1866.
Decrees of the Ecumenical Councils. Vol. 1. Ed. Norman P. Tanner. Washington, DC: Georgetown University Press, 1990.
Decretum Gratiani Universi Iuris Canonici. Venice, 1567.
The "Didascalicon" of Hugh of Saint Victor. Trans. Jerome Taylor. New York: Columbia University Press, 1991.
Dives and Pauper. Ed. Priscilla Heath Barnam. Oxford: Oxford University Press, 1980.
Durand, William. *Speculum judiciale*. Basel, 1574.
English Historical Documents, 1189-1327. Ed. Harry Rothwell. London: Eyre and Spottiswode, 1975.
English Lawsuits from William I to Richard I. Vol. 2. Ed. R. C. Van Caenegem. London: Selden Society, 1990-91.
English Metrical Homilies from Manuscripts of the Fourteenth Century. Ed. John Small. Edinburgh: W. Paterson, 1862.
The English Works of John Wyclif. Ed. F. D. Matthew. London: Keagan Paul, Trench, and Trubner, 1880; repr. 1902.
The Examination of William Thorpe. In *Two Wycliffite Texts*. Ed. Anne Hudson. Oxford: Oxford University Press, 1993.
Exposition of the Psalms, 33-50. Vol. 10. Trans. Maria Boulding. New York: New City Press, 2000.
Fasciculus Morum. Ed. and trans. Siegfried Wenzel. University Park: Pennsylvania State University Press, 1989.
Fasciculi Zizaniorum. Ed. Rev. Walter Waddington Shirley. London: Longman, Brown, Green, Longmans, and Roberts, 1858.
Fortescue, Sir John. *De laudibus legem Anglie*. Ed. and trans. S. B. Chrimes. Cambridge: Cambridge University Press, 1949.
Fouke le Fitz Waryn. Trans. Thomas E. Kelly. In *Robin Hood and Other Outlaw Tales*. Ed. Stephen Knight and Thomas H. Ohlgren. Kalamazoo, MI: Medieval Institute Publications, 1997.
Four Romances of England. Ed. Ronald B. Herzman, Graham Drake, and Eve Salisbury. Kalamazoo, MI: Medieval Institute Publications, 1999.
Foxe, John. *Acts and Monuments*. Princeton University, William H. Scheide Library. MS 11.2.1.
———. *Acts and Monuments*. Ed. George Townsend. London: Seeley, Burnside, and Seeley, 1843.
Gerhoh of Reichersberg. *Commentarius Aureus in Psalmos et Cantica Ferialia*. Patrologia Cursus Completus: Series Latina. Vol. 193. Paris, 1844-64.
Gower, John. *Confessio Amantis*. Vol. 2. Ed. Russell A. Peck. Kalamazoo, MI: Medieval Institute Publications, 2003.
Henryson, Robert. *The Testament of Cresseid*. In *The Poems of Robert Henryson*. Ed. Robert L. Kindrick. Kalamazoo, MI: Medieval Institute Publications, 1997.
The Heresy Trials in the Diocese of Norwich, 1428-31. Ed. Norman P. Tanner. Camden 4th Series. Vol. 20. London: Royal Historical Society, 1977.
The Historia Regum Britanniae of Geoffrey of Monmouth. Ed. Robert Ellis Jones. London: Longman, Green, and Co., 1929.
Hoccleve, Thomas. *The Regiment of Princes*. Ed. Charles R. Blyth. Kalamazoo, MI: Medieval Institute Publications, 1999.
Hoccleve's Works I: The Minor Poems. Ed. Frederick J. Furnivall. London, 1892.
Hoccleve's Works III: The "Regiment of Princes" and Fourteen Minor Poems. Ed. Frederick J. Furnivall. London, 1897.
Isidore of Seville. *Metalogicon*. Ed. C. C. J. Webb. Oxford: Oxford University Press, 1929.
Jack Upland, Friar Daw's Reply, and Upland's Rejoinder. Ed. P. L. Heyworth. Oxford: Oxford University Press, 1968.
Jacobus de Voragine. *Gilte Legende*. Vol. 1. Ed. Richard Hamer. Oxford: Oxford University Press, 2006.

Jerome. *Letter to Eustochium.* In *The Principal Works of St. Jerome.* Trans. W. H. Fremantle. Grand Rapids, MI: William B. Eerdmans, 1913.
Knighton, Henry. *Knighton's Chronicle.* Ed. and trans. G. H. Martin. Oxford: Clarendon, 1995.
Lais de Marie de France. Trans. Laurence Harf-Lancner. Paris: Lettres Gothiques, 1990.
The Lais of Marie de France. Trans. Robert Hanning and Joan Ferrante. Durham, NC: Labyrinth, 1978.
Langland, William. *The Vision of Piers Plowman.* 2nd ed. Ed. A. V. C. Schmidt. London: Everyman, 1995.
Lanterne of Li3t. Ed. Lilian M. Swinburn. London: Kegan Paul, Trench, Trubner, & Co., 1917.
De lapsu Susannae. Ed. Ignatius Cazzaniga. Turin: G. B. Paraviae, 1948.
The Lay Folks' Mass Book. Ed. T. F. Simmons. London: Trubner, 1968.
Love, Nicholas. *The Mirror of the Blessed Life of Jesus Christ.* Ed. Michael G. Sargent. Exeter: University of Exeter Press, 2005.
Matthew, F. D. "The Trial of Richard Wyche." *The English Historical Review* 5.19 (1890): 530–44.
The Middle English Charters of Christ. Ed. M. C. Spalding. Bryn Mawr: Bryn Mawr College, 1914.
Middle English Verse Romances. Ed. Donald B. Sands. New York: Holt, Rinehart and Winston, 1966.
The Minor Poems of the Vernon MS. Vol. 1. Ed. Carl Horstmann. London: Kegan Paul, Trench, Trubner, & Co, 1892.
Mozley, J. H. "Susanna and the Elders: Three Medieval Poems." *Studi Medievali* new series 3 (1930): 27–52.
Musurillo, Herbert, trans. *The Acts of the Christian Martyrs.* Oxford: Clarendon, 1972.
De officiis. Vol. 1. Ed. and trans. Ivor J. Davidson. Oxford: Oxford University Press, 2001.
Oxfordshire Forests, 1246–1609. Ed. Beryl Schumer. Oxfordshire: Oxfordshire Record Company, 2004.
Patrologia Latina. Vols. 1–221. Ed. Jacques-Paul Migne. Paris, 1844–64.
The Pistel of Swete Susan. Ed. Russell A. Peck. In *Heroic Women from the Old Testament in Middle English Verse.* Kalamazoo, MI: Medieval Institute Publications, 1991.
Pilii, Tancredi, Gratiae, Libri de iudiciorum ordine. Ed. Friedrich C. Bergmann. Bottingen, 1842.
The Poems of the Pearl Manuscript. Ed. Malcolm Andrew and Ronald Waldron. Exeter: University of Exeter Press, 2002.
Powicke, F. M. and C. R. Cheney, eds. *Councils and Synods with Other Documents relating to the English Church II: 1205–1313.* Oxford: Clarendon, 1964.
Pyers plowmans exhortation unto the lordes, knightes and burgoysses of the parlyamenthouse. London: Imprinted by Anthony Scoloker dwelling in the Sauoy tentes without Templebarre, 1550.
Registrum Johannis Trefnant. Ed. William W. Capes. London: Canterbury and York Society, 1816.
Richard de Bury, *The "Philobiblon" of Richard de Bury.* Ed. Michael Maclagan. Trans. E. C. Thomas. Oxford: Basil Blackwell, 1960.
Robert Mannyng of Brunne. *Handlyng Synne.* Ed. Idelle Sullens. Binghamton, NY: Medieval and Renaissance Studies, 1983.
Rogeri Dymmok Liber Contra XII Errores et Hereses Lollardorum. Ed. H. S. Cronin. London: Kegan Paul, Trench, Trubner, & Co, 1922.
Rotuli parliamentorum; ut et petitiones, et placita in parliamento. Vols. 1–3. Ed. J. Strachey. London, 1767–77.
Rymes of Robyn Hood. Ed. R. B. Dobson and J. Taylor. Pittsburgh, PA: Sutton, 1976.
Sancti Ambrosii Mediolanensis, De officiis. Ed. Mauritius Testard. Turnhout: Brepols, 2000.
Select Cases in the Court of King's Bench under Edward III. Vol. 5. Ed. G. O. Sayles. London: Selden Society, 1958.
Select Cases of Defamation to 1600. Ed. Richard Helmholz. London: Selden Society, 1985.
Select Pleas of the Forest. Ed. G. J. Turner. London: Bernard Quaritch, 1901.

The Shewings of Julian of Norwich. Ed. Georgia Ronan Crampton. Kalamazoo, MI: Medieval Institute Publications, 1993.
Speculum vitae. Ed. Ralph Hanna. Oxford: Oxford University Press, 2008.
The Statutes of the Realm. Vols. 1–11. Ed. A. Luders et al. London: Dawsons, 1810–28.
Supra Danielem XIII. In *Commentariorum in Danielem, Libri III, S. Hieronymi Presbyteri Opera.* Brepols: Turnhout, 1964.
Susannah: An Alliterative Poem of the Fourteenth Century. Ed. Alice Miskimin. New Haven, CT: Yale University Press, 1969.
Tilley, Maureen. "An Anonymous Letter to a Woman Named Susanna." In *Religions of Late Antiquity in Practice.* Ed. Richard Valantasis. Princeton, NJ: Princeton University Press, 2000. 218–29.
Tractatus de legibus et consuetudinibus regni Anglie qui Glanvilla vocatur. Ed. and trans. G. D. G. Hall. Oxford: Oxford University Press, 1993.
The Vision of Pierce Plowman, Now Fyrste Imprynted. Short-Title Catalogue 11906. Ed. A. W. Pollard et al. London, 1926.
Wyclif, John. *De Eucharistia Tractaus Maior.* Ed. J. Loserth. London: Trubner & Co, 1892.
———. *Tractatus de apostasia.* Ed. Michael Henry Dziewicki. London: Trubner & Co, 1889.
———. *On the Truth of Holy Scripture.* Trans. I. C. Levy. Kalamazoo, MI: Medieval Institute Publications, 2001.
———. *De Veritate Sacrae Scripturae.* Ed. R. Buddensieg. London: Wyclif Society, 1905.

Secondary Sources

Aers, David. *Sanctifying Signs.* Notre Dame, IN: University of Notre Dame Press, 2004.
———. "*Vox Populi* and the Literature of 1381." In *Cambridge History of Medieval English Literature,* ed. David Wallace. Cambridge: Cambridge University Press, 1999. 432–53.
———. "A Whisper in the Ear of Early Modernists; or, Reflections on Literary Critics Writing the 'History of the Subject.'" In *Culture and History, 1350–1600,* ed. David Aers. Detroit, MI: Wayne State University Press, 1992. 177–202.
Akbari, Susan Conklin. "Placing the Jews in Late Medieval English Literature." In *Orientalism and the Jews,* ed. Ivan Davidson Kalmar and Derek J. Penslar. Waltham, MA: Brandeis University Press, 2005. 32–50.
Alford, John A. "Literature and Law in Medieval England." *PMLA* 92.5 (1977): 941–51.
———. *Piers Plowman: A Glossary of Legal Diction.* Cambridge: D. S. Brewer, 1988.
Allmand, Christopher. *The Hundred Years War: England and France at War, c. 1300–1450.* Cambridge: Cambridge University Press, 1988.
Amodio, Mark. *Writing the Oral Tradition: Oral Poetics and Literate Culture in Medieval England.* Notre Dame, IN: University Notre Dame Press, 2004.
Amsler, Mark C. "Rape and Silence: Ovid's Mythography and Medieval Readers." In *Representing Rape in Medieval and Early Modern Literature,* ed. Christine Rose and Elizabeth Robertson. New York: Palgrave, 2001. 61–96.
Astell, Ann W. "Response to 'Langland and Allegory: A Proposition.'" *Yearbook of Langland Studies* 15 (2001): 43–46.
Aston, Margaret. *Lollards and Their Books.* London: Hambledon, 1984.
Baker, Denise. "The Pardons of *Piers Plowman.*" *Neuphilologische Mitteilungen* 85 (1984): 462–72.
Baker, J. H. *The Order of Serjeants at Law.* London: Selden Society, 1984.
Baldwin, John W. "The Intellectual Preparation for the Canon of 1215 Against Ordeals." *Speculum* 36 (1961): 613–36.
Bale, Anthony. *The Jew in the Medieval Book: English Antisemitisms, 1350–1500.* Cambridge: Cambridge University Press, 2006.

Barney, Stephen A. *The Penn Commentary on "Piers Plowman."* Vol. 5. Philadelphia: University of Pennsylvania Press, 2006.
Barr, Helen. *Signes and Sothe: Language and the Piers Plowman Tradition.* Cambridge: D. S. Brewer, 1994.
Bartlett, Robert. *Trial by Fire and Water: The Medieval Judicial Ordeal.* Oxford: Clarendon, 1988.
Beckwith, Sarah. *Signifying God: Social Relation and Symbolic Act in the York Corpus Christi Plays.* Chicago: University of Chicago Press, 2001.
Bennett, Michael. "Edward III's Entail and the Succession to the Crown, 1376-1471." *English Historical Review* 113 (1998): 580-609.
Birkholz, David. "Biography After Historicism: The Harley Lyrics, the Hereford Map, and the Life of Roger de Breynton." In *The Post-Historical Middle Ages.* New York: Palgrave, 2009. 161-90.
Birnes, William J. "Christ as Advocate: The Legal Metaphor of *Piers Plowman.*" *Annuale Mediaevale* 16 (1975): 71-93.
Bostick, Curtis V. *The Antichrist and the Lollards.* Leiden: Brill, 1998.
Bowers, John M. "*Piers Plowman*'s William Langland: Editing the Text, Writing the Author's Life." *Yearbook of Langland Studies* 9 (1995): 65-94.
Bradbury, Nancy Mason. "The Erosion of Oath-Based Relationships: A Cultural Context for *Athelston.*" *Medium Aevum* 73 (2004): 189-204.
Bynum, Caroline Walker. *Metamorphosis and Identity.* New York: Zone, 2001.
Camille, Michael. "The Book as Flesh and Fetish in Richard de Bury's *Philobiblon.*" In *The Book and the Body,* ed. Dolores Warwick Frese and Katherine O'Brien O'Keeffe. Notre Dame, IN: University of Notre Dame Press, 1997. 34-77.
———. *The Gothic Idol.* Cambridge: Cambridge University Press, 1991.
Campbell, Mary B. *The Witness and the Other World.* Ithaca, NY: Cornell University Press, 1988.
Cannon, Christopher. "*Raptus* in the Chaumpaigne Release and a Newly Discovered Document Concerning the Life of Geoffrey Chaucer." *Speculum* 68 (1993): 74-94.
Carruthers, Mary. "Allegory without the Teeth: Reflections on Figural Language in *Piers Plowman.*" *Yearbook of Langland Studies* 19 (2005): 27-44.
Cheney, C. R. *Notaries Public in England in the Thirteenth and Fourteenth Centuries.* Oxford: Clarendon, 1972.
Clanchy, M.T. *From Memory to Written Record: England, 1066-1307.* 2nd ed. Cambridge, MA: Blackwell, 1993.
Clifton, Nicole. "The Romance Convention of the Disguised Duel and the Climax of *Piers Plowman.*" *Yearbook of Langland Studies* 7 (1993): 123-28.
Clopper, Lawrence M. "Langland and Allegory: A Proposition." *Yearbook of Langland Studies* 15 (2001): 32-45.
Coghill, Nevill K. "The Pardon of Piers Plowman." In *Style and Symbolism in "Piers Plowman,"* ed. Robert J. Blanch. Knoxville: University of Tennessee Press, 1969. 40-86.
Cohen, Jeffrey Jerome. *Medieval Identity Machines: Hybridity, Identity, and Monstrosity in Medieval England.* Minneapolis: University of Minnesota Press, 2003.
———. "Midcolonial." In *The Postcolonial Middle Ages,* ed. Jeffrey Jerome Cohen. New York: Palgrave, 2001. 1-18.
———. *Of Giants: Sex, Monsters, and the Middle Ages.* Minneapolis: University of Minnesota Press, 1999.
Cohen, Jeremy. *Living Letters of the Law: Ideas of the Jew in Medieval Christianity.* Los Angeles and Berkeley: University of California Press, 1999.
Cole, Andrew. *Literature and Heresy in the Age of Chaucer.* Cambridge: Cambridge University Press, 2008.
Coleman, Janet. "Aurality." In *Middle English,* ed. Paul Strohm. Oxford: Oxford University Press, 2007. 68-85.

———. *Public Reading and the Reading Public in Late Medieval England and France.* Cambridge: Cambridge University Press, 1996.

Colman, Rebecca V. "Reason and Unreason in Early Medieval Law." *Journal of Interdisciplinary History* 4.4 (1974): 571–91.

Cooper, Helen. "Gender and Personification in *Piers Plowman*." *Yearbook of Langland Studies* 5 (1991): 31–48.

———. *The Structure of the "Canterbury Tales."* Oxford: Clarendon, 1989.

Copeland, Rita. *Pedagogy, Intellectuals, and Dissent in the Later Middle Ages: Lollardy and Ideas of Learning.* Cambridge: Cambridge University Press, 2005.

———. "Sophistic, Spectrality, Iconoclasm." In *Images, Idolatry, and Iconoclasm in Late Medieval England,* ed. Jeremy Dimmick, James Simpson, and Nicolette Zeeman. Oxford: Oxford University Press, 2002. 112–30.

———. "Why Women Can't Read: Medieval Hermeneutics, Statutory Law, and the Lollard Heresy Trials." In *Representing Women: Law, Literature, and Feminism,* ed. Susan Sage Heinzelman and Zipporah Batshaw Wiseman. Durham, NC: Duke University Press, 1994. 253–86.

———. "William Thorpe and his Lollard Community." In *Bodies and Disciplines: Intersections of Literature and History in Fifteenth-Century England,* ed. David Wallace and Barbara A. Hanawalt. Minneapolis: University of Minnesota Press, 1996. 199–221.

Correale, Robert M. and Mary Hamels, eds. *Sources and Analogues of the "Canterbury Tales."* Vol. 2. Cambridge: D. S. Brewer, 2009.

Craun, Edwin D. *The Hands of the Tongue: Essays on Deviant Speech.* Kalamazoo, MI: Medieval Institute Publications, 2007.

Curry Woods, Marjorie and Rita Copeland. "Classroom and Confession." In *Cambridge History of Medieval English Literature,* ed. David Wallace. Cambridge: Cambridge University Press, 1999. 376–406.

Dagenais, John and Margaret R. Greer. "Decolonizing the Middle Ages." *Journal of Medieval and Early Modern Studies* 30 (2000): 431–48.

Dahmus, Joseph H. *The Prosecution of John Wyclyf.* New Haven, CT: Yale University Press, 1952.

Davlin, Mary Clemente. "Kynde Knowyng as a Major Theme in *Piers Plowman* B." *Review of English Studies* new series 22 (1971): 1–19.

Delany, Sheila, ed. *Chaucer and the Jews.* New York: Routledge, 2002.

Dembrowski, Peter. "Learned Latin Treatises in French: Inspiration, Plagiarism, and Translation." *Viator* 17 (1986): 255–69.

Derrida, Jacques. *Demeure: Fiction and Testimony.* Trans. Elizabeth Rottenberg. Stanford, CA: Stanford University Press, 2000.

———. *Limited, Inc.* Trans. Samuel Weber and Jeffrey Mehlman. Evanston, IL: Northwestern University Press, 1988.

———. *Specters of Marx: The State of Debt, the Work of Mourning, and the New International.* Trans. Peggy Kamuf. New York: Routledge, 1994.

Dinshaw, Carolyn. "Pale Faces: Race, Religion, and Affect in Chaucer's Texts and Their Readers." *Studies in the Age of Chaucer* 23 (2001): 19–41.

Donaldson, E. Talbot. "Chaucer the Pilgrim." *PMLA* 69.4 (1954): 928–36.

———. "The Grammar of Book's Speech in *Piers Plowman*." In *Studies in Language and Literature in Honor of Margaret Schlauch,* ed. Mieczyslaw Brahmer, Stanislaw Helsztynski, and Julian Krzyzanowski. Warsaw: Polish Scientific Institute Press, 1966. 103–9.

Donohue, Charles. "Biology and the Origins of the Jury." *Law and History Review* 17.3 (1999): 591–96.

———. "Proof by Witnesses in the Church Courts: An Imperfect Reception of the Learned Law." In *On the Laws and Customs of England,* ed. Morris S. Arnold et al. Chapel Hill: University of North Carolina Press, 1981. 127–58.

Dove, Mary. *The First English Bible: The Text and Context of the Wycliffite Versions*. Cambridge: Cambridge University Press, 2007.
Duffy, Eamon. *Stripping of the Altars*. 2nd ed. New Haven, CT: Yale University Press, 2005.
Edwards, A. S. G. "'I Speke in Prose': *Man of Law's Tale*, 96." *Neuphilologishe Mitteilungen* 92 (1991): 469–70.
Enders, Jody. *Rhetoric and the Origins of Medieval Drama*. Ithaca, NY: Cornell University Press, 1992.
Erler, Mary C. *Women, Reading, and Piety in Late Medieval England*. Cambridge: Cambridge University Press, 2002.
Federico, Sylvia and Elizabeth Scala. "Getting Post-Historical." In *The Posthistorical Middle Ages*. New York: Palgrave, 2009. 1–12.
Florschuetz, Angela. "'A Mooder He Hath, but Fader Hath He Noon': Constructions of Genealogy in the *Clerk's Tale* and the *Man of Law's Tale*." *Chaucer Review* 44.1 (2009): 25–60.
Fowler, David C. *Piers the Plowman: Literary Relations of the A and B Texts*. Seattle: University of Washington Press, 1961.
———. "*Piers Plowman*: Will's 'Apologia pro vita sua.'" *Yearbook of Langland Studies* 13 (1999): 35–47.
Fowler, Elizabeth. *Literary Character: The Human Figure in Early English Writing*. Ithaca, NY: Cornell University Press, 2003.
Fradenburg, L. O. "Criticism, Anti-semitism, and Chaucer's *Prioress' Tale*." *Exemplaria* 1 (1989): 69–115.
———. "Pro Patria Mori." In *Imagining a Medieval English Nation*, ed. Kathy Lavezzo. Minneapolis: University of Minnesota Press, 2003. 3–38.
———. *Sacrifice Your Love: Psychoanalysis, Historicism, Chaucer*. Minneapolis: University of Minnesota Press, 2002.
———. "Simply Marvelous." *Studies in the Age of Chaucer* 26 (2004): 1–27.
Freeman, Thomas S. and Thomas F. Mayer, eds. *Martyrs and Martyrdom in England, c. 1400–1700*. Suffolk: Boydell, 2007.
Frisch, Andrea. "The Ethics of Testimony: A Genealogical Perspective." *Discourse* 25.1 (2004): 36–54.
Fuchs, Barbara and David J. Baker. "The Postcolonial Past." *Modern Language Quarterly* 65 (2004): 329–40.
Galloway, Andrew. "Intellectual Pregnancy, Metaphysical Femininity, and the Social Doctrine of the Trinity in *Piers Plowman*." *Yearbook of Langland Studies* 12 (1998): 117–52.
———. *The Penn Commentary on "Piers Plowman."* Vol. 1. Philadelphia: University of Pennsylvania Press, 2006.
———. "*Piers Plowman* and the Subject of the Law." *Yearbook of Langland Studies* 15 (2001): 117–28.
Gellrich, Jesse M. *The Idea of the Book in the Middle Ages: Language Theory, Mythology, and Fiction*. Ithaca, NY: Cornell University Press, 1985.
Giancarlo, Matthew. *Parliament and Literature in Late Medieval England*. Cambridge: Cambridge University Press, 2007.
Gill, Miriam. "From Urban Myth to Didactic Image: the Warning to Swearers." In *The Hands of the Tongue: Essays on Deviant Speech*, ed. Edwin D. Craun, Kalamazoo, MI: Medieval Institute Publicatioms, 2007. 137–60.
Gillespie, Vincent. "Vernacular Theology." In *Middle English*, ed. Paul Strohm. Oxford: Oxford University Press, 2007. 401–20.
Given, James Buchanan. *Society and Homicide in Thirteenth-Century England*. Stanford, CA: Stanford University Press, 1977.
Grady, Frank. *Representing Righteous Heathens in Late Medieval England*. New York: Palgrave, 2005.

Grafton, Anthony. *Forgers and Critics: Creativity and Duplicity in Western Scholarship*. Princeton, NJ: Princeton University Press, 1990.

Green, Donald C. "The Semantics of Power: *Maistrie* and *Soveraynetee* in *The Canterbury Tales*." *Modern Philology* 84.1 (1986): 18–23.

Green, Richard Firth. *A Crisis of Truth: Literature and Law in Ricardian England*. Philadelphia: University of Pennsylvania Press, 1999.

———. "John Ball's Letters: Literary History and Historical Literature." In *Chaucer's England: Literature in Historical Context*, ed. Barbara A. Hanawalt. Minneapolis: University of Minnesota Press, 1992. 176–200.

———. "Medieval Literature and the Law." In *Cambridge History of Medieval English Literature*, ed. David Wallace. Cambridge: Cambridge University Press, 1999. 407–31.

Greenblatt, Stephen. *Renaissance Self-Fashioning*. Chicago: University of Chicago Press, 1980.

———. *Will in the World: How Shakespeare Became Shakespeare*. New York: Norton, 2004.

Greetham, D. C. "Textual Forensics." *PMLA* 111.1 (1996): 32–51.

Grennen, Joseph E. "Chaucer's Man of Law and the Constancy of Justice." *Journal of English and Germanic Philology* 84.4 (1985): 498–514.

Hanawalt, Barbara A. "Ballads and Bandits: Fourteenth-Century Outlaws and the Robin Hood Poems." In *Chaucer's England: Literature in Historical Context*, ed. Barbara A. Hanawalt. Minneapolis: University of Minnesota Press, 1992. 154–75.

———. "Whose Story Was This? Rape Narratives in Medieval English Courts." In *Of Good and Ill Repute: Gender and Social Control in Medieval England*. Oxford: Oxford University Press, 1998. 124–41.

Hanna, Ralph. *London Literature, 1300–1380*. Cambridge: Cambridge University Press, 2005.

Harding, Alan. *The Law Courts of Medieval England*. London: Allen & Unwin, 1973.

Hatcher, John. "England in the Aftermath of the Black Death." *Past and Present* 144.1 (1994): 3–35.

Helmholz, Richard. *The Oxford History of the Laws of England*. Vol. 1. Oxford: Oxford University Press, 2004.

———. "*Quoniam contra falsam* (X 2.19.11) and the Court Records of the English Church." In *Als die Welt in die Akten kam*, ed. Susanne Lepsius and Thomas Wetzstein. Frankfurt: Vittorio Klostermann, 2008. 31–49.

Heng, Geraldine. *Empire of Magic: Medieval Romance and the Politics of Cultural Fantasy*. New York: Columbia University Press, 2003.

Hiatt, Alfred. *The Making of Medieval Forgeries: False Documents in Fifteenth-Century England*. Toronto: University of Toronto Press, 2004.

Highley, Christopher, and John N. King, eds. *John Foxe and His World*. Suffolk: Ashgate, 2002.

Hoffman, Richard L. "The Burning of 'Boke' in *Piers Plowman*." *Modern Language Quarterly* 25 (1964): 57–65.

Holsinger, Bruce W. "Medieval Studies, Postcolonial Studies, and the Genealogies of Critique." *Speculum* 77 (2002): 1195–1227.

———. *Music, Body, and Desire in Medieval Culture: Hildegard of Bingen to Chaucer*. Stanford, CA: Stanford University Press, 2001.

Hornbeck, J. Patrick. *What Is a Lollard?: Dissent and Belief in Late Medieval England*. Oxford: Oxford University Press, 2010.

Hudson, Anne. "The Examination of Lollards." *Bulletin of the Institute of Historical Research* 46 (1973): 145–59.

———. *The Premature Reformation: Wycliffite Texts and Lollard History*. Oxford: Oxford University Press, 1988.

Hyams, Paul R. *Rancor and Reconciliation in Medieval England*. Ithaca, NY: Cornell University Press, 2003.

———. "Trial by Ordeal: The Key to Proof in the Early Common Law." In *On the Laws and Cus-*

toms of England: Essays in Honor of Samuel E. Thorne, ed. Morris S. Arnold et al. Chapel Hill: University of North Carolina Press, 1981. 90–126.
Ingham, Patricia Clare and Michelle R. Warren, eds. *Postcolonial Moves: Medieval through Modern*. New York: Palgrave, 2003.
Ingham, Patricia Clare. *Sovereign Fantasies: Arthurian Romance and the Making of Britain*. Philadelphia: University of Pennsylvania Press, 2001.
Jackson, Bernard. "Susanna and the Singular History of Singular Witnesses." *Acta Juridica* 37 (1977): 37–54.
Jackson, J. A. "The Infinite Desire of *Pearl*." In *Levinas and Medieval Literature: The "Difficult Reading" of English and Rabbinic Texts*, ed. Ann W. Astell and J. A. Jackson. Pittsburgh, PA: Duquesne University Press, 2009. 157–84.
Jansen, Sharon L. "British Library MS Sloane 2578 and Popular Unrest in England." *Manuscripta* 29 (1985): 30–41.
———. "Politics, Protest, and a New *Piers Plowman* Fragment: The Voice of the Past in Tudor England." *Review of English Studies* new series 40.157 (1989): 93–99.
Jeffrey, David Lyle. "Victimization and Legal Abuse: The Wycliffite Retelling of the Story of Susannah." In *Retelling Tales: Essays in Honor of Russell Peck*, ed. Thomas Hahn and Alan Lupack. Cambridge: D. S. Brewer, 1997. 161–78.
Justice, Steven. *Writing and Rebellion: England in 1381*. Berkeley and Los Angeles: University of California Press, 1994.
Jurkowski, Maureen. "The Arrest of William Thorpe in Shrewsbury and the Anti-Lollard Statute of 1406." *Historical Research* 75 (2002): 273–95.
Kane, George. *Chaucer and Langland: Historical and Textual Approaches*. London: Athlone, 1989.
Kaske, R. E. "The Speech of 'Boke' in *Piers Plowman*." *Anglia* 77 (1959): 117–44.
Kay, Sarah. "Analytical Survey 3: The New Philology." *New Medieval Literatures* 3 (1999): 295–326.
Kelly, H. A. *Inquisitions and Other Trial Procedures in the Medieval West*. Aldershot: Ashgate Variorum Series, 2001.
Keen, Maurice. *The Outlaws of Medieval Legend*. New York: Routledge, 1961.
Kelen, Sarah A. *Langland's Early Modern Identities*. New York: Palgrave, 2007.
Kendall, Ritchie D. *The Drama of Dissent*. Chapel Hill: University of North Carolina Press, 1986.
Kennedy, Kathleen E. *Maintenance, Meed, and Marriage in Medieval English Literature*. New York: Palgrave, 2009.
———. "Retaining a Court of Chancery." *Yearbook of Langland Studies* 17 (2003): 175–89.
Kennedy, V. L. "The Moment of Consecration and the Elevation of the Host." *Mediaeval Studies* 6 (1944): 121–50.
Kerby-Fulton, Kathryn. "Langland and the Bibliographic Ego." In *Written Work: Langland, Labor, and Authorship*, ed. Steven Justice and Kathryn Kerby-Fulton. Philadelphia: University of Pennsylvania Press, 1997. 67–143.
King, John N. *English Reformation Literature: The Tudor Origins of the Protestant Tradition*. Princeton, NJ: Princeton University Press, 1982.
———. *Foxe's "Book of Martyrs" and Early Modern Print Culture*. Cambridge: Cambridge University Press, 2006.
Knapp, Ethan. *The Bureaucratic Muse: Thomas Hoccleve and the Literature of Late Medieval England*. University Park: Pennsylvania State University Press, 2001.
Kolve, V. A. *Chaucer and the Imagery of Narrative*. Stanford, CA: Stanford University Press, 1984.
Krug, Rebecca. *Reading Families: Women's Literate Practice in Late Medieval England*. Ithaca, NY: Cornell University Press, 2002.
Kruger, Steven F. *The Spectral Jew: Conversion and Embodiment in Medieval Europe*. Minneapolis: University of Minnesota Press, 2005.
LaCapra, Dominick. *History and Memory after Auschwitz*. Ithaca, NY: Cornell University Press, 1998.

Lampert, Lisa. *Gender and Jewish Difference from Paul to Shakespeare.* Philadelphia: University of Pennsylvania Press, 2004.
Lander, Jesse M. *Inventing Polemic: Religion, Print, and Literary Culture in Early Modern England.* Cambridge: Cambridge University Press, 2006.
Landman, James H. "'The Doom of Resoun': Accommodating Lay Interpretation in Late Medieval England." In *Medieval Crime and Social Control,* ed. Barbara A. Hanawalt and David Wallace. Minneapolis: University of Minnesota Press, 1999. 90–123.
———. "Proving Constant: Torture and the *Man of Law's Tale.*" *Studies in the Age of Chaucer* 20 (1998): 1–39.
Laub, Dori and Shoshanna Felman. *Testimony.* New York: Routledge, 1992.
Lavezzo, Kathy. "Beyond Rome: Mapping Gender and Justice in the *Man of Law's Tale.*" *Studies in the Age of Chaucer* 24 (2002): 149–80.
Lawton, David. "On Tearing—and Not Tearing—the Pardon." *Philological Quarterly* 60 (1981): 414–22.
Lea, H. C. *History of the Inquisition of the Middle Ages.* New York: Russell & Russell, 1955.
Leicester, Jr., H. Marshall. "The Art of Impersonation: A General Prologue to the *Canterbury Tales.*" *PMLA* 95 (1980): 213–24.
Levinas, Emmanuel. *Totality and Infinity: An Essay on Exteriority.* Trans. Alphonso Lingis. Pittsburgh, PA: Duquesne University Press, 1969.
Levy, I. C. *John Wyclif: Scriptural Logic, Real Presence, and the Parameters of Orthodoxy.* Milwaukee, WI: Marquette University Press, 2003.
Levy, Leonard W. *Origins of the Fifth Amendment.* Oxford: Oxford University Press, 1968.
Lindenbaum, Sheila. "London Texts and Literate Practice." In *Cambridge History of Medieval English Literature,* ed. David Wallace. Cambridge: Cambridge University Press, 1999. 284–309.
Little, Katherine C. *Confession and Resistance: Defining the Self in Late Medieval England.* Notre Dame, IN: University of Notre Dame Press, 2006.
Machan, Tim. "Medieval Multilingualism and Gower's Literary Practice." *Studies in Philology* 103 (2006): 1–25.
MacNair, Mike. "Vicinage and the Antecedents of the Jury." *Law and History Review* 17.3 (1999): 537–90.
Maitland, F. W. and Frederick Pollack. *The History of English Law Before the Time of Edward I.* 2 vols. Cambridge: Cambridge University Press, 1899.
Marcus, Ivan G. "Images of the Jews in the *Exempla* of Caesarius of Heisterbach." In *From Witness to Witchcraft: Jews and Judaism in Medieval Christian Thought,* ed. Jeremy Cohen. Wiesbaden. Harrassowitz Verlag, 1996. 247–56.
Matthews, David. "Recent Chaucer Criticism: New Historicism, New Discontents?" *Modern Philology* 106.1 (2008): 117–27.
Middleton, Anne. "Acts of Vagrancy: The C-Version 'Authobiography' (C.5.1–108) and the Statute of 1388." In *Written Work: Langland, Labor and Authorship,* ed. Steven Justice and Kathryn Kerby-Fulton. Philadelphia: University of Pennsylvania Press, 1997. 208–317.
Minnis, A. J. "Langland's Ymaginatif and Late Medieval Theories of Imagination." *Comparative Criticism* 3 (1981): 71–103.
Moore, Michael Edward. "Meditations on the Face in the Middle Ages (With Levinas and Pickard)." *Literature and Theology* 24.1 (2010): 19–37.
Morrin, Margaret J. *John Waldeby, O.S.A., 1315–1372: English Augustinian Preacher and Writer.* Rome, 1975.
Morris, William A. *The Frankpledge System.* London: Longman, Green, & Co., 1910.
Musson, Anthony. *Medieval Law in Context: The Growth of Legal Consciousness from Magna Carta to the Peasants' Revolt.* Manchester: Manchester University Press, 2001.

Musson, Anthony and W. M. Ormrod. *The Evolution of English Justice: Law, Politics, and Society in the Fourteenth Century.* Hampshire: Macmillan, 1999.
Nichols, Stephen G. "Editor's Preface." *Romanic Review* 79.1 (1988): 1–3.
———. "Philology in a Manuscript Culture." *Speculum* 65.1 (1990): 1–10.
Niebrzydowski, Sue. "Monstrous (M)othering: The Representation of the Sowdanesse in Chaucer's *Man of Law's Tale*." In *Consuming Narratives: Gender and Monstrous Appetite in the Middle Ages and the Renaissance,* ed. Liz Herbert McAvoy and Teresa Walters. Cardiff: University of Wales Press, 2002. 196–207.
Nolan, Maura. "Historicism after Historicism." In *The Post-Historical Middle Ages,* ed. Elizabeth Scala and Sylvia Federico. New York: Palgrave, 2009. 63–86.
———. "'With tresone withinn': *Wynnere and Wastoure*, Chivalric Self-Representation, and the Law." *Journal of Medieval and Early Modern Studies* 36.1 (1996): 1–28.
O'Brien, Bruce. "Forgery and the Literacy of the Early Common Law." *Albion* 27.1 (1995): 1–19.
Oliver, Kelly. "Witnessing and Testimony." *Parallax* 10.1 (2004): 79–88.
———. *Witnessing: Beyond Recognition.* Minneapolis: University of Minnesota Press, 2001.
Ormrod, W. M. *The Reign of Edward III: Crown and Political Society in England.* New Haven, CT: Yale University Press, 1991.
Owst, G. W. *Literature and Pulpit in Medieval England.* Cambridge: Cambridge University Press, 1933.
Palmer, J. J. N. "The Parliament of 1385 and the Constitutional Crisis of 1386." *Speculum* 46.3 (1971): 477–90.
Palmer, Robert. *English Law in the Age of the Black Death, 1328–1381: A Transformation of Governance and Law.* Chapel Hill: University of North Carolina Press, 1993.
Patterson, Lee. *Chaucer and the Subject of History.* Madison: University of Wisconsin Press, 1991.
———. "Chaucerian Confession: Penitential Literature and the Pardoner." *Medievalia et humanistica* new series 7 (1976): 153–73.
———. *Negotiating the Past: The Historical Understanding of Medieval Literature.* Madison: University of Wisconsin Press, 1987.
Paxson, James J. "Gender Personified, Personification Gendered, and the Body Figuralized in *Piers Plowman.*" *Yearbook of Langland Studies* 12 (1998): 65–96.
———. "The Personificational Face: *Piers Plowman* Rethought through Levinas and Bronowski." In *Levinas and Medieval Literature: Literature: The "Difficult Reading" of English and Rabbinic Texts,* ed. Ann W. Astell and J. A. Jackson. Pittsburgh, PA: Duquesne University Press, 2009. 137–56.
———. *The Poetics of Personification.* Cambridge: Cambridge University Press, 1994.
Phillips, Susan E. *Transforming Talk: The Problem with Gossip in Late Medieval England.* University Park: Pennsylvania State University Press, 2007.
Poos, L. R. "Sex, Lies, and the Church Courts of Pre-Reformation England." *Journal of Interdisciplinary History* 25.4 (1995): 585–607.
Powell, Edward. *Kingship, Law, and Society: Criminal Justice in the Reign of Henry V.* Oxford: Clarendon, 1989.
Putnam, Bertha Haven. *The Enforcement of the Statute of Laborers During the First Decade after the Black Death, 1439–1359.* New York: Columbia University Press, 1908.
———. "The Transformation of Keepers of the Peace into the Justices of the Peace, 1327–1380." *Transactions of the Royal Historical Society,* 4th ser., vol. 12 (1929): 19–48.
Rabin, Andrew. "Bede, Dryhthelm, and the Witness to the Other World: Testimony and Conversion in the *Historia ecclesiastica.*" *Modern Philology* 106.3 (2009): 375–98.
———. "The Wolf's Testimony to the English: Law and the Witness in the *Sermo Lupi ad Anglos.*" *Journal of English and Germanic Philology* 105.3 (2006): 387–414.

Ramsay, Nigel. "Forgery and the Rise of the London Scriveners' Company." In *Fakes and Frauds: Varieties of Deception in Print and Manuscript,* ed. Robin Myers and Michael Harris. Winchester: St. Paul's Bibliographies, 1989. 99–108.

———. "Scriveners and Notaries as Legal Intermediaries in Later Medieval England." In *Enterprise and Individuals in Fifteenth-Century England,* ed. Jennifer Kermode. Gloucester: Alan Sutton, 1991. 118–31.

Raskolnikov, Masha. *Body Against Soul: Gender and "Sowlehele" in Middle English Allegory.* Columbus: The Ohio State University Press, 2009.

Ray, Roger. "Bede's *Vera Lex Historiae.*" *Speculum* 55.1 (1980): 1–21.

Rex, Richard. "Thorpe's *Testament:* A Conjectural Emendation." *Medium Aevum* 74.1 (2005): 109–11.

Reyerson, Kathryn and Debra A. Salata, eds. and trans. *Medieval Notaries and Their Acts: The 1327–1328 Register of Jean Holanie.* Kalamazoo, MI: Medieval Institute Publications, 2004.

Reynolds, Susan. *Kingdoms and Communities in Western Europe, 900–1300.* Oxford: Oxford University Press, 1997.

Rice, Nicole R. *Lay Piety and Religious Discipline in Middle English Literature.* Cambridge: Cambridge University Press, 2008.

Riggs, David. *The World of Christopher Marlowe.* New York: Henry Holt, 2004.

Robertson, Elizabeth. "The 'Elvyssh' Power of Constance: Christian Feminism in the *Man of Law's Tale.*" *Studies in the Age of Chaucer* 23 (2001): 143–80.

Rubin, Miri. *Corpus Christi: The Eucharist in Late Medieval Culture.* Cambridge: Cambridge University Press, 1991.

Saul, Nigel. "The Kingship of Richard II." In *Richard II: The Art of Kingship,* ed. Anthony Goodman and James Gillespie. Oxford: Clarendon, 1999. 37–57.

Scanlon, Larry. *Narrative, Authority and Power: The Medieval Exemplum and the Chaucerian Tradition.* Cambridge: Cambridge University Press, 1994.

———. "Personification and Penance." *Yearbook of Langland Studies* 22 (2008): 1–29.

Scarry, Elaine. *The Body in Pain: The Making and Unmaking of the World.* Oxford: Oxford University Press, 1985.

Scase, Wendy. *Literature and Complaint in England, 1272–1553.* Oxford: Oxford University Press, 2007.

Schibanoff, Susan. "Worlds Apart: Orientalism, Antifeminism, and Heresy in Chaucer's *Man of Law's Tale.*" *Exemplaria* 8.1 (1996): 60–96.

Schirmer, Elizabeth. "William Thorpe's Narrative Theology." *Studies in the Age of Chaucer* 31 (2009): 267–99.

Schmitt, Jean-Claude. *L'exemplum.* Typologie des sources du Moyen Age occidental 40. Turnhout: Brepols, 1982.

Schofield, Phillip R. "The Late Medieval View of Frankpledge and the Tithing System: An Essex Case Study." In *Medieval Society and the Manor Court,* ed. Zvi Razi and Richard Smith. Oxford: Clarendon, 1996. 408–49.

Shuffleton, George. "*Piers Plowman* and the Case of the Missing Book." *Yearbook of Langland Studies* 18 (2004): 55–72.

Simpson, James. "Desire and the Scriptural Text: Will as Reader in *Piers Plowman.*" In *Criticism and Dissent in the Middle Ages,* ed. Rita Copeland. Cambridge: Cambridge University Press, 1996. 215–43.

———. *Piers Plowman: An Introduction.* Exeter: University of Exeter Press, 2007.

Smith, D. Vance. *Arts of Possession: The Medieval Household Imaginary.* Minneapolis: University of Minnesota Press, 2003.

Somerset, Fiona. "'Al the Comonys with o Voys Atonys': Multilingual Latin and Vernacular Voice in *Piers Plowman.*" *Yearbook of Langland Studies* 19 (2005): 107–36.

———. *Clerical Discourse and Lay Audience in Late Medieval England*. Cambridge: Cambridge University Press, 1998.
———. Review, *Pedagogy, Intellectuals, and Dissent in the Later Middle Ages*. *Medium Aevum* 72 (2003): 140–41.
Spencer, H. Leith. *English Preaching in the Late Middle Ages*. Oxford: Oxford University Press, 1993.
Spiegel, Gabrielle M. "History, Historicism, and the Social Logic of the Text in the Middle Ages." *Speculum* 65.1 (1990): 59–86.
Spolsky, Ellen, ed. *The Judgment of Susanna: Authority and Witness*. Atlanta, GA: Scholars Press, 1996.
Staley, Lynn. "Susanna and English Communities." *Traditio* 62 (2007): 25–58.
———. "Susanna's Voice." In *Sacred and Profane in Chaucer and Late Medieval Literature*, ed. Robert Epstein and William Robins. Toronto: University of Toronto Press, 2010. 46–67.
Stanbury, Sarah. *The Visual Object of Desire in Late Medieval England*. Philadelphia: University of Pennsylvania Press, 2007.
Steiner, Emily. "Commonalty and Literary Form in the 1370s and 1380s." *New Medieval Literatures* 6 (2004): 199–221.
———. *Documentary Culture and the Making of Medieval English Literature*. Cambridge: Cambridge University Press, 2003.
——— and Candace Barrington. *The Letter of the Law: Legal Practice and Literary Production in Medieval England*. Ithaca, NY: Cornell University Press, 2002.
Stock, Brian. *Listening for the Text*. Baltimore: Johns Hopkins University Press, 1990.
Stones, E. L. G. "The Folvilles of Ashby-Folville, Leicestershire, and Their Associates in Crime, 1326–1347." *Transactions of the Royal Historical Society*, 5th ser., no. 7 (1957): 117–36.
Strohm, Paul. *England's Empty Throne*. New Haven, CT: Yale University Press, 1998.
———. *Social Chaucer*. Cambridge, MA: Harvard University Press, 1989.
Tolmie, Sarah. "The *Prive Scilence* of Thomas Hoccleve." *Studies in the Age of Chaucer* 22 (2000): 281–309.
Von Nolcken, Christina. "A 'Certain Sameness' and Our Response to It in English Wycliffite Texts." In *Literature and Religion in the Later Middle Ages*, ed. Richard G. Newhauser and John A. Alford. Binghamton, NY: Medieval and Renaissance Texts and Studies, 1995. 191–208.
———. "Richard Wyche, a Certain Knight, and the Beginning of the End." In *Lollardy and the Gentry in the Later Middle Ages*, ed. Margaret Aston and Colin Richmond. New York: St. Martin's, 1997. 127–54.
Waldenfels, Bernard. "Levinas and the Face of the Other." In *The Cambridge Companion to Levinas*, ed. Simon Critchley and Robert Bernasconi. Cambridge: Cambridge University Press, 2002. 63–81.
Wallace, David. *Chaucerian Polity: Absolutist Lineages and Associational Forms in England and Italy*. Stanford, CA: Stanford University Press, 1997.
Waters, Clare M. "Talking the Talk: Access to the Vernacular in Medieval Preaching." In *The Vulgar Tongue: Medieval and Postmedieval Vernacularity*, ed. Fiona Somerset and Nicholas Watson. University Park: Pennsylvania State University Press, 2003. 31–42.
Watson, Nicholas. "Censorship and Cultural Change in Late-Medieval England: Vernacular Theology, the Oxford Translation Debate, and Arundel's Constitutions of 1409." *Speculum* 70.4 (1995): 822–64.
Weisberg, David. "Telling Stories about Constance: Framing and Narrative Strategy in the *Canterbury Tales*." *Chaucer Review* 27.1 (1992): 45–64.
Wenzel, Siegfried. *Latin Sermon Collections from later Medieval England*. Cambridge: Cambridge University Press, 2005.

———. *Macaronic Sermons: Bilingualism and Preaching in Late-Medieval England*. Ann Arbor: University of Michigan Press, 1994.

Whatley, Gordon. "The Uses of Hagiography: The Legend of Pope Gregory and the Emperor Trajan in the Middle Ages." *Viator* 15 (1984): 25–63.

White, Stephen D. "The Problem of Treason: The Trial of Daire le Roux." In *Law, Laity, and Solidarities: Essays in Honor of Susan Reynolds*, ed. Pauline Stafford, Janet L. Nelson, and Jane Martindale. Manchester: Manchester University Press, 2001. 95–115.

Wittig, Joseph. "The Middle English 'Absolute Infinitive' and 'The Speech of Book.'" In *Magister Regis: Studies in Honor of Robert Earl Kaske*, ed. Arthur Groos et al. New York: Fordham University Press, 1986. 217–40.

Woodbine, George E. "The Language of English Law." *Speculum* 18.4 (1943): 395–436.

Woolf, Rosemary. "Tearing the Pardon." In *"Piers Plowman": Critical Approaches*, ed. S. S. Hussey. London: Methuen, 1969. 50–75.

Woolley, R. M. "Constitutions of the Diocese of London, c. 1215–22." *English Historical Review* 30 (1915): 285–302.

Wormald, Patrick. "Neighbors, Courts, and Kings: Reflections on Michael MacNair's *Vicini*." *Law and History Review* 17.3 (1999): 597–602.

Žižek, Slavoj, Eric L. Santner, and Kenneth Reinhard, eds. *The Neighbor: Three Inquiries in Political Theology*. Chicago: University of Chicago Press, 2005.

index

abjuration: by heretics, 159, 161, 164; William Thorpe's refusal of, 164, 170
accusation, as court procedure, 17; oral and written, 73
Acts and Monuments (Foxe), 182–88
Adam Bell, 111
adultery: laws concerning, 21–22, 68–69; Susanna accused of, 61, 69–70
Aers, D., 174n, 195
Alla (*Man of Law's Tale*), 26–27, 30, 34, 36, 39–40, 43–45, 49, 50–53, 84
Allmand, C., 45n
Ambrose, on Susanna, 62–63
Amodio, M., 11
Anima (*Piers Plowman*), 122–23, 134, 136, 138; authority of, 123–24; names of, 122
Apology for Lollard Doctrine, 152–53
Arundel, Archbishop Thomas, 23, 80–82, 151, 153–56, 159, 161–64, 166, 168–70, 175–78, 180, 188
assizes, use of, 15, 19. *See also* law; trials
Athanasian Creed, 137–38
Athelston, 7
audiences: for the *Canterbury Tales,* 36; Christian, 61; for documents, 78; Lollard, 81; for Thorpe's interrogation, 162–64, 166, 170, 176–80; as witnesses, 1, 3, 177
Augustine, Saint: on Susanna, 60–61; on witnessing, 163, 189–90
authenticity, and witnessing, 189–90, 197

authority: absent, 82; of Anima, 123–24; centralized, 88–90; Christian, 58; of the Church, 79, 87, 169–70; critique of, 7–8; editorial, 183–84; and gender, 73; of God, 112; juridical and legal, 13, 15–16, 26–27, 56; of the Man of Law, 24; metaphors of, 74–75; moral, 56; of prophecy, 78; resistance to, 9, 87–88, 90, 112, 154, 160, 170; royal, 7, 20–21, 25–27, 87–88, 99, 101, 103, 110, 112; suspicion of, 95; as threat to community, 84; and witnessing, 1, 20; and writing, 2. *See also* resistance
autobiography, testimony as, 8–9, 81, 163, 179–80. *See also* biography

Badby, John, 185–86
Baker, J. H., 42n
Ball, John, 139
Barney, S. A., 125n, 126n
Barr, H., 144
Baxter, Margery, 160–61, 173, 195 bearing witness. *See also* testifying; testimony
Beckwith, S., 4n
Bede, Saint, 4–5
Bennett, M., 46n
biography: and history, 8–9; and literature, 10; and witnessing, 197–98. *See also* autobiography
Birkholz, D., 197–98

213

Blanchot, Maurice, 8
blasphemy, 21, 89
bodies: of Book in *Piers Plowman*, 116, 126, 135–36; of Christ, 3–4, 37–38, 174–75, 177; destruction of, 156; and documents, 54, 124, 160–61, 170; Lollard, 155–56, 159–62, 170; of martyrs and saints, 2–3, 12, 34; and royal power, 48–49, 52; as sites of resistance, 160; as sites of truth, 51; of Susanna, 59, 66–67; and testimony, 12–13, 22–23; of William Thorpe, 178, 183; as witnesses, 2, 54; and writing, 75
Boitani, P., 58n
Book (*Piers Plowman*), 23, 116–17, 124–26, 129–30, 134–36, 138, 140, 149, 156; body of, 116, 126, 135–36; oaths of, 135–36; social status of, 126–27; as text, 130; voice of, 116
Book of Daniel, 21–22, 55–56, 59, 64–66
Book of Leviticus, 139
Book of Revelation, 127, 129
books: bags of, 144–45; and salvation, 132–33; as source of knowledge, 130; as speaking, 127–28; as witnesses, 127–29, 132–34; of William Thorpe, 168
Bowers, J. M., 198n
Bracton, Henry de, 19–20, 47
Bradbury, N. M., 135n
bribery, 120. *See also* corruption
bureaucracy, documents produced by, 12, 18, 21, 28, 50, 75, 144–46. *See also* clerks; documents

Camille, M., 128n
Campbell, M. B., 2n
Charter of the Forest, 108
chastity: female, 22, 55, 59–60, 64, 66, 73; and silence, 57; of Susanna, 62, 64
Chaucer, Geoffrey, 2, 10, 39–43, 55, 72–73, 79; *Balade de Bon Conseyl*, 42–43; *Legend of Philomela*, 72–73, 78; *Man of Law's Tale*, 24–54; narrative persona of, 10; and parliamentary politics, 41–42; as pilgrim, 10; and royal succession, 46–47; and rumor, 18
Chester Emmaus play, 4
Chism, C., 112n
Christ, body of, 3–4, 37–38, 174–75; face of, 32–33; life of, 127; Passion of, 27, 32, 37–38, 50–51, 116, 124–25, 127, 129–30, 134–35; resurrection of, 3, 27; as witness, 196; witnessing of, 3, 127
Chrysostom, John, 168–69
Church Elders (Susanna story). *See* Elders
clamor, as voice of the community, 41–42. *See also infamia*; rumor
Clanchy, M. T., 12, 47–48
Clergie (*Piers Plowman*), 93, 128, 130–31
clerks, 12, 18, 75–76, 122–23. *See also* notaries; transcription
Cohen, J. J., 105, 107n, 113n
Cole, A., 151
Coleman, J., 11
communities: beliefs of, 4–6; in the *Canterbury Tales*, 25; Christian, 16–17, 22, 27, 28, 36, 37, 41, 44, 52, 53–54, 55, 57, 58, 84–85, 87, 89–90, 92; collective voice of, 41–43; as complainants, 17, 41–42; doctrinal, 3–4, 8, 11, 16, 17, 18–19, 21–22; formation of, 2, 6–8, 11, 13, 20, 25, 35–36, 41, 44, 53–54, 55, 57–58, 84–85, 87, 190; as guarantors of justice, 19; heterodox, 152, 154; legal, 11, 21; loyalty to, 87; and neighbors, 89–90, 94–95; non-Christian, 26–27; and oath-taking, 13, 16, 190–91; orthodox, 154; and outlaws, 105, 109–10, 113; of pilgrims, 25; political, 11, 19; sanctity of, 26; textual, 154; and witnessing, 1, 7, 13–14, 16–17, 26–27, 124
complaints, legal: by communities, 41–42; documentary, 65; initiated by cries, 62, 65, 67, 69, 96; oral and written, 68; in the *Pistel of Swete Susan*, 62, 73
compurgation, 13, 17, 119. *See also* oaths
Constance (*Man of Law's Tale*), 21, 25–27, 28–30, 39, 49, 50–53; face of, 30–32, 34–36; trial of, 30–31, 37–38, 43, 70
conversion, to Christianity, 30, 36, 40, 44–45, 53, 132–33
Copeland, R., 82n, 153, 161n, 165n, 178, 188
corruption: of the Church, 79–80, 93, 174–75; of the law, 55, 79, 93, 98, 102–3, 106–7, 119, 120
counterfeiting. *See* forgery
courts. *See* law; justice; testimony
Cresseid, 76–78
Crowley, Robert, 146–48
Cruel Constitutions (Arundel), 151, 156, 157, 159, 163

cry: as part of legal process, 62, 65, 67, 69, 96; of Susanna, 65, 67, 83–84
Cuthbert, Saint, 4–5

Daniel, in the Susanna story, 56, 70, 78
De heretico comburendo, 149–50, 153–54, 156, 159, 161, 170
de la Pole, Michael, 41
De lapsu Susannae, 63–64
defamation, law of, 89. See also *fama publica*; *infamia*; rumor
Derrida, J., 8, 9, 81–82, 83
Dinshaw, C., 31, 36
Dives and Pauper, 93–95
doctrine, of the Church, 1, 152–53, 165
documents: and bodies, 54, 124, 160–61, 170; bureaucratic, 21, 50, 75, 144–46; and false witness, 80–81; formulaic, 68–69, 73; in inquisitions, 158–59, 161; legal, 11–12, 18–20, 125; literary, 11–12; and male authority, 78; as present, 178; royal, 27; and silence, 76–77, 79–80; in the Susanna story, 78–85; as testimony, 18, 80–81, 85, 163–64; as witnesses, 1, 77–78, 163, 166, 170, 177, 189–90
Donaldson, E. T., 10, 135n
Donegild (*Man of Law's Tale*), 46–47, 49–50
Donohue, Jr., C., 96n
Doye, M., 152n
dreamers: authority of, 141, 147; in *Piers Plowman*, 115–16, 124–25, 131–32, 137
Duffy, E., 173n
Durand, William, 34, 101–2

Edward III, 45–46
Elders (in the Susanna story), 55–56, 58–59, 61–62, 65; approach to Susanna by, 69–70; authority of, 56; legal standing of, 66; oaths of, 70; perjury of, 71, 78; as specters, 82–83; testimony of, 63, 80; and writing, 69
Enders, J., 4n
England, as Christian community, 28–29
eschatology, Christian, 116, 130, 134
Eucharist, 170–75; Lollards' views of, 172–73; as miracle, 176; poetry concerning, 173–74; presence of, 171, 176–77; and vision, 173; William Thorpe on, 177–78. See also host; transubstantiation

evidence: in inquisitions, 157; material, 68; and oaths, 190–91; procedures and rules for, 42, 64, 71; and witnessing, 191–92
Examination of William Thorpe. See *Testimony of William Thorpe*
experience: as basis for witnessing, 125, 130–31, 132–33, 136, 149; contrasted with knowledge, 115–16, 194; in *Piers Plowman*, 140; and the vernacular, 138. See also eyewitnesses
eyewitnesses, 3–4, 22–23, 140, 147–48; metaphorical, 197; reliability of, 51

faces: of defendants, 34; and desire, 33; and divine justice, 39; as sites of truth, 53; as witnesses, 30–36, 39, 50. See also Constance
faith: and communities, 4, 26; and silence, 56; witnessing of, 2–3, 10
false witness, 21–22, 25–27, 39, 32, 34, 38–39, 44, 46–47, 54–55, 59, 64, 78–79, 87, 89, 93–94, 106, 114, 165; and documents, 80–81; of the Elders, 83; and forgery, 47–48, 50; as treason, 100–101. See also oaths; perjury
fama publica, 68. See also defamation; *infamia*; rumor
Fasciculus Morum, 32, 38, 91–92, 94
Federico, S., 194
Felman, S., 8–9
fiction, and evidence, 23
flattery, of kings, 142–43
Florschuetz, A., 45, 46
forests: liminality of, 107–9; in outlaw literature, 107–9; royal control of, 108–9
forgery, 28; as false witness, 47–48, 50; and the royal body, 48–49; as treason, 47–50, 52
Fouke le Fitz Waryn, 107–8, 109–10
Fourth Lateran Council, 16–18, 135n, 156
Foxe, John, 179–88, 195–96
Fradenburg, L. O., 88
frankpledge, 96–97, 102. See also oaths
Freeman, T. S., 181n
Frisch, A., 2n

Galloway, A., 120, 161n
Gellrich, J., 127–28

216 · Index

gender: and authority, 73; and authorship, 78; and witnessing, 78
Geoffrey of Monmouth, 5–6
Gerhoh of Reichersberg, 48
Giancarlo, M., 42
Gill, M., 37n
Glanvill, Ranulph de, 15–16, 19, 68, 97
gloss, defined, 74–75
Gluttony (*Piers Plowman*), 121–22, 134, 136, 138; and false oaths, 121–11
Good Samaritan, 105, 124
Gower, John, 31, 39–40, 72
Grady, F., 132n, 133, 140–41
Green, R. F., 8n, 13, 88, 99, 106, 110n
Greenblatt, S., 193, 195–96
Greetham, D. C., 191–92
Guillaume de Dole, 6

Halpern-Amaru, B., 58n
Hanawalt, B. A., 68n, 112
Hanna, R., 99
healing, of Lollard bodies, 159
Helmholz, R., 18, 89n
Heng, G., 29, 36
Henry II, 15
Henryson, Robert, on writing, 76
heresy, prosecution of, 23, 152, 154, 157–59, 165–66, 170; punishment of, 156. See also *De heretico comburendo*; inquisitions
hermeneutics, of witnessing, 189–91
heuristics: of texts, 192; of witnessing, 189–91
Hiatt, A., 47
Hippolytus, Saint, on Susanna, 59–60
Hocclve, Thomas, 73, 75–76, 185–86
Hoffman, R. L., 135n
Holsinger, B. W., 61n
host, consecration and witnessing of, 171, 173–75. See also Eucharist; transubstantiation Host, in the *Canterbury Tales*, 24–25
Hudson, A., 178, 179
hue and cry. See cry
Hugh of St. Victor, on writing, 74
Hyams, P. R., 7n, 15n, 97n

infamia, in inquisitions, 17–18, 156–58, 164. See also defamation; *fama publica*; rumor

Innocent III, 156, 157n
inquisition: in absentia proceedings in, 157–59; distinguished from trial, 156–57; growth of, 17; as legal process, 17–18, 23; procedures for, 156–59, 162–64. See also Thorpe, William
interrogation: of heretics, 153; of Lollards, 151–52; of William Thorpe, 161–70
Isidore of Seville, on writing, 74, 76

Jack Upland, 93
Jack Upland's Rejoinder, 174–75
Jackson, J. A., 33
Jeffrey, D. L., 81n
Jerome, Saint, on Susanna, 57, 60
John of Salisbury, on writing, 74, 76
Julian of Norwich, 32–33
juries, 16, 19; composed of neighbors, 97, 103–4. See also law; trial
Jurkowski, M., 153n
justice: divine, 2, 16, 25–27, 29–30, 34, 36–37, 39–44, 50–51, 55, 87, 98, 134, 190–91; human, 34, 36, 39–40, 51, 54; local vs. royal, 8, 19, 99–100, 102, 113. See also law
Justice, S., 12, 193

Kane, G., 10n
Kaske, R. E., 126n, 134–35n
Kean, M., 108n
Kelly, H. A., 156–57n, 157n
Kendall, R. D., 154n
Kennedy, K. E., 38n, 120n
Kennedy, V. L., 173n
King, J. N., 181
kings: fidelity to, 22; flattery of, 141–42; juridical power of, 19, 43–44. See also justice; law, royal
Knapp, E., 76n
Knighton, Henry, 155
knowledge: contrasted with experience, 115–16, 194; in *Piers Plowman*, 140; sources of, 130–3; and witnessing, 133, 149, 177
Kolve, V. A., 34n
Krug, R., 159

Lady Mede (*Piers Plowman*), 22, 118–22, 136

laity: contaminated by heresy, 155; education of, 154–55; Eucharist received by, 171, 173–74; literacy among, 12; in martyr narratives, 186–88; piety among, 115–16; spiritual authority of, 118. *See also* Lollards; preaching, unauthorized; Wyclif
Lander, J. M., 146
Landman, J. H., 51, 104
Langland, William, 2, 18, 22, 32, 93, 105, 114–16, 127, 130, 144–45; and prophecy, 147. *See also* Piers Plowman
Lanval, 6
Laub, D., 8–9
Lavezzo, K., 40
law: administration of, 40, 43, 67–68, 93, 99; canon, 15–16, 89, 151; Christian, 26; common, 15, 151; corruption of, 55, 79, 93, 98, 102–3, 106–7, 119, 120; didactic texts concerning, 92–93; discourse of, 141; English, 6, 11; fallibility of, 34–35; language of, 66–67, 149; royal control of, 8, 15, 20–21, 41–42, 51, 89, 101, 103; sovereign, 25–26, 28; and truth, 94; and witnessing, 1–2, 6, 13, 149. *See also* communities; documents; justice; oaths; rape; testimony; treason; trials
Lea, H. C., 157n
Leicester, H. M., 10
letters: forgery of, 49–50, 52; read during Mass, 73; as witnesses, 47–48
Levinas, E., 35–36
Lindenbaum, S., 67n
literacy: growth in, 12; and the law, 12, 66; of Susanna, 65–66; in vernacular languages, 23
Little, K. C., 121n
Lollards, 1–2, 23, 57, 80–81, 149, 154; bodies of, 159–60, 170; on the Eucharist, 171–73; as martyrs, 180–81; persecution of, 151–52, 179; as plague, 154–55, 159; on transubstantiation, 172–73. *See also* inquisition; Thorpe, William; Wyclif, John
Love, Nicholas, 172

MacNair, M., 96n
Man of Law, 24–25, 26, 27, 29, 30, 31, 34–35, 40, 42, 44, 45, 49–50, 54; on forgery, 49–50; as model, 198

Man of Law's Tale, 21, 24–54, 55, 71, 84, 87, 114, 190–91; politics of, 36
Mannyng, Robert, 92
Marie de France, 6
Martin of Tours, 110
martyrologies, 2–3, 23, 134, 156; and William Thorpe, 180; and witnessing, 182–83
martyrs: bodies of, 12; Lollard, 151; testimony of, 29–30, 182. *See also Acts and Monuments*
Mary, as witness of Christ's Passion, 50–51
Mauricius (*Man of Law's Tale*), 52–53
mediation: by clerics, 20, 81; of divine knowledge, 114. *See also* laity; preaching, unauthorized
Mee, C., 196–97
memory: and community, 9; and testimony, 5, 9
Mercy (*Piers Plowman*), 125
miracles: and divine justice, 40–41, 71; of the Eucharist, 176
Miskimin, A., 70–71
Moore, M. E., 34n
More, Thomas, 195–96
mouths: of Anima, 123; as site of false testimony, 54; as site of heresy, 165; as site of transgression, 121; as site of truth, 70, 72–75. *See also* bodies; silence; voice
Mozley, J. H., 58n
Mum and the Sothsegger, 117, 141–45
Musson, A., 88
mystery plays, 1, 3

narratores, 24, 198
nations. *See* communities
neighbors: and class, 100; and communities, 87, 89–90, 94–95; defined, 22, 85, 87–90, 94–95, 113; as jurors, 97, 103–4; legal status of, 95; loyalty to, 88; and outlaws, 90, 107–8; and royal authority, 100–102; and witnessing, 89–91, 94–95, 97–99, 102, 104, 113
New Criticism, 193
New Historicism, 23, 193–96; on witnessing, 196
New Philology, 23, 192–94
Nicholas of Lyra, on Susanna, 64–65
Nichols, S. G., 192
Nolan, M., 113n

218 · Index

Northumberland (*Man of Law's Tale*), 26–27, 29, 35, 44–45, 52–53; as pagan community, 29–30; and Rome, 53
notaries, 79–81, 122–23; as intermediaries, 81; transcription by, 154

oaths, 1, 13, 16–17, 19, 21, 37–40, 89; and class distinctions, 92; in common law, 119; and communities, 13, 16, 190–91; and contracts, 117; and evidence, 190–91; false, 21, 44, 92; in heresy inquisitions, 165; misuse of, 39, 92, 98, 101; and ordeal trials, 135; in outlaw literature, 110; and personifications, 117; in *Piers Plowman*, 117–19, 121–24, 135–37, 139, 191; in *Pistel of Swete Susan*, 70; and writing, 139; Wycliffite attitudes toward, 166–68; William Thorpe on, 167–68. *See also* compurgation; perjury; testimony
obedience, female, 21–22, 26, 55, 57, 59, 61, 73, 78, 84; of Susanna, 60
O'Brien, B., 15n
Of Prelates (Lollard treatise), 56, 79
Oliver, K., 9
Omnis utriusque sexus decree, 16–17
On the Feast of Corpus Christi, 174
Ong, W. J., 11
orality: and literacy, 11; and testimony, 11, 18, 20; and witnessing, 73. *See also* documents; silence; writing
ordeal, trial by, 1, 7, 13–17, 19, 135
Ormrod, W. M., 103n
Other, the, and transcendence, 35
Outlaw's Song of Trailbaston, 106–7
outlaws: and communities, 105, 109–10, 113; depictions of, 8, 22, 90, 104–14; equality and hierarchy among, 110, 111–12; God compared to, 89–90, 104–5, 112; and neighbors, 90, 107–8; and witnessing, 1, 111
Ovid, 72
Ovide moralisé, 72

Palmer, J. J. N., 41n
Palmer, R. C., 88, 103
Pardon (*Piers Plowman*), 137–39
Parliament: conflict of with the King, 41–42; in the *Piers Plowman* tradition, 148; and the prosecution of heresy, 155–56; Wonderful, 41
Passion, of Christ, 27, 32, 37–38, 50–51, 116, 124–25, 134–35; Book's narration of, 127, 129–30, 134–35; witnesses to, 125–26
patristic authorities: and Scripture, 168–69; on Susanna, 59–64
Patterson, L., 121n, 192n, 193n, 194, 195
Paxson, J. J., 35, 123n
Peace (*Piers Plowman*), 119–20
Pearl, 33
Peck, R. A., 70n
perjury, 21, 28–30, 37–40, 43, 71, 89, 91–92; in the *Pistel of Swete Susan*, 71
Perpetua, Saint, 2–3
personification, in *Piers Plowman*, 116–18, 127, 136–37, 145–46, 191; limits of, 143–44; and oaths, 117; and witnessing, 144, 146 Philomela, silence of, 72–73
Piers Plowman, 11, 22–23, 93, 115–50; date of, 148; and the idea of the text, 194; ideological uses of, 146–50; as model, 198; prophecy in, 147–48; Protestant readings of, 146, 148–49; tradition of, 117–18, 140–45; witnessing in, 120–21, 124, 149. *See also* Anima; Book; Clergie; dreamers; Gluttony; Lady Mede; Mercy; Pardon; Peace; Trajan; Truth; Ymaginatif
pilgrims: communities of, 25; as witnesses, 34
pistel: defined, 73; as witness, 78
Pistel of Swete Susan, 11, 18, 21–22, 54, 56–59, 65–76, 78, 82–85, 87, 191
Pizan, Christine de, 65n, 72
Plato, on writing, 74
politics: of *The Man of Law's Tale*, 36; in vernacular poetry, 144; of witnessing, 140–41, 144–45, 150. *See also* authority; resistance
Poos, L. R., 68n
preaching, unauthorized, 80, 153, 155–58, 160–63, 166–67, 175
printing: ideology of, 146; and the *Piers Plowman* tradition, 145–50; and Protestantism, 146
Proclamation of 1258, 99–100
prophecy, in *Piers Plowman*, 147–48

proximum, definition of, 95–96. *See also* neighbors; *vicinum Pyers Plowmans Exhortation*, 148–49

Qualiter et quando decree, 17–18
Quoniam contra falsam decree, 18

Rabin, A., 6
rape: common law treatment of, 22, 65, 67–68; of Philomela, 72; prosecution of, 67–69
Raskolnikov, M., 123n
readers, as witnesses, 1, 3, 163. *See also* audiences
Reformation: *Piers Plowman*'s role in, 146, 148–49; politics of, 146–50
reportage: in the *Piers Plowman* tradition, 146–49; and witnessing, 147–49
resistance: to authority, 9, 87–88, 90, 112, 154, 170; bodies as sites of, 160; silence as, 84
Rex, R., 184n, 188
Reynolds, S., 88
Rice, N. R., 167n
Richard de Bury, 128–29
Richard II, 25
Richard the Redeless, 141
Riggs, D., 197
Robin Hood, 111–12
romances: testimony in, 6; and trial by ordeal, 7
Rome (*Man of Law's Tale*), 52–53
Rubin, M., 170
rumor: in Chaucer, 18; and legal procedures, 17–18, 20, 68. *See also* defamation; *fama publica*; *infamia*

saints: faces of, 32; lives of, 1, 5, 21. *See also* martyrs; martyrologies
Sautre, William, 154, 155, 161, 186
Scala, E., 194
Scanlon, L., 121
Scarry, E., 136
Scase, W., 12, 41, 67n, 77n
Schirmer, E., 176
Scripture: citation of, 22–23, 27, 32, 82, 91, 119, 125, 130–31, 133, 168–69; personified in *Piers Plowman*, 131; Wycliffite attitudes toward, 167
seals: bureaucratic, 49; royal, 52. *See also* forgery
Shakespeare, William, reception of, 196–97
Short Charter of Christ, 126
Shuffleton, G., 128n, 130, 131n
silence: and chastity, 57; contrasted with flattery, 142; in the courtroom, 143; of crowds, 42–43; and documents, 76–77, 79–80; and faith, 56; female, 55–59, 69, 78; as fidelity, 104; as metaphor, 63–64; as refusal to testify, 87; as resistance, 84; and royal counsel, 142–43; as self-destructive, 143; of Susanna, 56–64, 75, 78–79, 80–82; as testimony, 65, 71; of William Thorpe, 80–81, 166; and writing, 75–77
Simpson, J., 116, 119, 138, 139n
Somerset, F., 153n, 169n
Somme le Roi, 91
sovereignty: in the *Canterbury Tales*, 25, 36; Christian, 27, 44, 46–47, 53
spectrality, 81–84
Speculum Vitae (William of Nassington), 38
Spiegel, G. M., 193, 197
Staley, L., 58n, 70n
Statute of Marlborough, 100
Statute of Westminster, 100–101
Steiner, E., 12, 126n, 128n, 144, 145n, 161n
Stephen, Saint, 32
Stock, B., 154n
Stones, E. L. G., 112
Strohm, P., 194
succession, royal, 45–46
Susanna, 21–22, 55–83; chastity of, 62, 64; cited by William Thorpe, 80–82; cry of, 69, 83–84; as exemplum in sermons, 73; legal knowledge of, 66–67; literacy of, 65–66; literary treatments of, 58–59; obedience of, 60; prayers of 61–62; silence of, 60–64, 75, 78–79, 80–82; trial of, 70–73; voice of, 58–59, 62, 64
Syria (*Man of Law's Tale*), 26, 28–29

Tale of Gamelyn, 110–11
Tertullian, 57
Testament of Cresseid (Henryson), 76–78

testifying: among neighbors, 22, 87, 91; refusal of, 22, 87
testimony: alteration of, 157n; and autobiography, 8, 81, 163; and biography, 179–80; bodily, 12; compurgatory, 13; distinguished from witnessing, 149; documentary, 80–81, 85; as factual, 8; female, 55, 56–57, 84; flexibility of, 153; and history, 4–5, 8–9; in inquisitions, 152–55, 157–59; legal, 1, 13–14, 79–80, 132, 143–44; and memory, 5, 9; oral, 5, 12, 18, 20, 78, 85; and personification, 146; as political, 145; private, 72; silence as, 65, 71; and subjectivity, 195;texts as, 68; Thorpe's recasting of, 154; varieties of, 84; written, 5, 18, 20, 69–70. *See also* compurgation; false witness; inquisition; law; oaths; Thorpe, William; trials
Testimony of William Thorpe, 11, 153–54, 161–70, 188; audience for, 177–78; and internal subjectivity, 195; manuscript history of, 183–84; text of, 178–79; witnesses to, 177
texts: distinguished from contexts, 193–94; heuristics of, 192; iterability of, 84; legal, 68; Lollard, 151–52; materiality of, 168, 193; origins of, 192; stability of, 18; types of, 194; as witnesses, 147, 149, 162, 181–82, 192; Wycliffite, 151–52
Thomas, as witness of Christ, 4
Thorpe, William, 2, 23, 80–81, 114, 153–54, 159n, 161–70; audience for, 179–80; authorial presence of, 183; autobiography of, 179–80; body of, 178; books of, 168; citation of Susanna by, 80–82; compared to Christ before Caiaphas, 195–96; on the Eucharist, 175–76, 177–78; historicity of, 153–54; New Historicist readings of, 195–96; as martyr, 179–88; as model, 198; on oaths, 166–68, 191; silence of, 80–81; on transubstantiation, 175–76; uncertain fate of, 178–79, 181, 187–88; voice of, 184; as witness, 188; on witnessing, 154
Tolmie, S., 75–76
tongues. *See* mouths
torture, and truth, 51–52. *See also* bodies
trailbaston, 102, 106–7
Trajan (*Piers Plowman*), 132–33, 135, 138
transcendence, divine, 35, 37

transcription, by clerks and notaries, 76, 79–80, 122–23
transubstantiation, 152, 170–72; Lollard views on, 175; Thorpe's views on, 175–76. *See also* Eucharist
treason, 6–7; false witness as, 27, 100–101; forgery as, 47–49, 52; of outlaws, 111
trespass, 106
Trevet, Nicholas, 31, 40
trial: by assize, 15, 19; of Constance, 30–31, 37–40; distinguished from inquisition, 156–57; by ordeal, 1, 7, 13–17, 19, 135; procedures for, 17–18; of St. Perpetua, 3; of Susanna, 70–73; types of, 17–18; use of documents in, 19–20; witnesses at, 1, 13–14. *See also* law; testimony
truth: and the body, 51; divine, 20, 29–30, 34, 43; and the law, 94; mouth as site of, 70, 72–73, 74–75; Scriptural, 167; telling of, 142–44; and torture, 51–52; and witnessing, 10, 20, 140
Truth (*Piers Plowman*), 137–40
Tyndale, William, 183–84

Valla, Lorenzo, 192
venue, rules concerning, 98–99. *See also* juries; law; neighbors
vicinum, definition of, 95–97. *See also* neighbors
voice: absence of, 77; female, 78; of Susanna, 58–59, 62, 64
Von Nolcken, C., 151, 180n
vox populi, 43

Wakefield Resurrection play, 3–4
Waldeby, John, 2, 22, 86–87, 89–91, 95–96, 102, 104–5, 112–13; audience for, 90–91
Wallace, D., 42n, 107
Watson, N., 156n
Whatley, G., 132n
Wife of Bath, 115
William of Conches, on writing, 74
William of Nassington, 38–39
wisdom, experiential, 116. *See also* experience; knowledge
Wittig, J., 135n
women: and inheritance law, 45–46; silence of, 69; witnessing by, 56–57. *See also* chastity, female; gender; obedience,

female; silence, female; testimony, female; voice, female
Word, divine, 21, 54, 117, 125, 127–28, 129–30, 134, 136, 149, 167, 190–91
Wormald, P., 96n, 97n
writing: and accusations, 73; and the body, 75; by clerks, 18; and oaths, 139; and silence, 75–77; and speech, 73–74; and the stability of texts, 18; and testimony, 5, 11; theoretical views of, 74–76; and transcription, 76

Wulfstan, 6
Wyche, Richard, 160, 165–66, 186; as martyr, 180–81
Wyclif, John, 146–47; 152, 154–55; banning of, 156; on the Eucharist, 171; and martyrdom, 181; on Scripture, 167. *See also* Lollards; Thorpe, William

Ymaginatif, in *Piers Plowman,* 133–34

INTERVENTIONS: NEW STUDIES IN MEDIEVAL CULTURE
Ethan Knapp, Series Editor

Interventions: New Studies in Medieval Culture publishes theoretically informed work in medieval literary and cultural studies. We are interested both in studies of medieval culture and in work on the continuing importance of medieval tropes and topics in contemporary intellectual life.

Fictions of Evidence: Witnessing, Literature, and Community in the Late Middle Ages
JAMIE K. TAYLOR

Scribal Authorship and the Writing of History in Medieval England
MATTHEW FISHER

Fashioning Change: The Trope of Clothing in High- and Late-Medieval England
ANDREA DENNY-BROWN

Form and Reform: Reading across the Fifteenth Century
EDITED BY SHANNON GAYK AND KATHLEEN TONRY

How to Make a Human: Animals and Violence in the Middle Ages
KARL STEEL

Revivalist Fantasy: Alliterative Verse and Nationalist Literary History
RANDY P. SCHIFF

Inventing Womanhood: Gender and Language in Later Middle English Writing
TARA WILLIAMS

Body Against Soul: Gender and Sowlehele *in Middle English Allegory*
MASHA RASKOLNIKOV

www.ingramcontent.com/pod-product-compliance
Lightning Source LLC
Chambersburg PA
CBHW030136240426
43672CB00005B/148